S. W. A. T.

Vance Jr. High 1986-87

Creating Effective Schools:

An In-Service Program for Enhancing
School Learning Climate and Achievement

Creating Effective Schools:

An In-Service Program for Enhancing
School Learning Climate and Achievement

Wilbur Brookover
Laurence Beamer
Helen Efthim
Douglas Hathaway
Lawrence Lezotte
Stephen Miller
Joseph Passalacqua
Louis Tornatzky

Learning Publications, Inc.
Holmes Beach, Florida

Library of Congress Number: 81-84659

Copyright 1982   Wilbur Brookover, Laurence Beamer,
                 Helen Efthim, Douglas Hathaway,
                 Lawrence Lezotte, Stephen Miller,
                 Joseph Passalacqua, and Louis Tornatsky

Co-Editors:
  Edsel L. Erickson
  Lois A. Carl

Learning Publications, Inc.
P.O. Box 1326
Holmes Beach, Florida 33509

Hardback: ISBN 0-918452-35-X

Paperback: ISBN 0-918452-34-1

Cover Designed by Melinda Frink Kabel

Printing: 4 5 6 7 8   Year: 5 6

Printed and bound in the United States of America

Preface and Acknowledgements

Creating Effective Schools is designed as an in-service training program for staff in schools desiring to improve the achievment of their students through modifications in the school learning environment. This program is the product of several years of work which has gone through several preliminary editions and has been used in the Pontiac, Michigan schools. This published edition is provided because of numerous requests for the materials. We do not consider it final, or definitive, but rather a work in process which has been developed through several stages.

Users of the school learning climate improvement materials may wish to consult with the authors who have been involved in the process of changing school learning climates. To do so please contact School Learning Climate, Inc., 930 Huntington Road, East Lansing, Michigan. Others may wish to use the materials without consultation. In either case the developers of these modules urge users to consider them as a functional whole rather than picking and choosing particular modules that may seem to serve their needs.

This school learning climate improvement program is indeed the product of cooperation among many people, therefore it is difficult to attribute authorship of any module to particular persons. Almost all of the major contributors have read and made suggestions for each of the several modules. A first version of these modules was produced by Wilbur Brookover and Associates at the Michigan State University Center for Urban Affairs. They were entitled, "School Climate Activities Training: A Program in Ten Modules," by Wilbur Brookover, Douglas Hathaway, Lawrence Lezotte, Joseph Passalacqua, and Louis Tornatzky. Subsequent versions have benefited from the staff of the School District of the City of Pontiac, particularly, Laurence W. Beamer and Helen Efthim. This edition is primarily the product of cooperative

v

efforts of Laurence Beamer, Pontiac Schools; Wilbur Brookover, Michigan State University; Helen Efthim,, Pontiac Schools; Stephen K. Miller, Michigan State University; and Joseph Passalacqua, Michigan State University.

Numerous other people have contributed to this work. Perhaps most important are the principals and teachers of the schools who have used the materials, reacted to them, and put into practice the beliefs and techniques identified here. Special recognition must also be given to the administrators of the Pontiac School System who have supported and encouraged the development of the school climate program. Specific mention should be made to Wesley Maas, the Executive Director of Secondary and Extended Education, who has been associated with the project throughout its existence. An effort to recognize all other administrators in the Pontiac schools who have supported the project would be inappropriate because of the likelihood that some persons would be overlooked. Emergency School Aid Act staff members in the Pontiac schools also made significant contributions to the development of this program. Patricia Flood edited the entire manuscript and made numerous contributions. Both Ronald Edmonds and Maureen McCormick Larkin read the manuscript and made appreciated suggestions. Special thanks are also given to Helen Felt, Janice Hill, Vickie Hubbard, Mary Ann Guerra, Alice Perrone, Karen Findlay, and Beth Rohrabacker who have facilitated the preparation of these materials.

Through the joint efforts of the Center for Urban Development at Michigan State University and the Pontiac Center for Research and Evaluation, a set of instruments designed to assess the school learning climate is being developed. These instruments will be available for use by school staffs in 1982.

This work was developed with support of a State administered grant of Federal Elementary and Secondary Education Act Title IV—C Funds and the Michigan Department of Education. The opinions expressed herein are those of the authors and do not necessarily reflect the position of the United States Department of Education or the Michigan Department of Education.

Contents

Creating Effective Schools

Introduction:
Important Principles

- **School Learning Climate**
- **The Goal of School Learning Climate Improvement**
- **Using the School Learning Climate Modules**
- **Additional Resources**

The quality of education provided for our children and youth is a major concern in American society. The level of achievement in basic skills and other areas of student behavior has been less than satisfactory in many American schools. This is particularly true for those serving low-income and/or minority students. This phenomenon has become so pervasive that many have concluded that high levels of student performance are impossible in schools with student bodies drawn from lower socio-economic status (SES) and/or minority families. Although the SES and minority composition of the school are statistically associated with level of student achievement, many exceptions exist which suggest the relationship is not a causal one. Although these schools are relatively atypical, the fact that some schools with educationally disadvantaged students do produce high achievement demonstrates that it is possible for other such schools to achieve that goal. The purpose of this volume is to assist any and all schools to produce high levels of achievement regardless of the socio-economic or minority composition of their student body.

For the past several decades educators, researchers and the public have usually sought to explain low student performance by either the characteristics of the individual student or the family background. Both of these explanations of student learning have largely ignored the influence of the principals and teachers with whom students interact. The discovery that some schools are effective in teaching students from disadvantaged family backgrounds makes plausible the conclusion that the nature of the school can make a difference in the level of student learning. Throughout this volume we assume that essentially all children can learn what any child can learn if we provide the appropriate teaching–learning environment in the school (Bloom, 1976). This set of school learning climate materials is designed to develop such a learning environment.

School Learning Climate

The concept "climate" has been used in many different ways in relation to schools. Organizational climate has commonly referred to the nature of the human relations among adult members of the organization. Others have used climate to refer to the degree of orderly discipline or violence in the school. Although both these and other concepts have some relevance, they do not describe school climate as used in these modules. In fact, there is considerable evidence that these various uses of "climate" either are not associated with levels of achievement or are negatively correlated to achievement (see Lezotte, Hathaway, Miller, Passalacqua, & Brookover, 1980, for a summary of this evidence). On the other hand, we have identified "climate" as the school learning climate. This is to emphasize that we are concerned with any aspect of the school social system that is associated with the level of student learning. School learning climates are, therefore, characterized by the degree to which they are effective in producing the desired learning outcomes among the students. Again, we stress that most uses of school climate do not pertain to achievement. Our use of school learning climate is specifically designed to explain and help increase student achievement. The reader should be aware of this distinction.

The characteristics of schools with effective learning climates may be classified under these general headings: the ideology of the school, the organization of the school, and the instructional practices. The identification of characteristics of effective school learning climates is based on a wide range of research in American and other schools. Although we have identified the characteristics of effective schools in three clusters for convenience of discussion, we emphasize that no one characteristic or any combination of two or three characteristics explains the degree to which schools are effective in producing high levels of student performance. Rather, the total complex of characteristics interact to produce effective learning environments.

The first cluster, which we have identified as the ideology of the school, refers to the general beliefs, norms, expectations, and feelings which characterize the school social system. The belief that students can learn and that teachers can teach is an important characteristic of an effective school learning environment. This belief must also be associated with the staff's expectation that all students can and will achieve at high levels. The expectations for students become generalized into norms, or standards of achievement. Research in Michigan elementary schools (Brookover, Beady, Flood, Schweitzer, & Wisenbaker, 1979) indicates that schools in which the staff evaluates students as slow or unable to learn and in which they hold low expectations for student achievement will be characterized by the students' high sense of futility in regard to school achievement. When the school is characterized by such feelings, it is likely that the level of achievement will be low.

Effective schools, therefore, must have student bodies that believe it is possible for them to learn in school. We hasten to add that the belief that the students can learn, even when accompanied by high expectations for them and low levels of student futility, is not sufficient to produce learning. A positive ideology of beliefs, norms, and expectations must be accompanied by a school social organization which defines learning as desirable and rewards effective teaching as well as successful learning. Furthermore, students do not learn simply because of these beliefs and expectations. Some type of effective instructional program must be directed toward the learning of specific kinds of behavior.

The second cluster of characteristics of effective schools is identified as the organization of the school. Schools organized in such a way that significant proportions of the students are identified as slow or non-learners, and are differentiated from other strata of students who are expected to learn, are not likely to be effective in teaching those students from whom little is expected. Many schools are stratified into different tracks, different sections, or different groups so that large proportions of the students are defined as unable to learn as much as other students. In such schools students may be recognized and rewarded for failure to learn at high levels. The role of the teacher in this type of school may be defined as one who differentiates readily among the students and who does a good job of identifying students who are not to be taught at the same levels as other students.

In order to have an effective school in which all students achieve at high levels, the student's role must be defined as a high achieving learner. The teacher's role must be defined as instructor of all students to high achievement. Both students and teachers must be rewarded for effective teaching and learning. The principal of an effective school must provide leadership in identifying the objectives and monitoring the success of the instructional program. A school in which a large proportion of the students do not achieve well and a smaller proportion achieve at very high levels is not effective.

It is readily apparent that the organizational characteristics of effective schools are highly related to the ideology that we have described above. A belief that many students cannot learn is commonly associated with schools in which there is a great deal of differentiation and stratification of students into many different level of expectations and achievement.

The third cluster of characteristics of effective schools is composed of instructional practices. These instructional practices are the subject of several modules in this set. They include effective instruction, reinforcement practices, student team learning, assessment, and time-on-task. We mention them at this point because effective school learning climates must be characterized by clearly recognized and accepted objectives which are common for all students, plus a directed instructional program that is designed for all students to master those objectives. Taken together, these modules on instructional techniques provide a framework for transforming the high expectations into actual high achievement.

Not all of the characteristics in the three clusters identified above are the subject of specific modules in this work. Several may be found in a single module and others will be the primary focus of a single module. Overall, the several characteristics of effective school learning climates as identified here will be mentioned and discussed in some detail. The research on which these characteristics are based will be discussed as they are identified.

It should be recognized that great variation exists in the extent and type of research upon which the characteristics of effective school learning climates are based. There is extensive research that demonstrates that the beliefs and evaluations concerning students' ability to learn, and the expectations which teachers hold for students, are highly related to the level of student achievement. Similarly, there is an extensive body of research to support the conclusion that student achievement is related to the amount of engaged time devoted to learning. The model of effective school learning climates presented in the following modules is therefore not the product of a single study demonstrating that high-achieving schools have all these characteristics, but rather from a series of studies of high-achieving schools.

There is some evidence that changes in schools in the direction of developing characteristics that are identified here do result in improved levels of student achievement, but definitive studies remain to be done. We cannot, therefore, categorically say that the kinds of school learning climate outlined here cause high achievement. However, there is an extensive body of correlational research which indicates that schools with characteristics such as we have identified have higher levels of student achievement than schools without these characteristics. We note too that the program outlined in these modules does not rely solely on changing the beliefs, attitudes, and expectations which characterize a school. Rather, this program includes efforts to raise achievement through modifying the organization, directly improving instructional practices, and altering the ideology of the school.

A further word of caution is appropriate concerning the characteristics of effective school learning climates. There is increasing evidence that some characteristics function differently in different school social systems. For example, we have emphasized the directed instructional practice in accord with the mastery model. Some would apply the mastery model to whole group instruction, while others might advocate individualized instruction. We have not advocated individualized instruction because we find little evidence to support this as a consistently effective teaching strategy. We think individualized instruction functions quite differently in different school contexts. If individualized instruction is used to assure that every student masters particular objectives, it would likely be quite effective. If, on the other hand, as is common in many schools, individualized instruction is used as a basis for differentiating among the students in a manner that identifies some students as not able to learn or not ready to learn the particular materials, the resulting outcomes are likely to be lower for a large proportion of the students.

This illustrates that no single variable or characteristic of school learning climates explains teaching effectiveness. All of the characteristics identified are interacting aspects of the total social system; some specific characteristics may function differently in different schools.

The modules which follow are designed to assist with in-service training of the staff that wishes to improve the learning climate of its school. We do not think it is appropriate or likely to be effective for the school to concentrate on only one or another of the following modules. Emphasizing a change in the level of expectations is certainly desirable, but changing the levels of expectations without the development of effective instructional programs is not likely to have the desired impact. All aspects of the school ideology, organization, and instructional practices interact to produce effective or ineffective school learning climate.

The Goal Of School Learning Climate Improvement

The goal of this entire program is to produce effective schools. An effective school is one in which essentially all of the students acquire the basic skills and other desired behavior within the school. Although many schools have demonstrated their effectiveness in teaching students from affluent families, most schools have not been effective in teaching students from lower socio-economic-status families, many of whom are members of racial and ethnic minorities. The goal of this program, therefore, is to produce a learning climate in which students will achieve, regardless of their socio-economic or minority background. Students from all types of family backgrounds have demonstrated their ability to learn the language of their associates, and we believe they can learn others skills and knowledge if provided the appropriate learning climate.

Any school in which a portion or all of the student body is failing to achieve at high levels should benefit from this in-service program. This program should however, be particularly helpful in improving achievement in low SES schools. As we have noted, some schools with students from poor families are achieving well, but most students in such schools are currently achieving below desirable levels. The goal of this in-service training program is to improve the achievement of all students through improvement of the school learning climate.

Using The School Learning Climate Modules

A school staff which decides to use this program must be aware of several of its features. Failure to take note of these features will reduce the effectiveness of the program and the chances of increased achievement.

1. The school learning climate is the COLLECTIVE norms, organization, and practices among the members of the social system. A combined effort by all of the staff is required to successfully establish an effective school learning climate.

2. Although various concepts and practices are explained in separate modules to facilitate understanding, a positive school learning climate is comprised of the UNITY of the entire set. The entire program must be used as a whole for maximum benefits. Using only certain modules ignores the fact that the different aspects of the school learning climate are interconnected and affect the other parts.

3. Using the program does not guarantee quick success. The program must be implemented completely over time if maximum results are to be achieved.

4. This program is designed to assist the principal and teachers of a building to bring almost all students to high levels of achievement in the curriculum for their grade, particularly for the basic skills areas of reading and mathematics.

The program is research based, using practices that have been related to increased achievement in repeated studies. In order to be consistent with standards of professional honesty and courtesy to other researchers, we have listed references where appropriate. We have also tried to summarize the basic research findings within the modules. For those who are not interested in the original references, the style of notation allows the reader simply to skim over the citations.

The following suggestions for using the School Learning Climate Program are based on the school as the unit of implementation. While the School Learning Climate Program can be implemented in different settings, e.g., district wide, in an individual school or by an individual teacher, the focus for change in this program is at the school level.

With this introduction we present a model for implementing the school learning climate program. Any program for school improvement must be used on a regular basis if change is to be expected. This program, like many others, will fail if not fully implemented. The following model is designed to facilitate the effective use of the concepts and practices explained in these modules. The essential elements for implementing the School Learning Climate Program are shown in the following model. The major components of the model and suggested means of implementing or operationalizing these components are presented in some detail in the next several pages.

A Model For School Learning
Climate Program Implementation

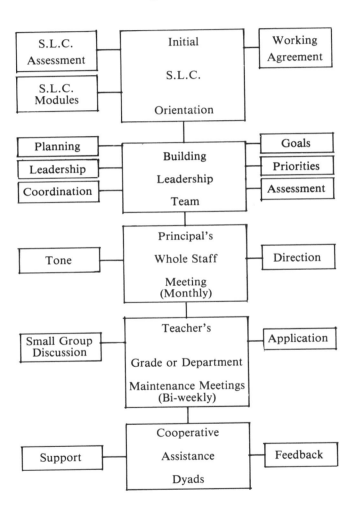

Initial Orientation

The purposes of the initial orientation are to:

1. Familiarize the staff with the total concept of School Learning Climate.
2. Present an overview of the School Learning Climate modules.
3. Assess the current level of School Learning Climate.
4. Establish and reach acceptance on a Working Agreement for conducting the School Learning Climate Program.

Ideally, the initial orientation should take place prior to the opening of school in September or at a time when the staff is released from regular school responsibilities. At least two (2) days should be devoted to the initial orientation, with additional time desirable if funds and schedules allow. The principal and teachers of the Building Leadership Team are responsible for conducting the initial orientation.

During the initial orientation, the principal and selected teachers present the total concept of School Learning Climate and briefly explain the individual modules comprising the program. In-depth study of School Learning Climate topics will occur each month as the staff works with one (1) module at a time.

The principal and teachers should also assess the current level of school learning climate by using the School Learning Climate Assessment Instrument (SLCAI). This instrument is designed to identify the strengths and weaknesses of the existing building learning climate so that a program of improvement can be identified for the year.

Finally, a Working Agreement should be developed and accepted by all staff participants. This agreement should identify what is expected from the principal and teachers who are to conduct the School Learning Climate Program. A suggested agreement follows:

Working Agreement For Implementing The School Learning Climate Program

I.   The Principal Agrees to:
   1. Participate in the School Learning Climate Training Program for the Building Leadership Team (BLT).
   2. Conduct the Initial Orientation Program for teachers with assistance of the Building Leadership Team.
   3. Act as chairperson of the Building Leadership Team and meet with its members at least once a month.
   4. Provide ongoing administrative leadership and support for project implementation.
   5. Participate in Maintenance Meetings of teachers.

II.   The Building Leadership Team Agrees to:
   1. Participate in the School Learning Climate Training Program for the Building Leadership Team.
   2. Assist the principal in conducting the Initial Climate Orientation Program for teachers.
   3. Attend a monthly meeting of the BLT.
   4. Participate in Maintenance Meetings of teachers.
   5. Provide ongoing instructional leadership and support for project implementation.

III.   Teachers Agree to:
   1. Participate in the Initial Climate Orientation Program for teachers.
   2. Allocate time for participation in biweekly Maintenance Meetings, as well as whole staff meetings for project implementation purposes.
   3. Participate in an Assistance Dyad with another teacher for cooperative follow-up on suggestions and tasks.
   4. Develop programs for classroom management, instructional delivery, and parent support, consistent with the School Learning Climate Program.

_____   _____
Principal   Date

_____   _____
BLT Chairperson   Date

_____   _____
Teacher Representative   Date

Building Leadership Team

The Building Leadership Team (BLT) is responsible for providing the leadership necessary to conduct the School Learning Climate Program. The BLT consists of the principal, who acts as chairperson, and three (3) or four (4) teachers. The teachers selected for the BLT should be opinion leaders among the staff and/or should represent important organizational structures, such as department heads, grade level chairpersons, etc.

This team's responsibilities include: a) identification of school goals and priorities related to school learning climate, b) preliminary planning for conducting the project, and c) setting up a program for assessing staff progress.

Matters of general planning, leadership, goal setting, and establishing priorities can then occur before the staff orientation. Following the initial staff orientation, the BLT meets monthly for planning, coordination, and evaluation. It is recommended that the BLT meet two (2) weeks prior to the principal's whole staff meeting to prepare for the climate topic and activities to be acted upon that month.

Principal's Whole Staff Meeting

Each month, the principal meets with the whole staff to discuss topics related to the School Learning Climate Program. According to the implementation calendar established by the BLT, one (1) topic or module is targeted for study and action each month. At the whole staff meeting, the principal reviews the selected topic or module and sets the tone and direction for staff activities that month.

Maintenance Meetings

The purpose of the maintenance meetings is to provide for

small group study or discussion related to topics or concerns of the School Learning Climate Program. These are intended as regular biweekly meetings to consider the practicality or implications of ideas or suggestions from the modules. Maintenance meetings should focus on application of suggestions from the modules or from the building staff.

Teachers should decide the best way to form maintenance groups. Usually this is done according to a common interest, such as by subject or grade level. For example, teachers might meet according to grade level in the elementary school while secondary teachers may wish to group accoring to departments or subjects. Once a maintenance group is formed, a chairperson should be selected and agreement should be reached on the dates and times for the biweekly meetings. It is recommended that members of the BLT *do not* act as chairpersons of maintenance groups. While BLT members should participate in these groups, they should not attempt to run or dominate them.

Assistance Dyads

Throughout the modules, teachers are encouraged to assist one another in following through with suggested activities, techniques, or tasks. The easiest way to do this is for teachers to form assistance dyads. For example, two (2) teachers from the same maintenance group would agree to work together for the year on activities from the School Learning Climate Program. This arrangement facilitates communication and understanding and also can develop into a valued support system for teachers. Teachers may be uncomfortable working closely with other teachers at first, but sharing and problem-solving should stimulate full cooperation toward common goals.

Time Commitments

Following the Initial Orientation, School Learning Climate activities should occur in a regular, planned manner. The implementation model described above identifies four (4) project functions that require time of staff each month. Each participant should expect to devote approximately one (1) hour each week to activities of the School Learning Climate Program. The actual time spent may be more or less than this; however, it is essential that all teachers and the principal commit time for these project activities:

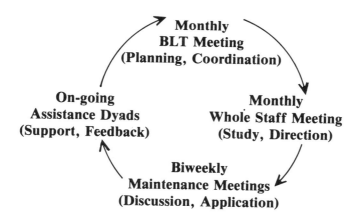

**Monthly
BLT Meeting
(Planning, Coordination)**

**On-going
Assistance Dyads
(Support, Feedback)**

**Monthly
Whole Staff Meeting
(Study, Direction)**

**Biweekly
Maintenance Meetings
(Discussion, Application)**

Project Implementation Schedule

The suggested schedule for implementing the School Learning Climate Program identifies monthly topics and activities for:

1. Building Leadership Team;
2. Whole Staff Meetings;
3. Maintenance Meetings; and
4. Staff In-Service.

The activities of the BLT, Whole Staff Meetings and Maintenance Meetings occur accordingly on a regular schedule each month. The released-time Staff In-Service, however, is scheduled as time and funds permit and involves either a half-day or full-day of staff time. The topics identified for Staff In-Service represent major implementation activities for the whole staff and are best addressed when students are dismissed from school. Your school may vary in the amount of released-time available to it for Staff In-Service in comparison to the suggested schedule. In case your staff needs released-time in addition to that recommended, it should be arranged by the BLT.

Suggested School Learning Climate Implementation Schedule

	Building Leadership Team Meeting	Whole Staff Meeting	Maintenance Meeting	Staff Inservice (Released Time)
August	School Learning Climate Training Program (Early August)			School Learning Climate Orientation (Late August)
September	Effective instruction (Module 5)	Organization for instruction: a mastery model	1. Requirements for using a mastery model 2. Instructional practices	Learning for mastery workshop
October	Discipline and classroom management (module 7).	Using a school-wide approach for discipline and classroom management	1. The classroom discipline plan 2. The school-wide discipline plan	Discipline and classroom management workshop
November	Student team learning (Module 8)	Using group dynamics to raise achievement	1. Academic competition 2. Teams-games-tournaments	Student team learning workshop
December	Mid-year evaluation of BLT activities	Evaluating our progress	Mid-year evaluation of maintenance activities	
January	Academic engaged time (Module 6)	Increasing time on task	1. Practices for increasing engaged time 2. Assessing time on task	
February	Motivation and reinforcement (Module 9)	Motivation and reinforcement principles	1. Motivation practices 2. Reinforcement practices	
March	Learning with retention (Module 5)	Increasing retention of learning	1. Retention practices 2. Review: motivation, Reinforcement, retention	Schedule as needed
April	Assessment practices for instruction (Module 10)	The Assessment-achievement connection	1. Formal and informal assessment 2. Test taking skills	
May	End-of-year evaluation of BLT activities	Evaluating our progress	End-of-year Evaluation of Maintenance meetings	
June	Planning for next year	Looking backward and looking forward	Planning for next year	

The BLT is responsible for scheduling and arranging for Staff In-Service. While the 2-day Orientation Session held at the beginning of the year is planned and conducted by the BLT, other In-Service activities should involve additional staff members or consultants.

The schedule of implementation activities is designed to permit a coordinated approach to project efforts. The BLT meets two (2) weeks prior to the monthly Whole Staff Meeting for planning and preparation. The principal sets the tone and direction for staff activities through presentations at the Whole Staff Meeting generally held during the first week of each month. Maintenance Meetings, scheduled for the second and fourth weeks of the month, deal with specific concerns of implementation related to the topic of the month established by the BLT. In the suggested schedule, two (2) topics are identified for each month, one (1) each Maintenance Meeting.

Presenting the School Learning Climate Modules

As stated earlier, the concept of School Learning Climate as described in the modules must be treated with unity for maximum benefits. The module presentation/discussion schedule can be organized as follows:

Initial Orientation (2 days in August)
First Day: Module 1 — Effective School Learning
                              Climate
              Module 2 —Expectations for Learning
              Module 3 —Organization, Role Defini-
                              tions and Rewards
              Module 4 —Grouping and Differentiation
Second Day:Module 6 —Academic Engaged Time
              Module 9 —Reinforcing Achievement
              Module 10 —Use of Assessment Data
              Module 11 —Parent Support and Involve-
                              ment

September:	Module 5 — Effective Instruction
October:	Module 7 —School Discipline and Classroom Management
November:	Module 8 —Student Team Learning

It is recommended that each project participant receive a full set of School Learning Climate Modules for browsing several weeks prior to the intitial staff orientation. In particular, Modules 1-4, 6, 9, 10 and 11 should be read before the orientation by each participant, as those modules will be presented during the 2 days of In-Service. Because Modules 5, 7, and 8 will be considered in detail in months subsequent to the orientation, reading of each of these modules should be done just prior to the month each topic is targeted for study.

The activities which appear at the end of each module are suggested ways to put into practice the content of the module. These activities are only some of the possible ways to follow through on the ideas presented in any module. Each staff is encouraged to develop additional activities that may better serve their needs.

Beginning in September and extending through the school year one (1) module should be targeted for study and discussion each month by the staff. Obviously, some modules deal with topics or activities that cannot be concluded in a month. However, it is recommended that the staff move on to the next topic as scheduled, initiating as many activities as possible and temporarily postponing remaining activities until a later date. In some cases, uncompleted work on a module can be continued while a new module is being investigated. If not, return to the unfinished activities as soon as possible. Studying modules and initiating activities according to a fixed schedule usually presents problems only during the first year in the School Learning Climate Program. Once understanding of the modules has been achieved, the need to schedule so tightly is lessened. Especially during the second year, less time will be needed for covering modules and more time should be available for follow-through activities.

Since limitations of time in the Initial Orientation prevent full consideration of the modules presented, it is necessary that general understanding of each module be achieved. Beginning in December, the remainder of the year should be divided between follow-up activities associated with the modules presented in the Initial Orientation and evaluation of project implementation. The BLT should develop a schedule of module topics for further staff investigation beginning in December and extending through the school year. (See Suggested Implementation Schedule.)

We are confident that this program will result in increased achievement if properly implemented and followed. However, staff members must agree that they want and are willing to work for positive change. Improving the school learning climate will not be easy, since it requires change in people, which is difficult at best. But the staff that is committed to raising achievement can do it. A thorough study of these modules will provide the understanding and guidance needed to begin that change.

Additional Resources

Bloom, B. S. *Human characteristics and school learning.* New York: McGraw-Hill, 1976.

This book provides the theoretical framework and empirical evidence for mastery learning. Stating that essentially all children can learn what any child can learn, Bloom's work is a fundamental challenge to the accepted belief that school learning is normally distributed because of individual differences in ability.

Bloom, B. S. News views of the learner: Implications for instruction and curriculum. *Educational Leadership,* 1978, 35(7), 563-568, 570-576.

Bloom summarizes his research and theory on the ability of virtually all children to learn well. This is concise, very understandable, and must reading for all educators.

Brookover, W., Beady, C., Flood, P., Schweitzer, J., & Wisenbaker, J. *School social systems and student achievement: Schools can make a difference.* Brooklyn: J. F. Bergin Co., distributed by Praeger Publishers, New York, 1979.

In study of 91 randomly selected Michigan elementary schools, school climate was found to explain as much of the variance in achievement between schools as SES and percent white. This research demonstrates that schools can and do make a difference in achievement outcomes over and above family background characteristics of the students.

Larkin, Maureen. *Milwaukee teacher expecation project guide.* Milwaukee Public Schools.

An earlier version of these In-Service materials has been used by Maureen Larkin in a successful program improving some inner city Milwaukee schools.

Lezotte, L. W., Hathaway, D. V., Miller, S. K., Passalacqua, J. & Brookover, W. B. *School learning climate student achievement: A social systems approach to increased student learning.* Tallahassee, Florida: National Teacher Corps, Florida State University Foundation, 1980.

This monograph provides a thorough discussion of school learning climate, a review of the literature, and problems of organizational change. The work is a comprehensive resource on how to increase achievement by improving school learning climate and furnishes important background to the information in these modules.

New York City Schools. *The school improvement project of the New York City Public Schools* (a mimeograph outline of the project); also Dennis McCarthy, Alan Lazarus, and June Conner, *School improvement project: A summary of the first annual assessment report.* Documentation Unit, Metropolitan Educational Development and Research Project, New York City Public Schools, New York, 1980.

The New York City school improvement project initiated by Ronald Edmonds has developed procedures for bringing about change in the school climate similar to those proposed in these materials.

Module 1

An Effective School Learning Climate

- **What Is An Effective School Learning Climate?**
- **Illustrations of Aspects of the School Learning Climate**
- **Improving School Learning Climate**
- **Measuring School Learning Climate**
- **Suggested Activities**
- **Additional Resources**

Every school has a learning climate. Some are effective; others are not. *Schools with effective learning climates have high achievement regardless of the type of community served by the school. By the same token, ineffective school learning climates are associated with low levels of achievement.*

Unfortunately, very few schools which serve low income and/or minority students have effective learning climates. The schools of the disadvantaged are beset with discipline problems, violence, poor attendance and, most of all, low achievement and failure to attain basic literacy skills. Other schools also experience these problems, but they are so concentrated in low SES areas that the accepted view among both educators and the public is that schools cannot overcome these environmental characteristics.

But this is simply not true. High achieving, low income/minority schools do exist, and they have been extensively studied (see Brookover et al., 1979; Edmonds, 1979; Hoover, 1978 for reviews). The implication put forth by these exemplary schools is consistent with extensive research by Bloom (1976) and his associates who conclude that "what any person in the world can learn, almost all persons can learn if provided with appropriate prior and current conditions of learning" (p. 7). These "appropriate conditions for learning" are what we identify as an effective school learning climate.

In the remainder of this module we will describe and explain effective school learning climates and address the issue of changing and improving the learning climate and level of achievement. In the modules that follow we will further expand on the attitudes, beliefs, structures, and instructional programs that characterize effective schools.

What is Effective School Learning Climate?

School learning climate refers to the attitudinal and behavioral patterns in a school which impact on the level of achievement. This includes such factors as teachers' expectations for and evaluations of students' learning, academic norms, students' sense of futility with respect to learning, role definitions, grouping patterns, and instructional practices. These and other factors which affect achievement can and do vary from school to school. In Lezotte et al. (1980), school learning climate is defined as "the norms, beliefs and attitudes reflected in institutional patterns and behavior practices that enhance or impede student learning (p. 4)." This definition emphasizes the positive or negative effect of various factors in the school on achievement.

In these modules we are particularly interested in the complex of interacting factors which characterize effective schools. By effective schools, we mean those which produce a high level of achievement for all students, regardless of family background. Therefore, effective school learning climate refers to the particular characteristics and patterns of attitudes, beliefs, norms, role definitions, structure, and instructional behaviors which are associated with high achieving effective schools.

Characteristics of Effective School Learning Climate

We have identified three clusters of characteristics of the school which make a difference in the level of achievement: ideology, organizational structure and instructional practices. We emphasize that these clusters are not separate and independent. There is an interactive relationship between them. Consequently, changes in one cluster are likely to result in concomitant changes in the others. (Perhaps these clusters are more useful for purposes of description than as distinct characteristics since there is considerable overlap between them.)

As previously noted in the introduction we distinguish between school learning climate and other uses of the term "school climate." That distinction bears elaboration: school climate, when used to indicate the physical environment, the professional climate, the organizational climate, or other related terms, identifies dimensions of the school other than achievement. These other "climates" are not unimportant, but research has shown them to be either not associated with achievement levels or negatively related to achievement. Again, the reader is cautioned that these other uses of school climate do not necessarily pertain to achievement.

The following points emphasize the distinction we make and further characterize our concept of a school learning climate:

1. School learning climate relates to student achievement and those factors within a school that affect achievement.
2. A school's learning climate is the collective set of attitudes, beliefs, and behaviors within a building. It

goes beyond the individual to the group norms of a school. These norms tend to be maintained over time with new members being socialized into the prevailing sets of behaviors.

3. The school learning climate describes the school as a social system. Since schools share a common function in society, there is some similarity in learning climates. On the other hand, different schools stress different "philosophies," instructional practices and methodologies, beliefs and expectations of students' abilities to learn. Consequently, school learning climate varies sufficiently to produce different levels of student achievement.

4. The school learning climate can be changed. Local and building norms do change, and the people who are members of the school social group are the change agents. Outsiders are unlikely to have much impact on the social group unless that group desires or is willing to change.

School Learning Climate and Student Achievement

The School Learning Climate Program for raising achievement by improving the learning climate is based on the study of effective schools. Previous research seemed to indicate that schools make little difference in the achievement outcomes of students beyond the influence of family background characteristics. Race and SES, used to represent family background, seemed to account for differences in achievement from school to school (Coleman, Campbell, Hobson, McPartland, Mood, Weinfeld, & York, 1966; Jencks, Smith, Acland, Bane, Cohen, Gintis, Heyns, & Michelson, 1972). However, more recent research indicates that schools can and do make a difference in student outcomes.

The existence of high achieving low income schools has been verified in case studies of these schools (e.g., Phi Delta

Kappa, 1980; Weber, 1971). Hoover (1978) lists common characteristics of black schools functioning at grade level. Edmonds (1979) reviews other studies of exemplary schools. Our own work includes a study of high and low achieving pairs of schools matched for SES, race, and rural-urban backgrounds (Brookover & Schneider, 1975) in which differences in school learning climate accounted for most of the achievement differences. Brookover and Lezotte (1977) studied schools that were improving or declining in achievement over a three year period. The factors that influenced their achievement were consistent with the concept of school learning climate identified here. Brookover et al. (1979) analyzed a random sample of 91 elementary schools in Michigan. In this study, they found that the school learning climate explained as much of the achievement differences among schools as did SES and race (see Lezotte et al., 1980, Chapter 4, for detailed analysis). Other studies relating to school learning climate and achievement are noted in the Additional Resources included with these modules.

Effective schools have been documented in other countries as well. Chen and Fresko (1978) studied Israeli junior highs. Madaus, Kellaghan, Rakow, and King (1979) looked at high schools in Ireland. Rutter, Maughan, Mortimore, Ouston, and Smith (1979) studied 12 inner city London high schools. The results of all of these studies are consistent with our own work, as are the studies of American high school academic climates by McDill, Meyers, and Rigsby (1967) and high school learning climates by Glasheen, Hadley and Schneider (1977).

We would be remiss if we did not also point out that several studies of classroom learning climates support the conclusion that school environment affects achievement (e.g., see Anderson, 1970; Moos, 1979; O'Reilly, 1975). The above review does not include the work on instructional practices which have proved effective in increasing achievement. Some of this work will be reviewed in subsequent modules on various aspects of the instructional program.

It is now clear that effective schools do exist, that schools can produce achievement in low income areas, and that the school learning climate is highly associated with levels of achievement. Since we are primarily concerned with effective school learning climates, we turn now to a synthesis of the above research: a profile of the exemplary high achieving low income school.

A Profile of an Effective School

We have briefly defined and described the school learning climate and documented the existence of exemplary schools. Now we will draw a profile of effective schools based on the studies noted above. In so doing, we will be further describing the school learning climate for effective schools.

We will synthesize the research findings into the three clusters of characteristics which we have identified as comprising the school learning climate: the ideology, the organizational structure, and the instructional practices of the school. The aspects which we include are positive features of effective schools. We are virtually profiling an "ideal" school. Though this is an ideal model, some schools do closely approximate this profile and are high achieving. The goal of our program is to create schools that match this profile as closely as possible.

A.   The Ideology of the School (see also the sample Statement of Purpose and Beliefs in the Activities section for this module).

1.   The professional staff holds the following beliefs and attitudes:

a.   All students can learn the school's objectives.

b.   All students are expected to reach high standards of achievement.

c .   Teachers can successfully instruct all students in the school's objectives.

d.   Individual and schoolwide performance on achievement tests is an appropriate goal and measure of school success.

   e. Norms of high performance for staff promote achievement and in addition counteract apathy, negative attitudes and practices, and low performance.

   f. The staff is committed to the job of producing high achievement for all students, no matter what it takes.

  2. Students' perceptions of the school learning climate:

   a. Students perceive and reinforce norms that high achievement is expected of all students.

   b. Students have a high self-concept of academic ability. This is the student's self-assessment of his/her ability to learn. (Self-concept functions as a threshold variable: high self-concept does not guarantee high achievement but lack of an adequate self-concept may preclude good academic performance.)

   c. Students have a low sense of academic futility. Sense of futility is a perception by the student that nothing one does will make a difference in school, that trying to learn or succeed is hopeless because of the system. (Students with high futility are low-achieving and poorly motivated.)

B. The Organizational Structure of the School

  1. Role expectations for appropriate behavior are defined in terms of achievement.

   a. "Effective teacher" role defined as instructing all students to high achievement.

   b. "Good student" role defined as high achiever.

   c. "Effective principal" role defined as instructional leader who promotes effective instruction and high achievement for all students.

  2. Reward structures and systems in the school are centered on achievement.

   a. Teachers are recognized and rewarded for producing high achievements for all students.

      b. Students are recognized and rewarded for high achievement and improved performance.

      c. Principal is recognized and rewarded for promoting a high achieving school in which all students master instructional objectives.

  3. Stratification of students is minimal.

      a. Flexible heterogeneous grouping is used rather than homogeneous segregation of students by ability, race, or SES.

      b. Testing programs are used for diagnosis of learning rather than sorting and selecting between levels of students.

      c. Compensatory education and special education programs function to help students "catch-up" to grade level and are conducted in and coordinated with the regular classroom.

  4. Differentiation of the instructional program is minimal.

      a. Common instructional objectives are established for all students.

      b. Common expectations are set for all students.

      c. Common instructional materials are used for all students.

      d. Common role definitions are stated for all students.

  5. Parental support and involvement are structured by the school to facilitate the school's achievement goals.

C. The Instructional Practices of the School.

  1. School goals and instructional objectives.

      a. School goals, of which first priority is attaining mastery of identified instructional objectives by all students, are clearly stated.

      b. Standards for mastery of instructional objectives for all students, and procedures for certifying attainment of those standards, are clearly stated.

      c. Instructional objectives for each grade level are clearly stated and reflect the school's goal of basic skill achievement.

    d. Professional staff recognizes and accepts the priority of mastery of instructional objectives for all students.

2. An effective program of structured, direct instruction incorporated into a mastery learning strategy (Bloom, 1976) for achievement of objectives by all students (see Module 5).

3. An orderly, relatively quiet, work-oriented atmosphere reflecting effective school and classroom discipline (see Module 7).

4. Use of instructional program results in high percentage of the total school day as "academic engaged time" for all students (see Module 6).

5. Use of academic competition to promote peer learning and motivation (see Module 8).

6. Effective use of reinforcement principles, contingent upon expected learning conduct (see Module 9).

7. Effective use of assessment data (see Modules 5 & 10).

    a. Ongoing monitoring of student progress, including diagnosis and regular feedback to pupils, is carried out.

    b. Accurate record keeping of mastery of objectives by all students is required.

    c. Diagnostic information is utilized in planning corrective instruction.

    d. Schoolwide data is used for evaluating and improving the school's instructional program.

We reiterate that the above profile is a composite of successful schools. In reality many schools have beliefs and practices which impede rather than enhance achievement. Some positive and negative examples of what we mean by school learning climate and how it can affect achievement are presented as actual case histories in the next section.

Illustrations Of Aspects Of The School Learning Climate

The following cases represent both effective and ineffective school learning climates. Our experiences and research indicate strongly that teachers' expectations of students' academic achievement are a major factor in what happens within a school. The following vignettes illustrate this and other aspects of the school learning climate.

"We Are All In This Together"

The George Washington Carver School* is composed predominantly of black, working class children who are achieving well above the state average. On a recent visit, the Carver staff was asked, "How do you account for your success?" Mrs. Johns, an experienced teacher, answered for the staff, "We are all in this together. We have a job to do. If Johnny doesn't learn to read today, we will see to it that he learns to read tomorrow."

This explanation of their effective program summarizes what school learning climate is. It clearly assumes that all students can learn. The staff has accepted the responsibility for teaching them. No one person is responsible; they are all committed to do the job.

"Don't Make Us Look Bad"

A black fifth grade teacher, separated from her husband, moved herself and her three children from Louisiana to Illinois. Her job in a black inner city school had gone well. She had called or visited every parent of her students. Eighty percent of the parents responded that she was the first teacher to communicate positively with them. After a time she began hearing subtle hints about being a "do-gooder" and "apple polisher" from her fellow teachers. When these hints became less subtle, she was forced to start having lunch by herself in her room. It was not long before she was told that "the way it is here is not to make waves, keep the kids quiet with busywork, and read your paper while they copy out of the encyclopedia." She continued her remedial reading work, cooperation with parents and high quality teaching. Results began to show, even though most of her students were far below grade level. Remarks about a woman alone with three children being in a precarious situation

* All names are fictitious.

really shook her up, but she persevered with her teaching efforts. Finally, she was told outright to conform or to expect physical consequences to herself, her family, car, or home. She returned to Louisiana. The learning climate of the school remains unchanged and the achievement level remains extremely low.

This case history portrays starkly the negative sanctions and the power of the social group to set standards and norms for the school. Often if these norms are unprofessional, a good teacher must become a social isolate or finally conform to the negative standards.

"The Lounge Is For Working"

A low income, suburban school composed mainly of Appalachian whites has unusually high achievement; it has an effective learning climate and is a successful school. Observation of the teachers' lounge reveals that this particular school does not have a socially oriented atmosphere among the staff. Rather the teachers use the lounge as a serious work place. Conversations revolve around how to help a student improve his math, how to overcome a problem, or how to implement a new idea successfully. Students are not put down, compared to siblings, or "tagged" with a bad image that precedes them to the next grade. Teachers believe their children can learn and are quite visibly proud of their achievements. The students in the school are industrious, eager, well-behaved, and like to read.

This school is another example of the power of the social group to set standards—in this case highly positive ones. This building also illustrates that behavior in the lounge is often reflective of the overall school learning climate. The true feelings and beliefs about the children and the school are allowed to surface in the informal atmosphere among the staff.

"The Grass Is Greener on the Other Side"

An industrial city in Illinois is split by a river. The east side is low income and minority. A large elementary school is overcrowded (the old mansions of the rich are now subdivided into multiple apartments) and has gone from ninety percent white to eighty percent minority in six years. Many members of the staff are older and have experienced the turnover of student population. The school, formerly a model school, is now low achieving. Comments such as "If I had a class like those kids on the

west side of town, I'd really teach them," or "I've got the top
ability class this year; maybe if I'm lucky I'll have average
achievement," and "These kids' parents just don't care about
them so how can you expect them to learn?" are common. The
low expectations of the staff are reflected in the overall achievement levels.

This last example is a classic case of Ryan's argument in *Blaming the Victim* (1976). The staff has set up a defense
mechanism that projects the cause of failure onto the students
and parents rather than looking at the school learning climate
and at how lowered expectations affect achievement.

These four vignettes are extreme but true examples. Not
all schools have school learning climates as extreme as those
reported here. However, the learning climate unique to each
school does explain much of the achievement outcome.
Because of this relationship, we need to know how to change
the learning climate if we are to raise achievement. In the next
section we will address this issue and suggest some ways to
facilitate change.

Improving School Learning Climate

The nature of the learning climate that characterizes a
school may be affected by many factors, but the adult
staff—principal, teachers, aides and other staff personnel—is
the major determinant of the learning climate in schools. The
norms, beliefs, evaluations, expectations, organization, and
associated instructional practices that characterize a school
vary greatly from one school to another and are highly
associated with variations in students' learning. The adult
members of a school social system are the primary agents in
developing the learning climate which defines the appropriate
behavior for themselves and their students. The teachers and
the principal in a school, not the central administration or
others outside the building, determine the nature of the school
learning environment.

It is precisely because of this fact that the school learning climate and achievement levels in a school can change. What is created by the staff can be changed by the staff. Often, however, change does not come easily. The professional staff must assume the burden of initiating the process. This will require a commitment by the members of the social system to produce high levels of student achievement and to make a collective effort to develop the attitudes, beliefs, and behaviors that characterize effective schools.

If the staff is to be successful in changing the school learning climate, several issues need attention. First, the staff must be made aware of the existence of schools with high achievement and effective learning climates. The awareness must then progress to understanding and application in order to make an impact on achievement. These modules and the framework for implementing an in-service program described in the Introduction provide a way to do this. However, the changes contemplated by a staff should be based on actual needs. This requires assessing the current school learning climate; a thorough study of the results of this assessment can then give a realistic picture of needs, resistance to change, or other factors before a program is undertaken (see Measuring School Learning Climate, this module.)

We know that a school can change if the staff desires to improve or modify beliefs, structures, and instructional practices. Some form of written commitment (e.g., a staff working agreement) will clarify responsibilities and questions about time and effort involved. The principal or delegated instructional leader plays an important role in this process (see Module 3). The program to be implemented must be continually monitored to ensure that the instructional techniques and emphasis are consistent with the effective learning climate of the "ideal" school.

The problems and issues noted here can be managed. But no matter how committed the staff may be, changing norms and attitudes is never easy. In the following sections we suggest strategies to facilitate change. A more detailed treatment of change and resistance to change can be found in Lezotte et al. (1980).

Addressing Negative Attitudes and Behaviors

Our experience suggests that if the school learning climate is to improve, teachers must become more aware of the relationship between daily activities and the level of student achievement. The day-to-day routine is the school learning climate. It is communicated to staff and students in both subtle and direct ways. For example, many school faculties are, unfortunately, characterized by their negative and disparaging remarks about Mary's ability, Billy's family, or Joe's behavior. This tendency varies from school to school but is definitely a reflection of differing school learning climates. Some teachers may defend this behavior as merely "blowing off steam" or expressing frustration, with no harm intended. Our answer to that is, intended or not, this type of atmosphere leads to lower expectations and evaluations of student ability. Additionally, the very fact that there is need to "blow off steam" in one school while another school does not evidence the same frustration is itself a reflection of the differing levels of school learning climate.

Of course, the above example could be expanded to include extended breaks, leaving the classroom excessively, inadequately preparing for class, and the like. We are aware that teachers have many positive as well as negative traits. The point is that, if a school wishes to improve the learning climate and raise achievement, the staff will have to focus and improve on the behaviors and attitudes that retard student achievement, especially in the beginning stages of the change process.

We believe that teachers want to do a good job. Teachers do not intentionally set out to have certain students learn less or to create ineffective school learning climates. However, we sometimes unconsciously behave in ways that can keep some children from learning. We are much more likely to do this when dealing with poor or minority children, regardless of our own background. A major reason is the pervasive belief that low income and/or minority pupils cannot learn well. Many myths, stereotypes, and personal experiences reinforce this belief system. Such factors as personal frustrations in schools, socialization of new teachers by experienced staff, teacher education that emphasizes individual differences in ability, research indicating that family background is the primary determinant of pupil performance and common racial and ethnic stereotypes contribute to this belief. This belief system in turn has the effect of absolving educators of their professional responsibilities to be instructionally effective. (See Persell, 1977, for a review.)

Even when informed of the existence of high-achieving disadvantaged schools, entire faculties or individuals are sometimes highly resistant to suggestions for change or improvement. Fear of failure, unfamiliarity with new programs, staff members' insecurities about personal competency and rejection of research findings are some reasons why change is resisted (see Lezotte et al., 1980, Chapter 5 for further explanation).

This is why it is helpful to approach the process of improving the school learning climate on a collective basis. If the entire staff engages in the change program, the process is less threatening to individuals. Full discussion by the staff should precede any monitoring of the learning climate (see below, The Climate Watchers Process). It may also help to relieve tension and the reluctance to participate if some of this group self-monitoring is done as light-hearted bantering.

The school's responsibility for high achievement for all students raises two other problems with respect to changing local norms. First, what is the individual teacher's responsibility with reference to the building norms and commitment to student achievement? Can a teacher sit back and refuse to join or support others in establishing the collective norm for high achievement? Does a teacher have a responsibility to be a catalyst for improving the building norms? How much risk, in terms of being called a "rate-buster," must the teacher take? Does the responsibility of the teacher end with his or her own class? These are not easy questions. But given the research on the strength of group norms and the effect of school learning climate on student achievement within a building, it becomes very difficult to accept an individualist or isolationist stance. If there are "holdouts"—complacent, noncommitted, or highly skeptical staff members—the rest of the staff may have to ask them to refrain from interfering, keep an open mind on results of the change process, and apply peer pressure to get them to participate.

The importance of conflict over changing norms is illustrated strikingly by feedback from one of the educators who assisted in the preparation of these modules:

> If the analogy of "rate busting" in a unionized production shop is used, this whole question would be more understandable to teachers, particularly teachers in this city. It really needs to be out on the table, so that all parties to the change process know what's coming and can anticipate their roles in "creative conflict." The example you give in this module of the new teacher being forced out because she/he worked too hard is in no way extreme: it is the "norm," in fact. Probably every teacher could come up with a similar story. We are just more polite about it than blue collar workers. Principals get heat, too, for rate busting on achievement.

This comment illustrates the importance of the total staff becoming involved if the chances of successful change are to be increased.

A primary responsibility for school academic achievement falls squarely on the principal. The principal should take the role of instructional leader and change agent in improving the school learning climate. Since the adminstrator is also responsible for the ongoing academic program, there is the very real possibility of role conflict and stress. The principal may be faced with a choice between a stable, happy, but low achieving school and the path of change and improvement with its attendant conflict.

We can envision many instances in which efforts to improve a school may result in conflict. However, the point to be made is that the potential for conflict should be recognized in advance and put "out on the table." In this way, it will be understood as a necessary and valuable part of the change process and any personal reactions will be minimized. The Changing Schools study (Brookover & Lezotte, 1977) found that the schools with rising achievement were often characterized by staff dissension, disagreement, and dissatisfaction, while the schools with declining achievement were marked by complacent and satisfied staff.

On the other hand, not all of the concomitants of change are unpleasant. Change can be challenging and exhilarating. The perils of boredom and teacher burn-out can often be best overcome by involvement in a new program, especially if the rewards include knowing that the students are achieving much better.

The problems of changing norms, staff conflict, and discouraging negative acts or comments by staff members are best placed in the perspective of the purpose or goals of the school. If these processes relate to and reinforce the notion that the overriding purpose of the school is to produce high achievement for all students, then the result is very likely to be positive. When this happens, teaching becomes a deeply satisfying profession.

The Climate Watchers Process

Attitudes and behaviors are not easily changed. Even when an individual wants to change, it is often difficult to dispense with old habits. Yet change that is difficult for the individual is often accomplished with the support of a group that is engaged in a common goal. Various cooperative self-help groups are based on this concept.

The support for this approach to change goes back to the World War II experiments of Kurt Lewin (1952) involving efforts to change the eating and cooking habits of housewives. With the need for prime cuts of meat overseas, groups of women were encouraged to use less traditional parts of the animal (e.g., brains, kidneys, tongue, etc.). Various methods were tried including using university experts, providing demonstrations and lectures, and making visits to individual homes. In the end, the only system that worked well was the institution of a group decision process among women who mutually supported one another, followed by check-ups and monitoring to see if they achieved their goal.

We suggest a Climate Watchers process based on that research and the success of the self-help groups. The norms and beliefs about students that are a part of an ineffective school learning climate will not be easily changed. Beliefs that minority and poor students cannot learn well are deeply embedded in western education and often reinforced by teacher training. Practices such as ability grouping and individualized instruction that result in the sorting and differentiation of students are also based on strongly held beliefs. Attempts by individuals to alter these beliefs and behaviors will very likely result in little or no change for the school as a whole. Suggestions or efforts at change by an individual often result in negative sanctioning pressures from the rest of the staff to conform to existing group standards. (The vignette on the teacher from Louisiana clearly illustrates this principle.)

The Climate Watchers can be set up as a process of supportive interaction to accomplish a common goal; to change negative beliefs and behaviors in the school learning climate into effective norms that support high achievement for all students. The following are essential aspects of this process:

1) Identifying both ineffective and effective attitudes

and behaviors with respect to achievement.

2) Explaining why and how these factors relate to achievement.

3) Creating awareness of the existence of these ineffective behaviors in day-to-day routines and instructional practices.

4) Setting up a regular forum for discussion of these behaviors.

5) Instituting a checking-up procedure among the group to report progress (or lack of it) in changing ineffective behavior.

This type of group process provides the basis for the cooperative peer forces which yield such powerful results in changing behaviors. However, if the Climate Watchers process is to be completely effective, it must also operate at an informal level among the staff members. The informal monitoring of conversations and behavior takes place continously as the staff personnel meet each other in the lounge, the corridor, the office or at lunch. Aspects of this informal part of the Climate Watchers include the following:

1) Climate monitoring becomes a part of the ongoing, daily discussion among members of the school staff.

2) The group becomes aware of the consequences their beliefs, actions, and comments have on school achievement.

3) Staff members mutually discourage undesirable or ineffective attitudes, comments, and behavior and reward effective behavior as it occurs throughout the building.

4) This informal, ongoing monitoring of conversation and behavior also becomes a part of scheduled gatherings such as faculty or grade level meetings or mutual assistance dyads.

The combination of formal meetings for check-in and informal mutual monitoring of the group's behavior is more effective than either by itself. However, getting the informal group dynamics to function on an ongoing basis may be difficult. While the process can be explained and encouraged in the regular formal setting, the actual informal monitoring has a spontaneity that must somehow spark to life by itself. The first step is commitment of the staff to develop an improved learning climate, coupled with agreement to criticize or reward one another spontaneously. Hopefully, the behavior will then become a part of the informal norm.

The key question now becomes, what attitudes and behaviors specifically should be changed? What kinds of questions should the group ask of one another during check-in times and what activities should be monitored informally? Teachers, principal, and others on the staff should discuss such questions as: "What have you done this week to maximize learning for all students?" " What have you done today that might influence the way pupils evaluate themselves?" "Have you said anything that might prejudice another teacher toward a student's performance next year?" "What do remarks in this school indicate about expectations for students' achievement and evaluations of their ability?"

The complete answer to what topics should be monitored is further spelled out in this entire set of modules. Behavior and attitudes that are consistent with an effective school learning climate and effective instruction should be publicly acknowledged. Conversely, behavior which impedes high achievement or reflects negatively on students' ability to learn well should be rebuked. The staff should ensure, however, that praise is contingent on actual improved performance and changes in behavior; a mutual admiration society for continued low achievement or negative attitudes will hinder any improvement. These tough issues must be faced squarely. Failure to do so will, in all likelihood, result in an unimproved school learning climate.

Although a Climate Watchers process can produce powerful incentives for change, it will be much more effective if all the members of the group participate. The tradition of the autonomous teacher, responsible primarily to him/herself with respect to instructional matters, leaves many teachers unwilling to engage in any type of activity which may be perceived as critical of another. This is reinforced by the general reluctance to openly criticize another person in any setting. Because of these factors, we need to be aware of a possible reluctance or self-consciousness about joining in these activities. Reluctance may be reduced if the need for change and collaborative action are introduced and reinforced in the context of increased achievement and school improvement. Few professionals can be opposed to these goals.

Measuring School Learning Climate

The primary factor to consider when measuring the school learning climate is the achievement level in the building. If achievement is low, the learning climate is ineffective. However, building and classroom test results provide only a global indication of the level of the learning climate. Although these results, interpreted in terms of the learning climate, give an idea of how much improvement is needed, more precise instruments are necessary in order to know why a school learning climate is ineffective.

On the other hand, we should not downplay the amount of information that can be obtained from various test data. In Module 10, we discuss the use of assessment data to improve classroom instruction and the overall building program. Here we simply stress that student achievement results may be the only available source of information about the learning climate in a classroom or school. This is particularly true if an individual or small group of teachers is attempting to implement this program independently.

Assessment of both the current state of a school's learning climate and the changes that occur in that climate are desirable. The initial assessment provides diagnostic information about the three clusters of characteristics that describe the learning climate of the school. Based on the diagnosis, the school learning climate program can then be used to prescribe for improvement of those areas identified. It is then possible to determine the degree to which the needed changes in the school learning climate are being implemented. Hall and Loucks (1977) found that the level of use (LoU) of an innovation that had been "adopted" ranged from incorrect or no use at all to complete and correct implementation, with most schools somewhere in between. The periodic assessment of both the current learning climate and the level of use of the program designed to improve it will enhance the effectiveness of the program.[1]

Summary

Our studies, along with those of Dr. Benjamin Bloom and many other researchers, provide strong evidence that the academic failures common in low income and/or minority schools need not occur. Unfortunately, the social system of most low achieving schools is designed to accept failure. We should discard our belief in the inevitability of the normal or bell-shaped curve, which is used to justify differentiating and sorting students so that many fail. Instead, if we substituted the concept of the "J" curve (Allport, 1934), with its assumptions that nearly all can and will learn, we could then develop a mastery model of instruction in which the results would conform to those high expectations. We would foster and have an effective school learning climate that insures, or at least makes probable, mastery of minimum reading and math competencies. Adoption of this position does not mean we must ignore some hard realities of education. In fact, there may be some community and peer group norms and some economic facts of life that are contradictory to high academic achievement in low

[1]Instruments are being developed to assess the nature of a school's learning climate and the level of implementation of the school learning climate changes proposed in these modules. These assessment instruments should be available in 1982.

income and minority areas. However, there are also some norms in these communities that are more supportive of high achievement than some of those of higher income all-white communities. Furthermore, there is no evidence to show that negative community factors, where they exist, must result in low achievement in school.

As professionals we should stop trying to use a student's home environment or social status as an excuse for poor academic achievement. Instead, we should help our peers and our public to understand the real importance of the school social system, the classroom environment and our own teaching activities. As teachers we must recognize that high achieving, economically disadvantaged schools are living proof that poor children can be educated to high levels of achievement. We should get on with the business of creating classroom environments and school learning climates that promote high achievement.

Suggested Activities

1. Develop two written statements for your school:
    a. Statement of Purpose and Beliefs
    b. School Achievement Plan

As these documents should represent the position of the school staff, involvement of both teachers and the principal in developing them is essential. Both documents should be consistent with the concepts of effective school learning climate outlined in this module.

The statement of Purpose and Beliefs should reflect the major position of the staff on the mission of the school in maximizing the achievement of all students in the school. The School Achievement Plan identifies the building approach to instruction for staff and students.

It is suggested that a format of short, capsule statements be used instead of a lengthy narrative style.

Both documents should be informative, but concise, as they are working guidelines for making educational decisions. Examples of such documents follow.

1a. Suggested Statement of Purpose and Beliefs

(1) The purpose of the school is to educate all students to high levels of academic performance.

(2) To fulfill this purpose, the members of this school staff believe:

  (a) All students should have a challenging academic program.

  (b) All students should master their grade level objectives.

  (c) Teachers are obligated to prepare all students to perform at mastery level on the objectives for the grade.

  (d) Parents should understand the academic goals of the school and support their child and the teacher's efforts to reach those goals.

1b. Suggested School Achievement Plan
(Identify and Assess Achievement Objectives)

(1) Learning objectives to be mastered will be identified for each grade level.

(2) A standard for mastery performance for the school will be set by the staff each year and explained to students and parents. (See Module 3)

(3) Formal assessment of academic progress for all students will be conducted as follows:

  (a) Pretest at the beginning of the course.

  (b) Quarterly tests.

  (c) Posttest at the end of the course.

(4) Progress reports will be sent to parents following each

formal assessment of student learning.

(5) The teacher will certify at the end of the course that each student has or has not achieved according to the established standard for mastery. A copy of the certification will be sent to each student's parent(s) or guardian(s).

(6) To meet the school standard for mastery, it is expected that

   (a) Teachers will organize and conduct instruction so that mastery performance is possible for all students.

   (b) Students will exert whatever effort is necessary to learn their objectives.

   (c) Parents will support and assist their child's efforts to learn the objectives of the grade.

2. Document Student Achievement

The practice of certifying student achievement is consistent with the expectation that students will achieve at high levels. It is the logical consequence of setting performance standards. The purpose of certification of performance is to officially establish that a student has, or has not, achieved according to the expected standard for the grade.

The following guidelines are suggested:

   a. The course posttest or comprehensive test is the primary instrument for certification as it requires the student to demonstrate understanding of the entire course.

   b . When a student achieves the standard of mastery established for his/her grade level, the teacher can indicate this on a Certificate of Academic Performance. Conversely, if the standard of mastery is not attained, the teacher can indicate this as well, as illustrated in the example certificate.

   c. If the teacher feels that certain test results do not

accurately reflect the student's understanding of the objectives for the grade, the teacher can use other data for certification—if it is objective and verifiable.

d. The teacher should make a genuine effort to inform parents about the student's success, or lack of success, in meeting the standard for mastery in the subjects specified. A copy of the Certificate of Academic Performance should be sent home.

e. Records of certification should be available when a student goes to a new teacher or to a new school. A copy of the Certificate of Academic Performance should be included in the student's cumulative file.

Illustrative
Certificate of Academic Performance

The Standard of Mastery established for students of _____ School for 1981-82 is as follows:

Each student is expected to master _____ % of the official objectives for the grade in reading and mathematics.

★ ★
★ ★ ★
★ ★ ★ ★
★ ★ ★ ★ ★
★ ★ ★ ★ ★ ★
★ ★ ★ ★

_____   _____
(Student)   (Grade)

Mastery of _____ % of the grade level objectives for 1981-82 *was achieved in*

_____ Reading   _____ Mathematics

Mastery of _____ % of the grade level objectives for 1981-82 *was not achieved in*

_____ *Reading*   _____ *Mathematics*

_____   _____
(Teacher Signature)   *(Date)*

3.   Teachers and administrators of the school should complete their respective forms of the *School Learning Climate Assessment Instrument.* This is designed to produce a profile of strengths and deficiencies of the school's learning climate. (Available 1982.) The results of the learning climate assessment should be compiled focusing on the areas that need improvement. These results should be distributed to and discussed with the whole staff. The deficiencies identified in the school profile represent the areas of greatest concern and should be targeted for special emphasis for the year.

4.   Set Priorities: Don't try to change too many things at once as this can be overwhelming and defeating. Instead, list the areas requiring change or attention and then prioritize them:

   a. Needs immediate attention
   b. Complete by the end of this year
   c. Work on next year
   d. Needs further study or clarification

Reach consensus on a realistic, but challenging, program of change for the building.

5.   Create a "Climate Watchers" process. Essentially, this is a way to encourage the total building staff to publicly monitor itself so the beliefs, attitudes, and behaviors associated with effective school learning climate can become standard operating procedure. The climate watchers function should operate at both the formal and informal levels of school organization. The formal use of Climate Watchers occurs in meetings that are already held on a regular basis, usually the biweekly grade/departmental meeting. Climate Watchers becomes a fixed part of agenda for each meeting. A single topic/concern that has been identified by the group should be discussed. It is recommended that a topic/concern for discussion at the next meeting be identified at the current session. This allows time for staff consideration, preparation, or trial

of new practices. It is also recommended that one person in the group assume responsibility for overseeing the climate watchers function at each meeting. This involves leading the discussion and seeing that a topic/concern is established for the next meeting's agenda.

6. An important feature of each climate watcher session is the "check in" time where all members of the group report their success or lack of success in adopting or dealing with the topic/concern of the last meeting. Establish the expectation that all members will report at each meeting—not just those who volunteer. Positive reinforcement should be expressed often to encourage individual efforts. Also, negative sanctions should occur naturally as called for.

The staff must also spontaneously develop the mutual monitoring of daily behavior on an informal basis. Informal, continuous checking-up will increase awareness of unconscious remarks and practices that are contrary to an effective school learning climate. In order to help institute and support this informal climate watching, the staff should also discuss at the formal climate watchers sessions the extent to which the staff is monitoring one another on an ongoing basis, with the goal of increasing the extent of this informal process. Only when the informal process has become an accepted and regular part of the group norms will the climate watchers reach maximum effectiveness.

7. At meetings, use the vignettes from the module to generate staff discussion about factors that contribute to good or poor school learning climate. Encourage faculty to identify not only deficiencies or problems, but also suggestions for improvements. Also, sharing individual experiences involving the learning climate from working in other schools will add meaning to the discussion.

Additional Resources

Bloom, B. S. *Human characteristics and school learning.* New York: McGraw-Hill, 1976.

Annotated in Introduction.

Brookover, W., Beady, C., Flood, P., Schweitzer, J., & Wisenbaker, J. *School Social Systems and Student achievement: Schools can make a difference.* South Hadley, MA: J. F. Bergin Co., distributed by Praeger Publishers, New York, 1979.

Annotated in Introduction.

Brookover, W. B., & Lezotte, L. W. *Changes in school characteristics coincident with changes in student achievement* . East Lansing: Institute For Research on Teaching, Michigan State University, 1977.

Known as the Changing Schools study, 6 schools which are improving and 2 schools which are declining on the Michigan statewide assessment test over a three year period are described. Improving schools have higher expectations and evaluations of students and are much more goal focused on achievement for all students than declining schools.

Brookover, W. B., & Schneider, J. Academic environments and elementary school achievement. *Journal of Research and Development in Education,* 1975, *9,* 83-91.

This study analyzes 12 pairs of high and low achieving schools which are matched for SES, race, and rural-urban characteristics. Differences in school learning climate accounted for most of the high to low variance in achievement between the matched pairs of schools.

Coleman, J., Campbell, E., Hobson, C., McPartland, J., Mood, A., Weinfeld, F., & York, R. *Equality of educational opportunity.* Washington, D.C.: U.S. Government Printing Office, 1966.

Commonly known as the Coleman Report, this massive study of the American schools was commissioned by the Civil Rights Act of 1964. Its major conclusion was that schools have little influence on achievement that is independent of family background and social class.

Edmonds, R. R. Some schools work and more can. *Social Policy,* 1979, *9,* 28-32.

In a concise review of the research on effective schools, the author stresses that political and attitude considerations, rather than limited understanding of successful schools, prevents our society from having equitable schooling for the poor and minorities.

Hoover, M. R. Characteristics of black schools at grade level: A description. *The Reading Teacher,* 1978, *31,* 757-762.

This study contains a notable listing of reasons—blaming the student or parents and blaming the system—that most educators give to rationalize why they cannot teach minority students to read well. Successful schools reject those excuses and commit themselves to teaching all pupils to read well.

Lezotte, L. W., Hathaway, D. V., Miller, S. K., Passalacqua, J., & Brookover, W. B. *School learning climate and student achievement: A social systems approach to increased student learning.* Tallahassee, Florida: National Teacher Corps, Florida State University Foundation, 1980.

Further annotated in the Introduction, this monograph contains both an extensive review of the literature on school learning climate and more detailed Annotated Bibliography than is provided in these modules.

Persell, C. H. *Education and inequality: The roots and results of stratification in America's schools.* New York: The Free Press, 1977.

This is an extremely well-written review and analysis of the inequalities of social class and education in America.

Phi Delta Kappa. *Why do some urban schools succeed? The Phi Delta Kappa study of exceptional urban elementary schools.* Bloomington, Ind.: Phi Delta Kappa, 1980.

This work contains case studies of 8 atypically successful schools and an extensive review of the literature on effective schools.

Rutter, M., Maughan, B., Mortimore, P., Ouston, J., with Smith, A. *Fifteen thousand hours: Secondary schools and their effects on children.* Cambridge, Mass.: Harvard University Press, 1979.

In a longitudinal study of 12 inner city high schools in London, differences in school outcomes cannot be attributed to the characteristics of entering students. Rather, the overall school ethos, composed of educational practices and beliefs controlled by the staff, accounts for the variance.

Walberg, H. J. (Ed.). *Educational environments and their effects: Evaluation, policy, and productivity.* Berkeley, Cal.: McCutchan Publishing Corp., 1979.

This book of readings is an excellent source on the effects of environments in the home, school, and larger society on educational outcomes.

Weber, G. *Inner City children can be taught to read: Four successful schools* (Occasional Paper No. 18). Washington, D.C.: Council for Basic Education, 1971.

This case study of 4 successful, low income and minority elementary schools was the prototype of research to disprove the belief that schools do not make a difference. Weber's findings are detailed in Lezotte et al. (1980).

Module 2

Expectations For Learning

- Teacher Expectations and School Learning Climate
- The Self-Fulfilling Prophecy
- Improving Expectations and Student Learning Climate
- Suggested Activities
- Additional Resources

What teachers expect, students are likely to learn. That, briefly stated, is the essence of the importance of teacher expectations, commonly known as the self-fulfilling prophecy. Teacher expectations constitute a major part of the adult influence in setting the learning climate in a school. While we as educators commonly talk about teacher expectations and self-fulfilling prophecies, seldom do we realize the true extent to which our attitudes and behaviors, both directly and indirectly, influence our students. The processes by which expectations are formed and transmitted to pupils are largely unconscious, becoming a part of the school learning climate. Despite the unawareness of their actions and beliefs, teachers send strong messages to students concerning appropriate behavior, levels of expected achievement, and evaluations of student ability. The same beliefs also unconsciously affect teachers themselves with respect to their levels of expectations for students and evaluations of students' abilities to learn.

This module explores the relationship between teachers' evaluation and expectations and the learning climate created for the students. In the first part of the module, interactions between the two major groups within the school—the adult staff and the student body—are explained. The school learning climate reflects the influence of teachers' evaluations and expectations; it also reflects student perceptions of those evaluations and achievement expectations. In the second part of the module, we address the process by which teacher expectations become self-fulfilling prophecies. By understanding this process, teachers should be able to avoid the formation of negative self-fulfilling prophecies. Finally, some specific suggestions for improving the students' learning climate are given. These involve increasing students' motivation by reducing students' sense of academic futility.

Teacher Expectations and School Learning Climate

In the first module, we indicated that the adult staff of the school is the primary determinant of the school learning climate. The key to this statement is in the influence of teacher expectations—not only on the beliefs of faculty—but also on the way students behave toward one another and toward themselves.

The social system of the school is composed of various staff and student groups, each with its own rules, values and standards of behavior. There may also be subgroups or cliques within these groups, such as teacher bowling teams, student friendship circles, athletes, or band members. These groups interact with one another to produce the total school learning climate. Within a given school, these groups have somewhat unique characteristics and influence, thus accounting for differences in learning climates from school to school.

The amount of emphasis on academic work is not the same from one school to the next. However, the staff has the primary influence in setting the attitudes of various student groups in a school with regard to the appropriate norms for learning: how much time for studying, how much work is assigned, how many students are thought capable of learning well, how to behave, etc. One of the major factors in assessing the importance of academic concerns, as opposed to competing interests such as sports, boy-girl relations, faculty parties, or the latest gossip, is the emphasis put on learning and achievement. This emphasis is shaped primarily by the adult staff.

Among professional staff members, factors such as the level of expectations of achievement, percent of students expected to finish high school, number of students believed to be capable of going to college, and the like, are all related to the accepted purpose of the school. For example, if the purpose of a given school is social control rather than educational excellence, the achievement expectations and academic norms may be displaced or lowered.

Similarly, students' attitudes toward learning are related to the accepted purpose and academic standards as set by the adult staff. Students' perceptions of expected academic performance come primarily from the standards and cues provided by the staff. Students are also judged by their peers, who utilize many factors other than academics in the formation of social groupings and prestige rankings. Popularity, athletics, music, dating, cars, and even drugs are some important criteria. But much of the basis of the social comparison of peers still comes from success or failure as a student. There is evidence that various social judgments become more important as students' academic success declines (Faunce, 1979). In other words, students are aware that they go to school to learn. When students are not successful in that endeavor, or when academic work seems unrelated to current and future goals, students turn to other pursuits that meet their need for recognition.

Influence of Teacher Expectations on Student Achievement

The strong influence of the adult staff in setting appropriate levels of teacher expectations, evaluations of student ability, and even standards of achievement can be seen if we investigate the relationship between these aspects of the school learning climate and achievement. Teacher expectations and evaluations of students' ability—present and future— are doubly linked to achievement (Brookover et al., 1979).

First, teacher expectations and evaluations are directly linked to achievement through differing amounts of instruction, time spent interacting with students, quality of materials, etc. In short, high expectations produce more and better instruction; low expectations result in less instruction and attention. This difference in amount and quality of education and its impact on student achievement has been documented by many researchers (e.g., Brophy & Good, 1974; Finn, 1972; Rist, 1970). An analysis of how these expectations are transmitted to students is the essence of the self-fulfilling prophecy which is addressed later in this module.

Second, teacher expectations are indirectly linked to achievement through student learning climate characteristics. We must stress here that the term "student learning climate," is used only for convenience. The student learning climate is a part of the overall school learning climate. The norms, expectations, and attitudes that students hold come from their perceptions of what is appropriate in a given social setting. Thus, in a school, students' perceptions of teacher expectations and evaluations link these teacher characteristics to student academic norms, student sense of academic futility and student self-concept of academic ability. Teacher expectations and evaluations influence these student characteristics which are in turn highly related to achievement. The Brookover et al. (1979) study shows that one aspect of the student learning climate—student sense of academic futility— accounts for more than half of the variation in achievement. However, teacher expectations and evaluations are directly associated with student sense of futility. Thus the indirect influence of teacher beliefs and behaviors, through student sense of futility and other aspects of student learning climate, may last long after contact between teacher and students has ended and completes the double link to achievement.

Student Learning Climate and Achievement

Three major aspects of the student learning climate are student academic norms, student self-concept of academic ability, and student sense of academic futility. Each one is influenced by teacher expectations; their levels vary from school to school as a part of the effective and ineffective aspects of the learning climate. All are related to achievement and will be described in turn.

The particular feelings and attitudes of students toward learning differ from school to school. Appropriate behavior with respect to academics is defined by group norms among students. Within the school, some variation from the overall norms occurs in the various social cliques and friendship circles. These student academic norms include prevailing standards for emphasis on grades, amount of time devoted to homework and the importance of academic work compared to non-academic activities. These variations in academic norms are related to achievement and are in turn influenced by teacher expectations.

Numerous studies have shown that student self-concept of academic ability is related to achievement. Self-concept of academic ability apparently functions in a necessary but insufficient manner. A certain amount of confidence and belief in one's ability to perform is necessary. Most students with low academic self-concepts are low achieving. But a high academic self-concept is not sufficient for high achievement; some students with high academic self-concepts do not achieve well. In general the student's confidence in his or her ability to succeed in school is related to past experiences in school and to teachers' expectations for achievement. This perception of teacher expectations is a strong factor in the child's belief in his/her ability to be successful academically.

An aspect of student learning climate which is strongly related to achievement is students' sense of academic futility. Academic futility reflects a sense of hopelessness; high futility means that students experience strong feelings that the system is stacked against them, that no one cares about them, that they have to be lucky to succeed, that no matter what they do they cannot overcome racism, poverty, etc. Schools which have high levels of student futility have low achievement. Schools which are low in sense of futility generally have high achievement. This sense of hopelessness may be associated with a high student academic self-concept (as has been recently observed among certain categories of minority students). This apparent contradiction can be explained by the rationale, "I know I've got low grades and don't do well in school, but it's not my fault; I could do it, but the system keeps me down." Here we see one important factor in addition to a high academic self-concept that is necessary for high achievement; students have to not only believe in themselves, but also believe that their efforts can make a difference in school and later in life.

In this section we have stressed the impact of teacher expectations and evaluations of students' ability on the three aspects of the student learning climate. The importance of teacher expectations and evaluations can also be seen in other ways. First, teachers' expectations have greater influence on low income and/or minority students than on middle class students (Brookover et al., 1979). Second, parents' expectations and evaluations also influence their children. We speculate that well-meaning teachers sometimes influence lower or working class parents by "cooling out" parents' higher aspirations for their children (getting the parents to accept the "reality" of low status future for their children). Thus indirectly, teachers might have the effect of reducing disadvantaged parents' expectations and evaluations of their children.

It is important to remember that academic norms, levels of academic self-concept, and level of academic futility vary from school to school. These student learning climate characteristics appear to be major factors in the level of student learning. Climate characteristics can change and through this it is possible to improve motivation. Some strategies for improving motivation by changing student climate, especially levels of futility, are suggested in the last section of this module.

The Self-Fulfilling Prophecy

In the study of *Pygmalion in the Classroom,* Rosenthal and Jacobson (1968) concluded that the IQ scores of certain students, who had been earmarked by the researchers as academic "bloomers," went up more than scores of other students in the class. These students actually were not "bloomers," at all, but had been randomly selected. Their IQ's apparently went up because their teachers thought they were brighter and treated them as special.

Although the original Pygmalion study has been severely criticized on methodological grounds, massive amounts of evidence have been compiled recently testing this question: Does the level of teacher expectations influence the level of student achievement, i.e., do high expectations produce high achievement and low expectations produce low achievement? The answer, based on extensive research, is a clear-cut "yes." (Two excellent reviews of the literature are Brophy & Good, 1974; Persell, 1977, chapters 7 & 8).

Educators need to be aware of the specific mechanisms by

which the self-fulfilling prophecy is transmitted. Knowing this, teachers can consciously change their behavior to avoid transmitting lower expectations which in turn affect achievement.

General Perspectives

The "self-fulfilling prophecy" may be defined as a process in which an unsubstantiated judgment or evaluation (of a person, situations, etc.) is treated as though it were absolute fact. Subsequent actions are based on the distorted evaluation. The confirming behavior in turn convinces the person making the distorted judgment that his/her original assessment was correct. In education, a typical example of this process is a teacher's assessment of a student's ability as low. Because of this assessment, the student is given lower level instruction than appropriate. The student performs poorly on subsequent testing compared to students taught at a higher level. This confirms the original false diagnosis of ability.

Several generalizations regarding the self-fulfilling prophecy are given below. In any given case, some or all of the following may apply:

1. Self-fulfilling prophecies have two parts—the prophecy or false assessment and the process by which the false prophecy is brought about (Brameld, 1972).

2. Both the false assessment and the mechanism by which it is brought about are done unconsciously. Because of this, self-fulfilling prophecies can be difficult to end or discover.

3. The distorted assessment often occurs because of prejudice or some stereotype (usually of such a subtle nature that the person is not aware of it.)

4. Self-fulfilling prophecies can operate at the group level and/or the individual level. In education, the individual, a whole class, whole tracks, and often the entire school may be a victim.

5. Self-fulfilling prophecies usually result from small but consistent effects, leading to cumulative results. Thus over time, the effects build up with later distorted judgments based on earlier ones. Finn (1972) suggests that forces in society and schools which cause differentiation and evaluation are so strong that it may be impossible to get a true assessment of ability, uninfluenced by the process of judging and treating persons based on those judgments. This is especially true because the process starts in infancy. In other words, what we perceive and measure as ability or aptitude may in reality be cumulative, long term effects of self-fulfilling prophecies.

6. Bloom (1976) suggests that almost all students are capable of achieving age-grade level objectives. This implies that many students are being assessed below their potential abilities. Crano and Mellon (1978) and Rist (1970) provide strong evidence that students conform to the level of expectations that teachers set.

7. Because of the difficulties noted above, it is better to err on the positive than on the negative side when judging students.

8. Merton (1957) suggests one more way in which the self-fulfilling prophecy is maintained. By using a "double standard," behavior that is judged as a virtue for the in-group is judged as a vice for the out-group. For example, it is common stereotype that minority members are spendthrift status seekers when they drive a Cadillac, yet the same Cadillac is a mark of prestige for white persons.

With this general background, we can now turn to why teachers have distorted expectations for and assessments of particular types of students.

Sources of and Reasons for Teacher Expectations

This section will briefly present what Persell (1977) calls the genesis of teacher expectations (see also Braun, 1973; Brophy & Good, 1974). Persell gives four major sources of teachers' predispositions to certain expectations for students:

1. Certain personality traits of teachers;
2. Societal prejudices and socializing experiences both in the wider community and within the school;
3. Educational concepts and beliefs such as IQ or cultural deficits; and
4. Educational structures such as grouping practices or testing programs.

Our own experience suggests that the learned, socialized norms of a particular school's learning climate are an important factor in establishing teachers' perceptions of students' abilities. Teachers are strongly influenced by the accepted beliefs and practices in the school where they work.

Brophy & Good (1974) suggest that teachers' affective responses to pupils are another important source of teacher expectations. The key here is whether students' responses are rewarding to or punishing to the teacher's sense of competence or accomplishment. Student behavior which is achievement oriented, dependent, and compliant is rewarding to teachers. This type of behavior meets the needs of teachers for classroom control and is consistent with most teachers' ideal student. On the other hand, independent, creative, or unruly students do not meet most teachers' needs for success. Teachers often have low expectations for the latter. These expectations develop independent of the students' actual learning potential. Many researchers (e.g., Bowles & Gentis, 1977; Crano & Mellon, 1978) suggest that the major source of academic expectations is the social characteristics of students.

In addition to the general factors noted above, there are many specific cues which teachers utilize to assess students' ability. These cues are often drawn from the appearance and identity of a student and have no relation to the students' learning potential. Yet educators sometimes use such cues as dress, grooming, language or family identification as indicators of students' learning ability. All educators need to be aware of the possible biasing effect of such cues in forming lower expectations.

The following list of factors, which have been identified as sources of bias by many researchers, are taken from the reviews of Brophy & Good (1974) and Persell (1977). Lowered academic expectations are associated with the items as described. Thus teachers should guard against lowered expectations due to:

1. Sex—lower expectations for elementary boys and for older girls. This is a function of beliefs about boys' slower maturation and sex role discrimination for older girls;

2. SES—lower expectations for lower SES (including level of parental education, types of jobs held, place of residence, etc);

3. Race—lower expectations for minority status;

4. Test scores, permanent records—belief in "fixed ability" precludes possibility of improvement and higher expectations;

5. Negative comments about students—lounge talk, other teachers' or principal's evaluation result in lower expectations;

6. Type of school—rural, inner city, or suburban—the first two are associated with lower expectations;

7. Appearance—lower expectations associated with clothes or grooming that are out of style, cheaper material, etc.

8. Oral language patterns—negative cues from any non-standard English result in lower expectations;

9. Neatness—lower expectations associated with general disorganization, poor handwriting, etc.;
10. Halo effect—tendency to label a child's overall ability based on one characteristic (e.g., poor behavior becomes the basis of overall negative evaluation);
11. Readiness—negative effects of assuming that maturation rates or prior lack of knowledge or experience are unchanging phenomena, thus precluding improvement;
12. Seating position—lower expectations for sides and back of classroom;
13. Socialization by experienced teachers—tendency to stress limitations of students for new teachers;
14. Student behavior—lower academic expectations for students with poor behavior;
15. Teacher training institutions—perpetuation of myths and ideologies of individual limitations of students results in lower expectations;
16. Teacher education textbooks—same as #15 above.
17. Tracking or grouping—labeling effects and a tendency to accentuate differences between students result in lower expectations.

In addition to knowing the sources of biased expectations, we also need to be aware of the ways in which teachers' expectations are transmitted to students. These are described in the next section.

How Expectations Are Transmitted

Earlier we suggested that the self-fulfilling prophecy is transmitted by use of differing amounts of instruction, based on different levels of teachers' expectations, and by using a double standard to judge the same behavior in different ways. In this section we will list specific classroom behaviors by which teachers communicate certain expectations to classes or particular students. Unless otherwise indicated, the following are instances of decreased amount of instruction (i.e., fewer opportunities, less time-on-task, etc., associated with lower expectations). These studies reveal that teachers are unaware of the differences in how they react to various students or classes. Teachers are also largely unaware of how they are affected by different norms from school to school. Again these factors come primarily from Brophy and Good (1974) and Persell (1977).

Thus lower expectations result in reduction of teachers' activities in relation to:

1. Amount and quality of praise for correct answers;
2. Actual amount of teaching students receive;
3. Content covered;
4. Response opportunity factor—
   a) number of times students are called on
   b) extent to which the question is challenging;
   c) degree of cognitive demands;
5. Academic content (and more non-academic activities)
6. Verbal and non-verbal warmth and acceptance of the student in general (see #7 - 10 below);
7. Non-verbal cues—amount of
   a) eye contact;
   b) forward lean;
   c) affirmative head nods;
   d) smiles;
   e) physical contact (e.g., pat on shoulder, hugs);
8. General encouragement and support;
9. Teacher assistance and willingness to help;
10. Wait time (the amount of time a student is given to respond to a question before the teacher gives the answer or moves on to another student);
11. High academic evaluations—reflected by percent of students expected to:

a) master skills;
b) complete high school or attend college;
c) do A or B work;

12. Reinstruction of students in failure situations (i.e., probing, restating questions, giving hints, etc., until student arrives at correct answer);

13. Evaluative feedback and constructive criticism of school work;

14. Academically oriented teacher role definitions (i.e., lower expectations are associated with the belief that social control or other non-academic goals are the appropriate teacher objectives).

In addition, lower expectations tend to result in increased incidences of:

1. Actual negative comments or negative expressions about the student (increased occurrence);

2. Harshness and punitiveness of discipline techniques;

3. Rewarding or praising incorrect answers (see the Module on Reinforcement for further explanation of this);

4. Rewarding inappropriate behavior. (This and #3 above both communicate to the student the teacher's belief that the student is unable to respond appropriately and so must be praised for inappropriate work or behavior).

In addition, the double standard of responding differently to the same behavior from different students can be seen in the punishing responses of teachers directed at students who depart from teachers' expectations (Brophy & Good, 1974). This is directed primarily at minority or "slow" students who sometimes do better than the teacher has predicted. This is an effective censuring device that reinforces original negative expectations.

We should add that not all students are equally susceptible to selffulfilling prophecies. The extent to which students are influenced by teachers is related to the importance of the teacher as a significant other (an influential individual for a person) to students. Thus such factors as the student's age, the extent of peer affiliation, the degree to which the teacher is respected, community values, and the prevailing learning climate in a school all affect the degree of influence of a teacher. But regardless of this variation, the cumulative effect of teacher expectations on student learning is considerable. Since most educators are largely unaware of the lowered expectations that result in different instruction and lower achievement, the need for examining our behavior for possible biasing actions is great.

Throughout this module we have stressed the negative effects of lowered expectations. But teacher expectations can also have positive effects. In the last section we will suggest strategies for raising achievement through higher expectations.

Improving Expectations And Student Learning Climate

We noted earlier that there is a double link between teachers' expectations and student achievement. The direct link focuses on the teachers role in "creating" poor student performance through a series of behaviors which reflect their low expectations of students. Thus a teacher may be directly responsible for lower levels of student achievement when that teacher reduces the instructional time, and/or restricts the academic material because of low expectations. The indirect link refers to the students' role in making the self-fulfilling prophecy a reality. Some students perceive not only that particular teachers do not expect them to learn well but that success in their school system is not likely for students "like them." A student learning climate develops in which students come to expect the same poor achievement and behavioral results from themselves as the teachers evidently expect from them. This student perception of the school system as one which precludes their academic success, in spite of their efforts to achieve, represents the indirect link between teacher expectations and achievement.

The most obvious strategy for improving student self evaluations and reducing feelings of futility is to establish a positive self-fulfilling prophecy instead of a negative one. This involves raising the expectations for all students and especially poor or minority pupils for whom lowered expectations have been too often the case. For example, setting performance standards and expecting all students to master their age-grade level objectives clearly says to students, "You can learn and we'll see that you do learn." This also involves ensuring that the various sources of negative bias and possible means of transmitting those false judgments, described in this module, are not allowed to operate. Successfully implementing this strategy will mean an increase in the actual amount and quality of teaching for many students. The instructional practices reviewed in the remainder of this set of modules should facilitate this goal.

Some of the changes that will assist in improving the student learning climate may be summarized as follows:

1. *Raise teacher expectations and evaluations of students.* Teacher expectations influence students' perceptions of all three aspects of student climate, through the influence of the overall school learning climate and the more direct teacher-student interactions.

2. *Communicate the high teacher expectations and evaluations to all students.* Students are not likely to have low self-concepts of ability and a high sense of futility if teachers often communicate to them that they are able to learn and are expected to learn.

3. *Establish an instructional program that makes operative the high expectations for all students.* High expectations alone do not produce learning. Skills and knowledge are acquired through the teaching-

learning process. The acquisition of desired skills and knowledge demonstrates that it is possible for students to learn and that the school is committed to teaching them.

Evidence that student achievement is highly related to the expectations teachers hold for students, and the evaluations they make of students ability, is extensive and consistent. Students come to see themselves as others see them and teachers adapt their instruction to the level of expectations held for students. If little is expected and little is taught students develop feelings of hopelessness or futility in the school.

Summary

This module has investigated the relation between teachers' expectations, student perceptions of the expectations and evaluations, and student achievement. Teacher expectations are a part of a web of interacting relationships between the staff and students within the overall school learning climate. The importance of teacher expectations and evaluations of students is seen in the double link to achievement—a direct link through the self-fulfilling prophecy and an indirect link through students' self-concepts of their ability and their sense of academic futility.

The self-fulfilling prophecy is an unconscious process in which a false estimate of ability is acted upon as though it were true. This results in behavior, by the person evaluated, which conforms to the original distorted judgment, thus confirming the original judgment in the eyes of the person who made it. Different amounts of instruction, which correspond to the level of teacher expectations, and a double standard, in which the same behavior is judged positively for the favored and negatively for the disfavored, are the primary means by which self-fulfilling prophecies are carried out. Educators often are unaware of the degree to which false assessments are made, of teachers' sources of bias, and of the ways in which teacher expectations are transmitted to students. This module reviewed how those differing expectations are formed and transmitted to students.

Suggested Activites

1. The faculty should view the CBS (*60 Minutes*) film "Marva," which depicts a black teacher's private school in which students learn high-level classic literature (e.g., Shakespeare, Chaucer) as well as other basics. The students came from inner city public schools in Chicago where they were previously failing and had the usual negative attitudes about school. Yet these same students are now reading and writing far above grade level under Marva Collins' teaching.

    Discuss this film in terms of the learning climate in Marva's school. What are Marva's attitudes and expectations for her performance? For her students? Now compare that to your own school. What can be done to change you or your school?

2. View the film "Eye of the Storm" which depicts the blue eye, brown eye experiment on discrimination among third graders. The faculty should discuss the effects of discrimination in terms of expectations for learning: What are the effects over time? What factors are the focus of discrimination in real life? How do teachers and other adults transmit these cues to students? How do other students transmit cues? Where and how do students pick up on differences?

3. Use group problem solving to deal with issues of poor or negative expectations related to students, staff, parents, or the community. Topics of this kind should be brought up at whole staff meetings or the biweekly grade/departmental meeting. Dealing with

the problem or issue, not the individual, is generally the best approach. However, in some cases, identifying the person(s) is appropriate and effective for solving a problem, provided the discussion, remarks, and suggestions are kept objective and constructive. (Refer to the Climate Watchers process and the section on addressing negative behavior in Module 1.)
For example, a teacher may need help in understanding what can be done to counteract examples of negative self-concept displayed by students in his/her class. The group should try to suggest specific actions or strategies for attacking the problem. One suggestion might be for the teacher to try to eliminate negative cues that pupils receive from teachers, parents, and other students. Further suggestions for how to do this should come from the group. In this instance, increasing the academic proficiency of students through frequent success experiences would be a good start. Building self-esteem without effective instruction and remediation of skill deficits is *not* the answer.

4. Teachers are encouraged to get feedback on their classroom behavior to see if they are unconsciously communicating different levels of expectations to students. This can be done by an individual teacher using a tape recorder to record classroom remarks. Replaying the tape will be informative and can be done privately. Also, having another teacher observe your class for this purpose is encouraged.

5. The faculty should attempt to implement the strategies to improve student learning climate described in this module. If possible, some measure(s) of the student learning climate (e.g., tardiness, absenteeism, attendance on the day of a test, informal surveys of student attitudes, levels of motivation, amount of scapegoating, etc.) should be taken before and after the program to determine its effectiveness.

This is especially appropriate for junior high or secondary level students.

Additional Resources

ABC News (Producer). *The eye of the storm.* New York: ABC Merchandising, Inc., Film Library, 1970.

This film shows the experiment with Iowa 3rd graders in which they are told that children with blue eyes are superior to those with brown eyes and are treated accordingly. The results, in only 1 day, demonstrate the devastating effects of discriminatory behavior.

Bowles, S., & Gintis, H. *Schooling in capitalist America.* New York: Basic Books, Paperback, 1977.

The authors present an extensive analysis of the relation between SES and schooling in America. They contend that the major influence on schools is our economic system of capitalism.

Brookover, W., Beady, C., Flood, P., Schweitzer, J., & Wisenbaker, J. *School social systems and student achievement: Schools can make a difference.* So. Hadley, Mass.: J. F. Bergin Co., distributed by Praeger Publishers, New York 1979. Annotated in Introduction.

Brophy, J. E., & Good, T. L. *Teacher-student relationships: Causes and consequences.* New York: Holt, Rinehart, and Winston, 1974.

This is an extensive review and analysis of teacher expectations and student performance, written from the perspective of the individual teacher.

CBS (Producer). Marva. From *60 Minutes.* New York: Carousel Films, Inc., 1979.

This is a stark portrayal of a black woman's private school in which her students master Chaucer, Shakespeare, and other advanced work. Marva, who takes students who are doing poorly in Chicago's inner city, says that she can turn any student around by using high expectations and concentrated academic instruction.

Persell, C. H. *Education and inequality: The roots and results of stratification in America's schools.* New York: The Free Press, 1977.

Annotated in Module 1, Persell includes two excellent chapters on expectations and the self-fulfilling prophecy.

Module 3

Organization, Role Definitions, And Rewards

- School Organization
- The Principal's Role
- Other Staff Role Definitions for Improving Achievement
- Suggested Activities
- Additional Resources

We have emphasized that the school functions as a social system, a collective of various members occupying a range of roles, positions of status in a social organization. In this module we wish to identify the nature of a school organization and the major role definitions associated with effective schools.

School Organization

Every social organization has some purpose or goals which presume to direct and justify it. Social organizations, however, frequently have their original intent displaced by secondary or unintended purposes. Therefore, schools that wish to be effective in producing high levels or student learning should examine their goals and objectives carefully.

In recent decades the primary goal of teaching students basic communication, computation, cognitive skills, and knowledge has been partially displaced by other efforts. To some extent this shifting of goals rests on the assumption that it would facilitate the achievement of the primary goal. For example, the emphasis upon humanistic values and differentiated, individualized programs was intended to facilitate the achievement of basic cognitive skills and knowledge through developing personal and social skills. But these other objectives, no matter how desirable in their own right, result in reduced attention to academic goals and consequently may lower achievement. Examination of the goals of education leads to the conclusion that essentially all of the desired outcomes of education are facilitated by the mastery of the basic communication and computational skills (see *Measuring and Attaining Educational Goals,* Brookover, Ferderbar, Gay, Middleton, Posner, & Roebuck, 1980).

A primary task, therefore, in the development of effective schools is the clear identification and specification of the instructional goals and objectives held for the students. Furthermore, the effectiveness of the school can be determined only by assessing the degree to which the academic goals and objectives are achieved. Thus mastery of the basic cognitive skills by all students is a major portion of the school's goals. Other behaviors may be identified as essential at various levels, but the primary goal of basic skill achievement must not be displaced by non-academic or irrelevant purposes.

The Structure of the School

Achievement of the goals of an organization is highly related to the structure of the organization. The belief that there are vast differences in the ability of students to learn various skills and knowledge has become associated with the differentiation of objectives and expectations for different groups of students. This results in the stratification of a school organization into various levels. Elementary schools are frequently organized according to such concepts as high, average, and low sections—either by whole classrooms or by groups within a class. At the secondary school level, students are tracked into different curricula with different levels of courses. This stratification of the school is associated with differential expectation states for different students. Compensatory education programs, in contrast with the regular program, may also lead to stratification by setting up different levels of expectations, instruction and materials, and achievement outcomes (see Brookover, Brady, & Warfield, 1981). Although the kinds of strata or groups we have mentioned are not always officially identified in the organization of the school, students as well as adult members of the organization often recognize unofficial distinctions between pupils in different categories. Thus norms, expectations, and objectives are identified for some groups of students that are quite different from those identified for other groups of students.

The stratification of the school into different levels may be associated with differential prestige and different reward systems for teachers of various groups of students. In some districts special education, gifted, or compensatory education teachers may be rewarded in both prestige and salary at a higher level than teachers who work in regular classrooms; reduced class loads are further evidence of the differential rewards. Such rewards are likely to solidify and maximize the extent to which the school is stratified into different levels.

To the extent that differential goals are set for various groups of students and the school is stratified into dissimilar levels, the average level of achievement of the students is likely to be lowered (Brookover et al., 1979). Since the goal of an effective school should be to maximize the extent to which all students achieve mastery of basic skill objectives, the school should have one common set of objectives for all students and be organized to facilitate the achievement of those objectives by all students.

The Instructional Program

Several modules in this set are devoted to the practices which are effective in instructing students to high achievement levels. The emphasis is on practices that facilitate the mastery of intended objectives by all students. Schools and classrooms that are organized in such a way that some students are identified or labeled as slow or unable to learn are likely to set up a self-fulfilling prophecy regarding such labels (see Module 2). All instructional practices and the associated grouping of students, as well as classifications of teachers, should be oriented toward maximizing the achievement of the basic skill objectives by all students.

Reward Systems

We have noted above that sometimes prestige and other rewards of the school organization are differentiated on the basis of different objectives for various groups of students. The teacher of the gifted may get special recognition, higher status, or maybe even a higher salary than teachers of presumably less gifted students. Such a reward system makes it quite clear to all in the organization that the achievement of a select group of students is more highly valued than the achievement of others. In a similar fashion, special education and compensatory program teachers or school personnel such as counselors are given special recognition, status, and other rewards for identifying students who are not to be taught the same objectives that other students are expected to learn. All of these programs associated with sorting and selecting students may have higher status than regular classrooms despite the fact that overall achievement in the school is not raised and slower students' handicaps are not overcome. These examples illustrate the possibility that the system of recognition, prestige, and perhaps even salary can reward members of the organization for instructional practices that reduce rather than maximize the achievement of many students. Regardless of other aspects of the organization, the staff of a school should be recognized and rewarded for producing high levels of mastery by all of the students rather than the selection of a few students for high levels of achievement. The school, therefore, should be recognized and rewarded as a total organization, for its overall accomplishments rather than for the differentiation of student achievement.

The Principal's Role

Nearly all of the literature on effective schools (Brookover & Lezotte, 1977; Edmonds, 1979; Hoover, 1978; Phi Delta Kappa, 1980; Weber, 1971) emphasizes the importance of the school principal in bringing about high levels of student achievement. While we do not doubt its validity, we wish to make three observations about this generally accepted tenet. First, there are some effective schools in which someone other than the person occupying the principal's position provides the kind of leadership necessary for a successful school. This may be an assistant principal, an instructional leader, or an influential teacher who fulfills the role with the approval and support of the designated principal. Although it is easier for the designated principal to assume the strong leadership role necessary, other members of the school organization may be effective in this role.

Second, we would emphasize that there is little consensus on the exact nature of the behaviors involved in the strong principal leadership role. Therefore, it is difficult to specify at this time what principal role behaviors or personal styles will be effective in every school.

The third observation is that the principal can easily be distracted from the primary purpose of enhancing student learning. It is essential that the principal or other leader give primary emphasis to the role defined below.

Regardless of who fulfills the leadership role, the following discussion identifies tasks or activities that we think must be accomplished. The specific behavior of the principal or other leader doing these tasks may vary from school to school. We have examined the role under two general categories: the role of instructional leader and the role of the change agent. The latter assumes that the school is not as effective as it could or should be and that a program of planned change (using this set of modules) is anticipated and desired by some or all of the members of the school staff.

Instructional Leader

Although the principal may have many other functions in operating a school organization, the leadership role in establishing an effective instructional program in the school is foremost. The particular style of leadership is perhaps less important than the accomplishment of the tasks that need to be done by the instructional leader. Some may accomplish the task by directive methods. Others may be successful through indirect methods—by mobilizing other personnel to achieve the desired tasks.

Someone in the school organization, ideally the principal, must provide leadership to establish clearly identified and specific learning objectives at each grade level and for each course. Unless all members of the organization understand what is to be achieved at each grade level and for each course, they are likely to go in many different directions. Agreement on the objectives is essential for evaluating the school's effectiveness. It is unlikely that a single individual, even the most directive principal, can identify and specify all of the objectives at the various levels, but (s)he should provide the leadership to see that this is done.

Closely associated, of course, with identifying the instructional objectives at each level are the standards for mastery for the achievement of the objectives. The ultimate goal should be 100% mastery of all of the objectives established for each grade level and course in the school. The staff must first agree on the standards of achievement and then adopt an instructional program, consistent with an effective school learning climate, to insure that all students actually attain the standards of mastery for all objectives. The instructional leader plays a major role in developing and maintaining these high norms and expectations for all students.

In order to accomplish objectives set at a mastery level, all teachers must have the necessary instructional materials and resources to carry on the instructional program. The principal has a major responsibility for seeing that such materials are available.

Consistent with Module 5, Effective Instruction, both formative tests and summative tests should be available for teachers to measure all of the various objectives at appropriate times. Since the school should have common objectives for all students at each grade level and for each subject, the tests, both diagnostic and mastery, can be conveniently located in a central file covering all objectives. Teachers and other personnel in the school system can contribute to and facilitate the development of such tests, but someone, generally the principal, should make certain that the appropriate tests are available and are representative of the learning objectives which the school has established. At the secondary level, department heads or other instructional leaders may play the appropriate role in developing and supplying the test instruments.

The school testing program should also include, as indicated in Module 10, a regular evaluation of the instructional program. The accumulation of summative test records and periodic objective referenced tests should be important sources in the assessment of whether the instructional program is achieving the desired objectives. This involves the maintenance of records for each classroom and each grade level as a whole.

The primary basis for this evaluation should be the degree to which all of the students have mastered the objectives set for them. The principal should take primary responsibility for this evaluation.

In order to insure time to carry out the instruction for mastery of the objectives, the principal or designated leader should plan the school day so that adequate time is available for instruction in each of the various areas. Teachers can participate in planning the school day, but there must be a commitment on the part of the leadership that instruction and time-on-task will not be disrupted or invaded by other activities or diversions (see Module 6).

Teachers as well as students are likely to behave in ways for which they are reinforced. Although colleagues may contribute to the reward system among staff members, the principal has a major responsibility for giving positive or negative reinforcement to teachers and other staff members when performance merits either. Often school personnel are positively recognized and praised for not bothering the principal or for doing other pleasant and desirable things, such as having an attractive room, being well dressed, or being the life of the Friday after-school get together. To the extent that the activities for which the staff is recognized, praised, or rewarded do not assure the achievement of the designated objectives by the students, or become a means of displacing emphasis from achievement to other goals or processes, the staff is likely to devote its time and energy to nonproductive activities. Again, we are not stating that other activities are unimportant, but the primary goal of the school learning climate program is high achievement for all students; other activities should facilitate, not distract from or displace this ultimate goal. Unfortunately reward systems often reinforce these goals rather than the primary goal. The principal should also facilitate the development of appropriate grade level, classroom, and team rewards for students in accord with Effective Instruction and Team Learning, Modules 5 and 8.

Effective instructional leadership must encompass all of

the tasks which we have briefly identified above. They do not necessarily need to be done by the same person. A principal or assistant principal or other instructional leader may assume some of the functions, but these functions must be coordinated and become a recognized part of the organizational roles. (See the Activities for this module for a concise summary-listing of some instructional responsibilites of the principal.)

The Principal as Change Agent

If the students in school are not already achieving at high levels, the accomplishment of that goal will involve some changes in the school's operation. Throughout these modules we have identified characteristics of school learning climate that are associated with high levels of student achievement. The process of creating the kind of learning climate identified here cannot be stated as a simple formula. Studies of effective schools, however, indicate that school principals can be change agents in modifying the nature of the school and its effectiveness in bringing students to high levels of achievement. It is certainly not likely that a school will have high achieving students if the principal and other leaders in the school do not openly seek to achieve that goal. It is therefore essential that the principal provide strong leadership or at least actively support other staff to bring about the needed changes. The first step is for the principal to identify what is to be changed.

A leader who has support of his/her staff may accomplish much of this by personal influence and direction. This is likely to be facilitated by the formation and operation of a Building Leadership Team (BLT) including teachers and the principal (see the discussion of the BLT in the Introduction to these modules). The BLT must have a clear understanding of what it is trying to accomplish and then coordinate the efforts of the staff to enable all students to reach the standard of mastery set for the school.

Since the School Learning Climate Program requires action and time commitments from the principal and teachers, the principal and/or BLT should identify basic responsibilities of staff for conducting the program. This can be easily described in a Working Agreement that sets expectations for staff involvement (see example in the Introduction). Clear statement of, and mutual commitment to, the contents of the Working Agreement should be accomplished before attempting to carry out this program.

Many people think that changes in a school system necessitate the involvement of the entire staff in the process of deciding what changes are desirable. If everybody readily agrees that change is necessary and concurs on what goals are appropriate, such broad involvement may be helpful. There is evidence, however (Herriott & Gross, 1979), that involvement of everybody in the deciding of what changes should be made frequently results in no change. The only things that everybody can agree on may be the current practices. In contrast, change is more likely to occur if a strong leader specifies the changes to be made, involves a cross section of staff in planning those changes, and follows through on the compromises that might occur within an organization.

It is difficult for a school staff to reach consensus on both the need for change and the type of change needed. Furthermore, if consensus is reached it may be on the need to increase staff members' satisfaction with their jobs rather than high achievement for all students. Staff satisfaction is also desirable, emphasis on such goals may not facilitate the students' learning (Brookover & Lezotte, 1977; Conran & Beauchamp, 1976). Planned change in complex social organizations such as schools can easily be displaced from the intended goal.

The process of change envisioned in this set of modules involves many significant differences in idealogy, structure, and instructional program of in-service education is likely to be necessary. Out experience indicates that school principals sometimes are able to effectively carry on the in-service education themselves with staff participation. If this is feasible and the principal or other leadership persons are effective in doing the in-service education, it is probably more expedient than bringing in outside consultants.

It is unlikely that significant changes will occur in the school if the central administration does not support the change. The principal or other change agent in the school should therefore take whatever steps are necessary to obtain central administration support, so that the school as a whole is likely to be supported and rewarded for improvement in the school learning climate and student achievement.

Not only should the central administration provide support and recognition for significant change, but the building principal should be recognized and rewarded for participation in the change process. Likewise teachers who have developed effective instructional practices should be recognized for their success by the principal. For both principals and teachers, the greatest reward should be reserved not just for participation, but for improved results: higher achievement for all students.

Finally, the principal or change agent should develop a system of following through to determine to what extent the intended changes are being implemented. Innovative educational programs are often discussed but usually not fully implemented or conducted long enough to obtain a fair assessment of their impact. Thus it is necessary that the principal check on the extent to which the desired changes actually occur and encourage continued use of suggested practices from the modules for a 2-3 year period. Hall and Loucks (1977) note that higher levels of use of an innovation are associated with higher outcomes of intended goals. Therefore all the members of the school organization should have knowledge of the attitudes, beliefs, and practices essential for change. It is not sufficient to have given the staff this set of modules or any other pattern of in-service training and assume that all will be knowledgeable about them To determine the extent to which all members of the school staff know and understand how the school learning climate should be changed, consistent followup is necessary.

However, knowledge of a particular program, such as team games, does not assure that the program will be used. Some method should be developed to determine the extent to which the beliefs, attitudes, expectations, and instructional practices of the program are actually being used in the school. Contributors to this set of modules are developing an instrument to assess the level of use of these materials (see Module 1). Program leaders at school, however, by observation and various other methods, can determine that to some extent on their own. The school that accomplishes a high level of use and an associated high level of achievement should be recognized by the central administration and the total community. The principal or other change agent should develop a systematic procedure for determining the level of use of the proposed changes and see that the school's success in achieving high levels of student performance is known and recognized.

Other Staff Role Definitions
For Improving Achievement

For any given position in the school, the role definition and expectation, reflecting the formal rules plus the informal group norms and peer demands, provides the primary influence on individual behavior. Role prescriptions and expectations can vary considerably from school to school. In this section, we will discuss optimal role responsibilities and definitions for creating an effective school learning climate.

Two comments can be made regarding the possibility of changing individual role behavior. First, formal role prescriptions or definitions, when inconsistent with practices necessary for attaining high achievement for all students will need to be officially restructured to conform with the profile of an effective school (see Module 1). Second, informal role expectations and group norms may also be contrary to the set of beliefs and practices that promote high achievement for all students. Both formal roll definitions and informal norms can be highly resistant to change (see Lezotte et al., 1980, Chapter 5). We suggest that the reward system be closely inspected. Informal norms and role expectations are highly consistent with the social system members' perceptions of what they are rewarded for. Thus, before informal role expectations will change, reward systems may have to be altered to confer recognition for high student achievement.

In setting forth the following observations on appropriate role definitions for various staff members, it is important not to forget that the school functions as a system. Individual roles combine to create the school learning climate. And while individuals have responsibility to perform their own roles effectively, there remains a collective responsibility on the part of the staff to create the total learning climate which will insure that all students achieve well.

Department Head, Instructional and Grade Level Leaders

Most secondary schools have department heads who are charged with various administrative responsibilities for budgeting, scheduling, curriculum planning, etc. In some elementary and secondary schools, special roles for instructional leaders exist. Both department heads and instructional leaders act to assist the principal to develop and maintain an effective instructional program. For both positions all functions and duties must be considered as means to the end of high achievement for all students. Some key responsibilities for department heads and instructional leaders include:

1. Setting and planning objectives. The department head or instructional leader should insure that there is a common set of grade level objectives which all students are to master.
2. Implementing instructional policy. Many instructionally related duties are delegated by the principal. They include the following.

    a. Maintenance or departmental meetings. These should focus on activities and problems in getting all students to mastery of instructional objectives. Discussion of strategies and suggestions from these modules must occur on a regular basis.

    b. Monitoring informal norms. The leadership positions can have positive input in seeing that group norms of expectations and evaluations of students are maintained at a high level.

    c. Improving instructional programs. The department head/instructional leader will have major responsibility for the successful carrying out and improvement of instructional strategies for raising achievement (e.g., mastery learning, improved time on task, group learning games, etc.).

3. Setting reward structures. The department head/instructional leader should have primary responsibility for seeing that the types of academically oriented reward structures (listed in the Activities section for this module under "Creating Academic Reward Structures") are carried out for students.

Counselors

Counselors often have responsibilities for working with students with emotional and behavioral problems. But in most schools, counselors also have much, if not all, of the responsibility for placement and advisement of students with respect to curriculum choices. This responsibility involves both the choice of electives and the ability level or track for required courses. These factors are most relevant in secondary schools.

Our position on the role expectations of counselors is clear. Counselors should take primary responsibility so see that all students have equal opportunity to choose whatever further schooling or career they want upon graduation from high school, without being excluded from certain options because they do not have the required course background. The implication of the position is closely related to our position on ability grouping. For those in the middle and lower tracks, grouping and tracking limit the opportunity for attainment of the necessary cognitive skills required for further schooling. Furthermore, students are sometimes restricted from advanced classes because of not having the required sequence of prerequisite courses, even if the student has the required entry skills. Finally, students in lower or middle tracks rarely move upward. Almost all movement in tracking systems is downward (Rosenbaum, 1976). Especially since there is strong evidence that counselors currently contribute to the restrictions on further opportunity that students in lower and middle tracks experience (Rosenbaum, 1976; 1980), it is time that the counseling role be reappraised in the area of academic and vocational guidance. We should stress that like lowered expectations for low SES or minority students, the restrictions of the advisement/tracking system are often not a conscious process, but are a part of the structural system that feeds into state colleges and universities with unofficial quotas on the number of students allowed in the college prep track. Our point is that a conscious awareness and active effort to change the system are necessary for positive change.

More problems associated with ability grouping are described in Module 4; however, the following considerations regarding the advisement and placement functions of the counselor are noteworthy.

1. Counselors should be responsible for seeing that academic opportunities be maximized for all students. Counselors should be rewarded for maximizing the number of students who qualify for college rather than selecting and sorting students into stratified academic and occupational categories.

2. Communicating to students and parents information about future possibilities for college or different careers is essential. (See "Communicating to Parents

And Students'' in the Activities for this module.) For example, a decision by a student to take a shop or home economics elective instead of a foreign language in junior high can often be an irreversible choice of a whole sequence of prerequisites for the college preparatory track. The implications of a decision of that magnitude must be known by both students and parents.

Students, like adults, often take the path of least resistance. Students may track themselves because of the difference in work load of different classes, especially if unaware of the consequences. Parents may not wish to let a 12 or 13 year old's reluctance to take a more difficult class preclude their child from later options, if aware of the consequences.

3. Counselors should encourage positive student placements. Counselors sometimes contribute to the tracking within a school by advising students to avoid certain "difficult" classes or by making actual placements based on various test scores or teacher recommendations. The obvious communication to students is that "you aren't capable of doing better." Instead of limiting student options, counselors need to open up the system and concentrate on counseling strategies that provide the academic help for students to "make it" in the higher level classes, thus creating equial opportunity for success in college and later in life.

Teachers

Despite the influence of the principal and other staff members, the ultimate responsibility for delivery of the instructional program lies with teachers. The level of achievement in a school depends in large part on the effectiveness of the teachers' instruction. And the particular way in which instructional programs are carried out is strongly influenced by the role definition and expectations of the members of the school staff.

Role definitions of teachers do make a difference in achievement. Considerable evidence indicates that there are fundamental differences in the way teachers define their appropriate role behavior—and that these different role definitions result in differing levels of achievement for students (Brophy, 1979; Good, 1979).

The role expectations associated with the highest level of achievement define the teacher's task as seeing that all students master basic common instructional objectives. This role definition encompasses diagnostic testing and reteaching to insure that the students who do not learn the material on the first exposure will be given maximum opportunity to attain mastery. There is a sense of commitment that the job of teaching entails doing all that is necessary to see that all students learn the objectives.

Role definitions of teaching which do not emphasize the mastery of instructional objectives by all students are associated with lower achivement. the implications are obvious: What is not taught is not learned. Teachers who spend time on goals other than high cognitive achievement for all students are not as effective as teachers who have that goal and teach to attain it.

Finally, we would note that the instructionally effective teacher is one who is good at the instructional techniques explained in this set of modules. Teachers who wish to raise the level of their students' achievement can use these modules as a guideline for improving their effectiveness. Again, we emphasize that the achievement oriented role behavior advocated here is not likely to occur unless teachers are rewarded for it. Current reward systems will probably need to be changed.

Compensatory Education Staff

State and federal compensatory education programs such

as Title I are designed to give extra help to disadvantaged homes. While most of these programs have not been successful in that endeavor, a few have been. The following characteristics of the role definition of effective compensatory education staff are based on and consistent with successful programs and the research on effective atypical schools.

1. *Criteria of success.* The successful program is one in which the students enrolled are able to progress to age-grade level achievement. This means catching up. Many programs inappropriately set their goals so that students are only expected to attain a portion of a normal year's growth or the equivalent of a year's growth at their level. Consequently, these students never catch up and usually fall further behind. The success of the program should be measured by the percent of students who do catch up to age-grade level performance.

2. *Reward system.* Compensatory education teachers should be expected to get students to achieve at grade level for their age or above. Rewards and recognition should be given to teachers who accomplish this and not for continued below grade level performances or increasing the numbers in the program.

3. *Supplementary instruction.* Compensatory instruction should be supplemental to the regular instruction. Students who miss their regular reading or math instruction are prevented from being taught their grade level basic objectives. Again, what is not taught is not learned.

4. *Reinstruction.* Compensatory instruction should concentrate on helping students master the objectives of the regular program. For students who are behind, this can mean either reinstruction over the objectives, work on deficient prerequisite skills, or both.

5. *Coordination.* The need for reinstruction over the objectives of the regular program requires the coordina-

tion of the compensatory teacher's instruction with the regular classroom teacher. This requires communication on subject matter objectives as well as student progress over specific objectives.

6. *Responsibility for the student's achievement.* In many programs the responsibility for a student's achievement is shuffled between the regular teacher and the compensatory teacher. We recommend that the regular classroom teacher maintain responsibility for the child's learning. The compensatory program is to help the regular teacher, not relieve him/her of responsibility.

7. *Place of instruction.* Most compensatory instruction occurs in pullout programs. Immediately, a problem with labeling effects is faced. Students know that the "dummies" go to special reading or math class. There are also the problems of time lost to and from class and of scheduling around regular reading and math. We recommedn an in-class program in which the compensatory teacher joins with the regular teacher to provide extra reinstruction or work with deficient skills as needed. This format answers several of the problems raised in the foregoing points.

8. *State and Federal guidelines.* Some guidelines of state and federal programs contain provisions to insure that these monies are spent only on eligible students. This policy often results in rules that conflict with the effective program outlined here. But the conflict is more perceived than real. Effective compensatory education programs that do not violate policy guideline—and that achieve success—are possible and do exist.

9. *Paraprofessional Aides.* Many teacher aides are funded by compensatory education or special education programs. Yet research shows that aides often have low expectations for achievement and perceive their role as "cooling out" students, i.e., convincing the

students to accept their lower status in school because of less ability (Brookover et al., 1981). Paraprofessional aides should be given training which stresses high achievement for all. Appropriate activities center on reinstructing students who have not yet mastered objectives. Rewards and recognition for aides should be dependent on achieving success in helping students catch up to grade level.

Special Education Staff

Special education programs are designed to give special instruction to students considered unable to function adequately in the regular classroom. These students are considered to have personal deficiencies which restrict their learning. Unfortunately, special education programs often serve as a rationale for lower expectations and goals rather than specialized instruction to help the student function normally. While not all special education programs experience this shift in goals, many do, and the danger of this occurrence must be guarded against. We are concerned primarily with learning disabilities (LD), emotionally impaired (EI), educable mentally impaired (EMI). and physically impaired (PI) rather than programs for severely handicapped students. Some of the ways this unconscious shift in goals occurs are listed below.

1. Lowered expectations due to low program goals.

2. Labeling effects among peers of students who are designated "special education."

3. Permanence of the program, in which students are considered to be permanently enrolled in special education rather than trying to give the student sufficient help to be able to return to the regular classroom.

4. The "difference" syndrome, in which students in special education programs are viewed as so different from regular students that the usual methods for working with students are considered ineffective.

Hence, completely different methods must be used.

5. The "writing off" function, in which regular education teachers are "relieved" of the responsibility for teaching students who are identified as special education.

6. The "expanding numbers" trend, in which the number of identified special education students expands to fill the number of available slots. When this happens, more and more students are "identified" as special education students in response to pressures from regular classroom teachers to relieve themselves of "slow" students who can't learn. State and Federal funding based on the number of "identified" special education students also creates strong pressure for school districts to increase the number of students in the program—and thus the amount of dollars coming into the district.

The role definition of the effective special education teacher counteracts these negative trends by working to improve the total school learning climate: helping set up a program that enables "slow" students to learn well, thus reducing the demand for special education alternatives, and teaching those students in the program effectively so they are able to exit special education and function in the regular program.

Non-Instructional Support Staff

Schools require certain supportive services which facilitate the primary focus of the organization. Routines such as busing, lunchroom, maintenance, and secretarial-clerical procedures cannot be neglected. But these services must not detract time or effort from academic goals. Rather, these necessary routines must be planned and scheduled so that they facilitate high achievement for all students.

The implications for non-academic staff are twofold. One, secretaries, bus drivers, custodians, and other personnel must perform their roles in a generally courteous and efficient manner. If a particular activity continually detracts from instructional time (e.g., discipline problems at lunch or on the bus), the principal and the staff must establish a new routine which does not create further discipline problems. Two, support staff members must understand that their role is to support the instructional functions of the school. Their efficiency allows the school to run smoothly and learning to continue uninterrupted. Support personnel must be recognized and rewarded for this efficiency; both the principal and other instructional staff should communicate their appreciation for this service.

The key to effective non-instructional staff behavior is consistent with the concept of goal displacement: daily routines of support staff must not be allowed to become an end in themselves; rather they must be means to achieving high performance from all students.

Summary

The school functions as a social system. But within the social system, individuals hold various positions. The way in which a person behaves within a position is determined primarily by the role definitions and expectations of appropriate action for a particular school. These role definitions vary considerably from school to school and even within the same school.

Role behavior is also related to the group norms and values within a school. The process of change is highly influenced by how the members of the social group define roles and collectively alter norms and values. Relationships of the organization, structure, instructional program, and reward systems to the problem of change must be understood by the school staff.

Specific role definitions and responsibilities for various positions in the school should be examined in terms of behaviors which will maximize achievement for all students. The role of the principal is critical to establishing an effective school learning climate. Other staff role behavior can be either positively or negatively related to achievement. In summary, behavior that stresses mastery of age-grade level objectives for all students correlates the highest with achievement. Role behaviors that emphasize other goals do not yield equally high achievement. In addition, informal role expectations and norms are highly associated with staff members' perceptions of what they are rewarded for in a particular school. Informal norms will probably not change for the better unless the reward systems, both formal and informal, are tied to producing high achievement for all students.

Suggested Activities

1. *Working Agreement.* The Principal and/or BLT should develop a Working Agreement that specifies the major expectation for staff involvement for implementing the School Learning Climate Program (see p. 12 in the *Introduction*). This set of expectations should be presented to the teachers for approval and/or amendment.

2. *Goals and Policies.* Examine school and district goals and policies. Is high achievement for all students the number one priorty of the district? If not, steps should be taken to formally amend the school and/or board policies. In addition, written procedures of the school or district which are inconsistent with the priority of high achievement for all students should be changed.

3. *Public Information.* A strong public information program should be developed, emphasizing the goal of high achievement for all students. Public support from various community groups—business, labor,

churches, community organizations, etc.—should be sought in addition to a direct appeal for help from parents. The section in these Activities on Communicating to Parents and Students indicates several essential points for inclusion in the program.

4. *Reward structures.* Both administration and staff should list the kinds of activities, attitudes, and behaviors that are currently rewarded, through both formal recognition and informal praise and encouragement. How these facilitate or hinder high achievement for all students should then be analyzed and evaluated. The staff should establish reward systems that encourage high academic performance. For example, pep rallies are held before key athletic events. Are they held before major achievement testing? Does the school have intramural or interscholastic academic games and competitions? Why not? (See the section on reward structures in these Activities.) Reward structures not consistent with high achievement for students and teachers must be changed.

A major problem in many (most) school districts is that the reward structures for principals, through both the formal and informal channels, are not consistent with high achievement for all students. This is particularly true for the central office in which loyalty, team play, and keeping things quiet are rewarded. Often there are implicit messages that these are "real" requirements of a good principal. Likewise, teachers may implicitly reward the supportive disciplinarian principal. Again, these explicit and implicit rewards must be reviewed, analyzed, and changed where inconsistent with high achievement. This will require input and commitment from both the school(s) and the central office.

5. *Role definitions.* The school staff should examine the formal job descriptions of employees for discrepancies between job description and the staff responsibilities

identified in this module. Those job descriptions which are inconsitent with the academic focus on high achievement for all students should be formally amended by the central office administration. (See respective role definitions in this module and for Paraprofessional Aides in these Activities.)

6. *Changing informal norms.* Informal norms and procedures for carrying out the routines of the school may also be inconsistent with the goal of high achievement for all students. The Climate Watchers Process described in Module 1 is the best avenue for monitoring and changing informal norms that impede or hinder high achievement.

7. *Logs of daily activities.* The principal (and/or secretary) should keep a log of all activities and time spent for 2-3 days. This will provide basic information for improved planning and scheduling of work.

8. *Plan of action.* The principal should make sure the school has a "plan of action" that focuses all instructional responsibilities into a comprehensive set of activities. The principal must take the lead in seeing that this is done and that various staff members know and are held responsible for their respective role behaviors. This plan of action should be consistent with the outline for Effective School Learning Climate in Module 1 and the section of Principal's Instructional Responsibilities in these Activities (immediately below).

Principal's Instructional Responsibilities

We have alluded to several particulars for which the instructional leader must be responsible. The following outlines several of the activities and functions for which the principal must take the lead. The principal or designated instructional leader must focus the planning, goal setting, and setting up of routines which effectively accomplish these tasks.

1. *Instructional objectives.* The goals of the school, particularly high achievement for all students, must be translated into grade level instructional objectives. This must be done first for reading/language arts and math. Other subject areas can follow, but emphasis should be first on acquisition of language arts and math objectives and skills. The grade level or departmental staff should develop a common calendar for teaching these objectives (see Module 5).

2. *Student assessment.* Yearly achievement data over the grade-level instructional objectives, preferably with a criterion-referenced test, should be collected, analyzed, and discussed with the staff to pinpoint areas of strength and weakness (see Module 10).

3. *School learning climate assessment.* The principal should take the lead in utilizing and discussing with the staff both the formal instruments and the informal Climate Watchers Program (see Module 1).

4. *Comprehensive planning.* A comprehensive plan by which the staff will change and improve the school learning climate, consistent with the assessment results of #'s 2 and 3 above, must be articulated with staff cooperation.

5. *Efficient use of faculty meetings.* Faculty meetings are used for instructional issues. Administrative details should be handled through some form of written memoranda as much as possible.

6. *Concentration on instructional problems.* Departmental or grade level meetings must be organized around instructional problems. For example:
    a. Cooperation and sharing of teachers' ideas and materials, in connection with implementation of a mastery learning program (see Module 5).
    b. Monitoring academic progress of students.
    c. Discussing ways to increase time-on-task or improve classroom management (see Modules 6 and 7).

d. Discussing ways to help students, who are below grade level or who are not mastering materials, "catch-up."

7. *Establishing a file of objectives.* A file of objectives, which indicates the district goals and specific grade level instructional objectives for the school, must be developed. This should include instructional strategies, practice materials, and sample tests. The file should become the basis of the sharing of teacher materials for mastery instruction. This file should also be accessible to and contributed to by all staff. Finally, it should be under the direction of a staff member appointed by the principal, with responsibility to see that it is complete and is being used by the staff.

Creating Academic Reward Structures

Perhaps one of the most important aspects in creating an effective school learning climate is setting up a reward system that clearly "strokes" staff and students for academic success. In most schools, this will require a planned strategy to change the reward structure from informal, non-academic related norms to an ongoing, academically based norm. Some possible strategies include:

1. *Praise and encouragement.* The principal, for staff members, and teachers, for their students, must provide sincere praise for positive achievements that are related to the goals of the school (see Module 9 for a description of the principles of reinforcement).

2. *Games, competitions.* Group learning games within the classroom or between rooms foster a reward system based on cooperative, team-based academic achievement that results in highly visible trophies, banners, public recognition, etc. (see Module 8). This can be extended to the area of attendance.

3. *Formal recognition.* Recognition in newsletters, bulletin boards, school newspapers, etc., for various academically oriented activities, adds incentive for achievement.

4. *Academic displays.* Creating room and school bulletin boards and overall decor around academic activities. Displays of student work that show excellence or improvement can be very effective.

5. *Interscholastic teams.* Establishing interscholastic "academic" teams with all of the usual hoopla of student assemblies and school spirit—but based now on cognitive competition.

6. *Teacher rewards.* Rewarding teachers with public recognition, citations, etc., for having all students reach age-grade level goals or for displaying exceptional improvement through the year.

7. *Student rewards.* Providing picnics, ball game outings, etc., at the end of the year for all students who master grade level objectives or reach a set level of improvement through the year.

The above are merely suggestive of ways in which a faculty can change the reward structure in a school. Put simply, students must be rewarded for being good students and teachers must be rewarded for doing a good job of getting all students to achieve well. The principal should take the lead in this process.

Communicating to Parents and Students

For a social system to function effectively, all members of the organization must know the prescribed rules and regulations which define role expectations and appropriate behavior. Just as the principal is responsible for communicating goals and strategies for running the school to the staff, he/she is also responsible for the communication of policies, regulations, procedures, and expectations to both the students and their parents. This includes appropriate preparation for school, day-to-day rules and behavior, standards of excellence, goals and philosophy, and of course procedures for sanctioning inappropriate behavior.

An efficient means of communicating these general rules is through a Student Handbook and a Parent Handbook. Regular newsletters of some sort provide an update on school events and problems throughout the year. Instruction-related topics, which are essential to be included in the handbooks, include:

1. The school discipline plan explained in full detail;
2. Attendance and tardiness policies, also fully explained;
3. Explanation of grades, their implications, and methods of grade reporting. (Standards of excellence and school expectations for meeting these standards should be described);
4. What to expect at parent-teacher conferences;
5. Explanation of the school's testing program; interpretation of scores in terms of grade level, percentiles, and national and local norms; and the specific score of their own child should all be described to parents.

We believe strongly that an essential aspect of an effective school learning climate involves honest, accurate information on the likely consequences of student performance in school and decisions regarding curriculum. Clearly, for whatever reasons, many schools are now failing in this regard.

Role Definition for Paraprofessional Aides

The role of the paraprofessional aide is to assist the teacher to teach students. While the perceived role expectations for aides vary from school to school, some common positive role expectations concerning the use of aides include:

1. Teachers should be responsible for initial instruction of students and for monitoring the learning process.

2. Aides should help in the reinstruction of students who
    have not mastered objectives. Possible activities in-
    clude:
    a. Listening to students read;
    b. Conducting drill for practice sessions;
    c. Correcting practice exercises for students.
3. Aides may help students practice particular deficient
    skills which are prerequisite to the current instruc-
    tional objectives.

Additional Resources

Brookover, W., Beady, C., Flood, P., Schweitzer, J., &
Wisenbaker, J. *School social systems and student
achievement: Schools can make a difference.* So. Hadley,
Mass: J. F. Bergin Co., distributed by Praeger
Publishers, New York, 1979.

Annotated in Introduction.

Brookover, W. B., Brady, N. M., & Warfield, M. Educational
policies and equitable education: A report of studies of
two desegregated school systems. In R. L. Green (Project
Director), *Procedures and pilot research to develop an
agenda for desegragation studies* (Final Report). East
Lansing: College of Urban Development, Center for Urban Affairs, Michigan State University, 1981.

This study documents how educational policy and practices often contribute to segregation and lower achievement. Special education and Title I programs frequently
separate and isolate students, have reduced achievement
goals, and use lower level instruction and materials.

Brookover, W. B., Ferderbar, G., Gay, G., Middleton, M.,
Posner, G., & Roebuck, F. *Measuring and attaining to
goals of education.* Alexandria, Va.: Association for
Supervision and Curriculum Development, 1980.

This document outlines the importance of setting educational goals and measuring school outcomes. Mastery of basic skills in language arts and mathematics contributes to the attainment of other advanced goals and can thus be considered first priority for schools.

Brookover, W. B., & Lezotte, L. W. *Changes in school characteristics coincident with changes in student achievement* East Lansing: Institute for Research on Teaching, Michigan State University, 1977.

Annotated in Module 1, this study further demonstrates the importance of the principal as instructional leader in improving schools.

Hall, G., & Loucks, S. F. A developmental model for determining whether the treatment is actually implemented. *American Educational Research Journal,* 1977, *14* (2), 263-276.

The authors report that educational innovations approximate levels of use or the degree of implementation of the intended change. Ranging from no use at all through full implementation in 8 levels, the extent to which the program is fully implemented is associated with program outcomes.

Herriott, R. E., & Gross, N. (Eds.) *The dynamics of planned educational change: Case studies and analyses.* Berkeley, Cal.: McCutchan Publishing Corporation, 1979.

Five case studies of comprehensive educational change are presented along with analyses of the problems and factors involved in planned change.

Module 4

Grouping and Differentiation

- **Grouping Patterns**
- **Research and Grouping**
- **How to Group Students to Maximize Achievement and Simplify Classroom Management**
- **Suggested Activities**
- **Additional Resources**

Grouping students for instruction is a common educational practice. Grouping patterns are related to student achievement and are a major characteristic of the school learning climate. Grouping patterns and the related objectives and instruction for each group both reflect and influence the school staff's expectations of the various student groups. The students come to accept these expectations and evaluations of their learning potential and come to perform at the expected level (self-fulfilling prophecy).

This module will explain the various types of grouping, their relationship to student learning, and the research regarding the effectiveness of these forms of grouping.

Grouping Patterns

Two basic types of grouping (homogeneous and heterogeneous) are prominent in schools. There are many ways of using them separately or together.

Homogeneous Grouping

Homogeneous grouping, also known as ability grouping, clusters students of like "ability." For example, classroom reading groups are frequently homogeneous, in keeping with most reading textbook series that have various levels in which students are placed according to their reading performance. In some cases, whole classes may be grouped by performance at each grade level. Many schools have high, medium and low ability classrooms for students of the same age. Homogeneous grouping may occur with some forms of teaming: Teacher X may teach math to all the "slower" 2nd graders while teacher Y may teach math to all the "advanced" 2nd graders.

At the secondary level homogeneous groups are often based upon tracks labeled college bound, general, business, and vocational, with different curricula and expectations for each track. These grouping patterns strongly influence students' future education and career options.

As noted in Module 3, special education and compensatory education programs also represent a common elementary grouping pattern. Usually they are pull-out programs where students leave their classrooms for separate instruction. These programs often are not coordinated with regular program and the "special" student is generally placed in a curriculum other than the one taught in his/her regular classroom. This may lead to confusion for the child, and poor management of student time, which in turn may lead to lowered achievement in grade level skills.

Placement by track or homogeneous grouping placement is generally based upon prior school performance, teacher judgments, recommendations, and standardized achievement or aptitude test scores. Homogeneous or ability grouping tends to "lock-in" pupils at particular levels. Research by Rosenbaum (1976) indicates that, with rare exceptions, movement between groups or tracks generally is downward. Students seldom move to a higher group. This finding illustrates the irony of using ability grouping to increase achievement.

Homogeneous grouping communicates differentiated learning expectations to students. "High" group students often receive an entirely different educational experience from that of "low" group students. The result of such procedures is to produce vast differences in student achievement over time, although homogeneous grouping is promoted on the basis that it fosters achievement. Teachers may be surprised to learn that this widely used practice has not been supported by research evidence for over fifty years (Wilson & Schmits, 1978).

Heterogeneous Grouping

Heterogeneous grouping is the other basic grouping practice. It places students of different demonstrated achievement in groups by random assignment or by conscious design. Heterogeneous grouping frequently is used to form whole classes at each grade level. Reading and other instructional groups also may be formed heterogeneously. Cooperative group learning can be facilitated by heterogeneous groups, where those who have learned the course material become teachers to those who are having difficulty. (For more information regarding heterogeneous group learning see Module 8.) Furthermore, heterogeneous grouping does not have many of the negative effects associated with homogeneous grouping patterns. For example, groups do not become identified as slow or inferior; mixed grouping improves social relations between students; and most importantly, this form of grouping facilitates the use of common learning objectives and expectations. The benefits of heterogeneous grouping will be explained further in the section on Research and Grouping.

The following two types of instructional grouping are commonly observed in classrooms. They are related to the main grouping patterns discussed above, with implications for communicating differential learning expectations to students.

Individualized Instruction

Individualized instruction involves the management of many achievement levels and is based on self-paced learning at each students' performance level. Teachers often contrast this pattern to the more common homogeneous classroom. They indicate that with individualized instruction, they must sometimes manage twenty-five or more students working on different skills. Even though this is a self-paced method, it communicates varying expectations for learning based on the individual student's performance level. There are generally no common objectives which all students are expected to learn; also, some students are expected to take much longer to learn lower level objectives. A national study of innovative instructional practices found no evidence that individualized instructional programs enhanced achievement (American Institute for Research, 1976).

Whole-Class Instruction

Whole-class instruction tends to be more heterogeneous simply because of the number of students involved. This pattern works because new content can be provided to more students at the same time with economy of preparation. Many teachers feel that direct observation and management of student time and attention are facilitated. Some provision must usually be made for individual student needs, to assure that all students master the appropriate grade-level objectives. This process is outlined in Module 5 on Effective Instruction. Particular attention should be paid to the section on feedback and corrective/enrichment instruction, as these are essential characteristics of effective whole class instruction.

Research And Grouping

There has been much research done on the various types of grouping patterns and their relationship to student learning. Since the aim of this program is to enhance achievement, it is imperative that we know which grouping pattern or combination of patterns improves the level of learning for all students.

After an extensive review of the research on ability grouping, Findley and Bryan (1971) concluded that homogeneous ability grouping shows no consistent, positive value for helping students generally, or helping particular groups of students, to learn better. Other reviews of the effects of homogeneous ability grouping have come to similar conclusions. For example, the Wilson and Schmits (1978) review of data accumulated since 1928. Goldberg, Passow, and Justman (1966) explain that where research has found improved achievement in favor of homogeneous grouping, the results are usually explained by difference in instructional methods and materials, the development of educational objectives, or related factors. Yet, the practice of ability grouping continues to be widespread.

Research by Brookover et al. (1979) indicates that emphasis on different objectives for different elementary school groups is associated with lower achievement for the whole school. This suggests that the self-fulfilling prophecy is operating in many schools. Elizabeth Cohen (1980) reports that reading group level is a status characteristic in the classroom which leads to parallel expectations and a self-fulfilling prophecy regarding performance. She notes that in the desegregated classroom it is generally the minority student who will be negatively affected by status generalizations regarding competence.

In a tracking or homogeneous system, since the objectives

and the curricula are different for various groups of students, the outcomes of those groups are almost certain to differ. Rosenbaum (1975) found that on the average, intelligence tests scores of students in the college bound tracks tend to increase while those in the non-college-bound tracks tend to decline over a two year period.

Studies of both ability grouping and tracking indicate that placement or classification of students tends to be relatively permanent. Once students are placed in low ability or non-college tracks, it is unlikely that they will move into a higher group. Thus, ability grouping at the elementary level leads to placement in parallel tracks at the secondary level. What happens is that differential learning expectations with differing amounts and types of instruction produce varied achievement outcomes which accumulate: the gap increases over the years. For example, Coleman et al. (1966) found that at the third grade level, achievement for white and black students was quite close together but by the 12th grade the learning gap had increased greatly.

Rosenbaum (1980) indicated that secondary students in low ability or non-college-bound tracks are generally unaware that future life choices are limited or enhanced by track placement. Even when students are given a free choice of curriculum, the low achieving students are not fully informed of the consequences of selecting various courses. Rosenbaum finds that the students who select a college-bound curriculum are those who are most informed about the future consequences of their selection. He focuses on the role of high school guidance counselors as major contributors to student misperceptions of the future effects of class or curriculum selection. It is the responsibility of the school to insure that all students understand the consequences of course selection.

Tracking and homogeneous grouping practices usually result in a heavy concentration of students from low income families in low tracks or slow groups. Leila Sussman (1977) has documented this phenomenon. This pattern is a major concern for urban districts that have undergone desegregation because it is clear that, if those patterns of grouping are used, resegregation might well occur within the school building or classroom.

Tracking systems have on at least two occasions been declared illegal. The Judge in *Hobsen v. Hanson* (1967) declared that the tracking system in Washington, D.C. public schools was unconstitutional since it did not provide equal educational opportunities to all students. A similar decision has been made with respect to *Berry v. Benton Harbor* (1974). In California the use of standardized tests for student placement has been declared illegal due to placement decisions regarding minority students on the basis of presumed intellectual inferiority.

The above brief review may be disappointing to teachers who sincerely believe that ability grouping increases achievement. The studies cited, as well as other reviews (e.g., Esposito, 1973), acknowledge this conflict, but agree that the evidence cannot support the assumption that homogeneous grouping aids achievement. Persell (1977) reaches a similar conclusion after a careful analysis of the research.

How to Group Students to Maximize Achievement and Simplify Classroom Management

The important point to understand is that teachers' decisions about grouping can have significant effects on achievement. For example, how often have you heard the belief expressed that it is the *role of the teacher* to challenge the ability of high achievers while teaching to the ability of low achievers? The belief is often put into operation through use of different workbook assignments, basal reading levels, and practice materials—generally as a result of establishing different learning objectives for "high" and "low" ability students.

Students in different groups are expected to learn different skills and are taught through different instructional methods, using materials deemed appropriate for their particular achievement levels. If the teacher has three ability groups he/she must prepare three curricula. This process impedes classroom and school achievement by differentiating the curriculum and it makes the job of teaching more complex. It establishes superior-inferior attitudes among students, it increases the achievement gap between the groups, and it legitimizes below-grade level achievement. It can function to isolate and divide class members physically, mentally, and emotionally.

Teachers need not refrain from grouping students in their classes; rather they should use the variety of techniques outlined in the Effective Instruction Module 5 when appropriate. The negative effects of homogeneous grouping and goal differentiation can be avoided by using the following grouping patterns for the instructional purposes shown.

1. Use whole class grouping for:
   a. Initial instruction on common objectives.
   b. Initial practice.
   Note: Whole-class instruction should be the primary type of grouping method, supplemented with other types of grouping as needed.
2. Use heterogeneous student learning groups for regular practice and reinforcement of skills.
3. Use temporary homogeneous performance grouping for corrective instruction or remediation. This type of grouping is used selectively, based on identified common student deficiencies, and is short-lived.
4. Use personalized instruction for:
   a. Corrective, enrichment, or extension learning.
   b. Supplementing whole class instruction.

The above instructional purposes and grouping patterns sometimes overlap and can be adjusted to fit varying classroom needs. However, this is a generally useful framework for grouping decisions that will maximize student achievement and help to meet the teacher's instructional and management concerns. As Wilson and Schmits (1978) conclude, heterogeneous grouping limits the negative effects of ability grouping while still making possible effective management of the classroom. Heterogeneous small groups and teams also facilitate the mobilization of the powerful tools related to peer culture (peer instruction, peer modeling and peer reinforcement).

While the student learning teams (Module 8) may be kept together for considerable periods of time, it is important that instructional groups be flexible rather than permanent. In the initial stage of teaching a particular objective, the teacher probably will discover that some students are at or near mastery in this area while other students require a great deal of instruction. The groups for this particular task may then be heterogeneously formed to include students at different levels of mastery so as to utilize the forces of peer norms and instruction. Occasionally, limited use of homogeneous groups is advocated, but only for corrective or enrichment instruction. When a particular learning objective is completed, these performance groups are dissolved and new groups are formed for the next task. Research demonstrates that the same students will not always be the "fast" learners (Bloom, 1976). It is essential that instructional groups are (1) formed only for instruction in a specific objective, (2) usually contain a mixture of fast/slow performers; and (3) are dissolved when the class moves on to a new objective.

How to Reach Common Goals at Grade Level

Since, as the Coleman Report (1966) indicates, differences in student achievement tend to increase over time, the problem of coping with students who have wide differences in achievement is compounded in the upper elementary grades and secondary schools. There may be students in fifth and sixth grades who are reading at the first and second grade level. How can the teacher instruct students whose grade levels vary so greatly from the "norm" to master the appropriate age-grade basic skills? Some suggested techniques are given below.

1. If the grade level skills are the type which do not require prior knowledge, heterogeneous grouping and practice is recommended.

2. Students functioning below grade level can be homogeneously grouped for corrective instruction and still be instructed in the same grade level skills that all students are expected to master during heterogeneous or whole class instruction.

   For example, when grade level skills require prior knowledge, it may be necessary to instruct students temporarily on the basis of common prerequisite skills deficiencies. This form of grouping would be flexible, because it will not always be the same students who need remedial work. Further, it is only those essential prerequisite skills which need remediation. We often assume students must go page by page in the second, third, and fourth grade level basal readers and workbooks before being exposed to the fifth grade level objectives. The goal, however, is age-grade level achievement, not total content coverage below grade level.

3. Teach selectively only the skills necessary for grade level mastery that will help the student learn faster. A combination of both homogeneous and heterogeneous grouping patterns could be used. For example, two days a week use homogeneous groups for remediation and/or enrichment, and three days a week use heterogeneous groups or whole-class instruction for group learning on common objectives.

To reach common goals, flexibility in grouping is necessary. Teachers must have common grade-level learning expectations, and must use various forms of grouping to communicate these expectations and improve achievement. Common basic skill goals should be expected of all students, including those functioning below grade level.

Summary

The ways in which students are grouped and the associated academic expectations for each group have a great influence on student achievement. Homogeneous grouping by ability, or tracking, with associated differentiated goals and objectives, has a proven negative effect on overall student achievement, while heterogeneous grouping with high expectations for learning common objectives has a positive effect on student achievement. Therefore, grouping practices which have an inhibiting or limiting effect on students' learning basic skills should be reexamined and replaced with more appropriate and productive approaches.

In summation, teachers should use grouping practices that are designed to:

1. Communicate and model common expectations for student learning.
2. Facilitate mastery of basic skill objectives by all students.
3. Reduce prerequisite skill deficits as quickly as possible, to facilitate current grade level instruction.
4. Intellectually challenge all students.
5. Eliminate any justification for below-grade level achievement.

Suggested Activities

1. Discuss current grouping practices at a grade level or departmental meeting. Review the positive and negative effects of grouping practices from the module and try to arrive at a consensus as to the most productive grouping methods for all students.
2. Expect all students to master their grade level skills and communicate this clearly to both students and parents

at the beginning of the year/course.

3. Provide for "filling in the holes" for students below grade level, as well as teaching them current grade skills. Compensatory education teachers, such as those funded under the Federal Title I program, should target prerequisite skills required of identified students. This obligates the regular classroom teacher to specify the critical skills needed by his/her students to facilitate learning grade level skills. Regular, (at least weekly) ongoing communication must take place between the classroom teacher and special teachers about what should be taught in compensatory education. Obviously instruction, both in and out of the regular classroom, must be coordinated and directly linked.

4. Identify the sex/race composition of your instructional groups. If strict homogeneous grouping by performance has been used, groups may be composed largely of any one sex/race group rather than being mixed. For example, instruction for lower performing groups or whole classes may contain mostly minority students or boys. This should be remedied by switching to heterogeneous performance groups for instruction. Using a whole-class approach for basic skills grade level instruction eliminates the composition problem—as long as the class is balanced for sex/race.

Additional Resources

American Institute for Research, *Impact of educational innovation on student performance,* Project LONGSTEP. Final Report: Volume I, Executive Summary, Palo Alto, California: American Institute for Research, 1976.

This is the summary of a very extensive study of innovative

educational practices with specific emphasis on individualized instruction. Contrary to the beliefs of many educators the study found that individualized instructional programs did not enhance achievement in basic skills.

Persell, C. H. *Education and inequality: The roots and results of stratification in America's schools.* New York: The Free Press, 1977.

Annotated in Module 1, Persell has an excellent chapter on grouping.

Rosenbaum, J. E. *Making inequality: The hidden curriculum of high school tracking.* New York: John Wiley & Sons, 1976.

In a case study of a white, working class high school, Rosenbaum demonstrates the negative effects of tracking on the middle and lower tracks. This is a thorough treatment of the topic and contains an excellent review of the literature.

Module 5

Effective Instruction

- **Background**
- **Effective Instruction**
- **Dealing with Prerequisite Skills and Corrective Instruction**
- **Feasibility**
- **Suggested Activities**
- **Additional Resources**

The objective of this module is to familiarize the reader with instructional methods and related teacher behaviors that classroom studies have shown to be the most effective for increasing student achievement. Most of these studies have observed or experimented with the teaching of sequential language and mathematics skills in elementary and secondary classrooms. Sequential skills are also the focus of this module.

The choice of instructional methods communicates expectations to students and contributes to school learning climate. Teachers who expect all their students to learn are more directive than those who do not. They set high standards, present careful demonstrations, and provide feedback aimed at correcting rather than accepting student learning errors. Their daily behavior says to each student: You are here to learn these things and I am here to make sure you learn them well.

What is presented here as effective instruction is actually a combination of three major and compatible instructional methods. Each method has been shown to contribute to higher achievement when used alone. When used together, they form a comprehensive approach to instruction which multiplies the demonstrated success of each.

The components of effective instruction and their functions are:

1. Learning for Mastery, used for general instructional organization, structure and goal-setting, as well as its specific contribution of "mastery performance standards" and the "feedback-corrective" process which will be described in other sections of this chapter.

2. Direct Instruction, the techniques of which are used for the whole-class instruction phase of Learning for Mastery. Whole-class instruction includes initial presentation of content by the teacher and controlled practice opportunities.

3. Student Team Learning, used for reinforcement of instruction by the teacher, in practice-for-competition sessions. This is described more fully in Module 8, Student Team Learning.

Since only a brief outline of effective instruction is possible in this module, we have included an annotated bibliography with major references for the three approaches above.

Background

In recent years, converging lines of research from various disciplines, schools of thought, and regions of the country have begun to zero in on consistently effective methods of teaching language and math skills. Some of this research includes a whole spectrum of instructional behaviors and some is limited to one or two main factors, such as reinforcement and student time-on-task. Increasing the skills of inner city, low income and minority students has been an emphasis of these studies.

The contradictory nature and weakly-supported findings of some past research have helped lead to educational "faddism" and subsequent discouragement with achievement results, culminating in the conclusion that schooling itself does not have much real impact on student achievement. Now, however, improved research methods based on the close observation of successful teachers and schools are changing this picture. Consequently, coherent sets of instructional methods and behaviors which can be shown reliably to increase basic skills achievement are emerging.

That different groups around the country should independently and without consultation be obtaining complementary findings, resolving what seemed to be contradictions, and getting similar results with similar methods provides strong evidence of effectiveness. Teachers may try these methods with confidence and determine for themselves their practicality and degree of effectiveness in their own classrooms. Methods which get the best results can begin to replace those which so far have resulted in unsatisfactory student performance.

Bloom (1971) noted that the concept of a "normal or bell-shaped curve" distribution of ability/achievement has had a severely damaging effect on teacher expectations. If teachers assume that student achievement follows such a curve, they will expect high, average and low achievement—"winners" and "losers"—from each group of students they encounter. Grading practices follow this set of expectations, so that students internalize the expectations at an early age and come to think of themselves as A, B, C, D, or failing students. The effect of this expectation "curve" on student performance has already been discussed in the preceding modules.

Learning for Mastery (LFM) use the "J" curve as a more appropriate and realistic way of looking at classroom achievement: that is, nearly all students are capable of arriving at the

high end of the "J" curve at the conclusion of a course. LFM
is based on the assumption that the middle ninety-five percent
of students can learn any given subject to a high degree of
mastery, given sufficient time and appropriate instruction
(Bloom, 1978). "Aptitude" for a particular subject is seen not
as a predictor of final achievement level, but as a predictor of
the amount of time required by the student to reach an
established mastery level on new material (Carroll, 1963).
There may be slower learners and faster learners in various
subject areas, but they are not labelled "poor" students or
"good" students.

STUDENT ACHIEVEMENT UNDER TWO
CONDITIONS: Normal and J Curve Distributions

(Adapted from Bloom, 1976, p. 165)

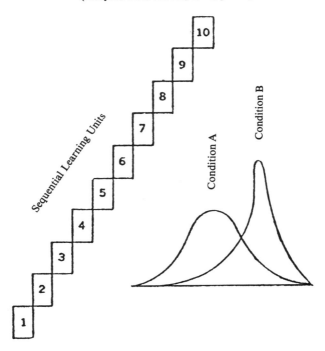

Under condition A, assume that 90 percent of the students learn Unit 1 adequately, while 10 percent do not. These 10 percent will not learn any of the later units (2-10) adequately because Unit 1 is basic to all that follows. Assume further that while 90 percent master Unit 1 adequately, some of these will not learn Unit 2 adequately. For each additional unit, more students fall by the wayside until by Unit 10, only 10 percent learn it adequately while 90 percent do not. If these students are given a summative test in which all 10 units are equally represented, the curve of achievement is likely to approximate a normal distribution with considerable individual variation.

Under condition B (mastery learning), assume also that 90 percent learn Unit 1 adequately while 10 percent do not. But these 10 percent are provided corrective instruction until at least 5 percent or more have adequately learned Unit 1, before entering Unit 2. This process is repeated on each unit and the goal is always to have 95 percent of the students achieve adequate learning before moving on. Using the same summative test as in condition A, over 90 percent of the students reach about the same level of achievement as the top 10 percent of the students under condition A. This is the J curve distribution.

Unlike the "ability level," which is often assumed to be fixed or unalterable, these aptitudes are subject to change. It has been demonstrated that if students learn how to learn, their rate of learning will increase. For example, students who take three or four times as long as other students to master a unit at the beginning of a course may take about the same time as the others to master the final unit of the course. Anderson (1980) notes that LFM students tend to become more similar to one another both in terms of the amount learned and the time needed to learn. The effect is cumulative as the learning skills are maintained and transferred to new courses or subject areas. In high-implementing mastery learning classrooms, eighty or ninety percent of students have performed "A" level work while in comparable classrooms using the same basic materials, only twenty percent have reached that level under traditional teaching conditions (Bloom, 1978).

Learning for Mastery has its most profound effect when used as a system, over time, by cooperating teachers using congruent objectives, materials, and tests. The achievement resulting from such a system is different qualitatively and quantitatively from that of other methods.

Effective Instruction

Effective instruction is based on teaching a common set of grade level skill objectives to the whole class, with the expectation that all students will reach or exceed a stated mastery performance standard. Because of differences in skill levels, aptitudes (time to learn), and expectations of entering students, some will need extra time and corrective instruction to reach the mastery performance standard: others will need enrichment instruction. This personalized help is given in practice, feedback, and reinstruction generally, subsequent to initial instruction of the class. Initial instruction is carefully planned to establish and model expected outcomes for the entire class. Although outside help may be used if available—and, under conditions described here, students will help each other—it is the teacher who directs the process, who structures and paces the learning, insures continuity and maintains maximum time-on-task for the students.

To sustain and increase motivation, it is important for all class members to have frequent success experiences. However, success is not accomplished by lowering standards, by using objectives and materials below the age-grade of students in the class, or by allowing excessive off-task behavior. Rather the objective to be learned is divided into small meaningful parts or "bites" for students experiencing difficulty. This process of identifying the prerequisite and component skills of an objective is called task analysis. Satisfaction for the students comes from mastering these small "bites" in succession.

Effective instruction has built-in mastery indicators. The teacher gets quick verbal feedback from all students as well as frequent progress test results. This feedback helps to identify the students who need additional time and corrective instruction. Equally important, it also signals when practice is becoming excessive and the time has come for the class to move on to new tasks.

The components of effective instruction are briefly described below.

Planning and Preparation for Effective Instruction

1. Identify a clear and measurable set of skill objectives for the course. Planning, teaching and evaluating should all relate to these objectives. Some schools or districts already have well-established course objectives. If not, the teacher, or teachers cooperatively, should develop or identify them.

2. Establish a mastery performance standard for the course. For example, if it is believed that students must master at least 8 out of 10 of the skill objectives (or 16 out of 20) in order to function effectively at the next grade level, the mastery performance standard is set at 80 percent. The teacher then aims for and anticipates that all students will reach or exceed the mastery performance standard of 80 percent.

3. Determine grades to be given for various levels of student mastery. For example, a student reaching or exceeding the mastery performance standard by the end of the course would get an automatic A or B, regardless of other factors such as level of participation in class or the amount of time spent. Students not reaching the mastery performance standard would receive grades below A or B, without regard to other factors. It is important here to make a direct connection between grades and the level of learning

attained by the student on the stated objectives of the course.

4. List the objectives of the course in a sequence beginning with the easiest and working toward the most difficult whenever possible. When listing the objectives in order, building in prerequisite skills for the next objective should always be considered so that a natural progression of learning takes place.

5. Using the school calendar, schedule the teaching of objectives for the semester or year. Be sure to allow extra time for the first objectives in order to bring students to mastery. Some students will have skill deficits to make up or will require more time to master the first objectives. If this extra time is planned for early in the course, the rest of the course will proceed more quickly and smoothly with less "backtracking."

6. Divide scheduled objectives into learning "units" of one or more week's duration. Each unit would focus on one or more main course objective and would include initial whole-class instruction, practice, progress testing, and corrective/enrichment instruction. These units may include sub-objectives leading to mastery of a main objective, following the principle of breaking down complex tasks into simple, discrete steps which students master in succession. Units may be built around a theme or a certain body of knowledge which is appropriate for the age and grade level of the students. In this way the teacher can plan for maximum content coverage and add richness and variety.

7. Plan initial whole-class instruction for each unit and gather the necessary instructional and practice materials. The teacher models academic behavior for the students by being well prepared for class and having materials ready for use or distribution.

8. Develop or obtain a brief test or procedure which will

measure only how students are progressing on the unit objective(s). This is the progress or formative test. It is considered a part of student practice. Although it may be scored and recorded, it is not used to help determine grades.

9. Identify alternative strategies for reteaching the unit objective(s) to students who did not reach mastery.

10. Identify enrichment/extension strategies for the unit objective(s) for those students who reach mastery earliest.

11. Develop or obtain a test which measures final mastery of the unit objective(s). This is the mastery or summative test used for grading students. Mastery tests may be given after each unit or after several units to conform to school marking periods. Test anxiety is reduced by having had the opportunity to take ungraded practice tests on the same objectives.

Note: Diagnostic or pretest information helps to focus planning, preparation, and time allotments on the greatest skill needs of students. However, it is possible to proceed without such information and use the progress tests for adjustment and modification of instruction as the course proceeds.

Student Orientation

It is during orientation that expectations are communicated to students for the first time. Plan in advance what to say to them and plan subsequent behavior to convince the most dubious and discouraged among them.

1. Present the objectives of the course to entering students. Put them in writing, post them on the classroom wall, send them to parents. This information is basic to students' sense of purpose, organization and self-management.

2. Describe the mastery performance standard established for the course. Tell the students that they are all expected to reach that standard, and describe the procedures to be followed which will help them to reach it. Stress individual and collective responsibility for learning, and the time and attention it will require.

3. Inform students of the grades to be earned by reaching the mastery performance standard (A or B). Stress the direct connection between learning and grades. There will be students in most classes who have never been able to earn an A or B in their school careers because of "curve" grading, of being graded before adequate practice and corrective instruction, because of behavior problems or various other factors. Make a promise to these students that if they learn, they earn. Keep the promise.

Initial Instruction and Controlled Practice

Initial instruction on the common objectives is provided by the teacher to the whole class at the same time. Some successful techniques gained from studies of "Direct Instruction" are used here to keep all students participating at a high level.

1. The teacher determines lesson objectives, materials and methods. Student choices are limited and are made within the framework for learning established by the teacher.

2. Students know what to expect and are given complete and clear directions. The classroom is organized and businesslike. Disruptions are kept to a minimum through good planning and management on the part of the teacher and the building staff.

3. The teacher models task orientation by being prepared for class, having materials ready, and by maintaining active and continuous teaching behavior.

4. The teacher is directly responsible for initial teaching of content. Students are not expected to learn or discover independently through the use of worksheets, texts, or any other means. The teacher presents, illustrates, explains or demonstrates what is to be learned. Assignments for practice are made following the teacher's lesson, and are consistent with lesson content. Materials and activities reinforce and supplement instruction from the teacher.

5. The lessons proceed in small steps. Each step is built on the last and builds toward the next. During initial presentation and during review, the teacher points out to students the logical sequence and the continuity of the lessons. Students are helped to see the meaning and the progression of their learning and to relate the skills they are learning to the larger objective.

6. Following instruction on content, the teacher conducts question-answer sessions with the class, making sure all students get chances to respond. Some practitioners suggest calling on students in order, so that students are not inadvertently or systematically left out. Hunter (1979) suggests posing questions to the class, waiting a few seconds so that all students must consider the correct response, and then calling on an individual to respond. The teacher uses a variety of group alerting techniques to keep all class members participating at a high level. The behavior to be avoided here is calling on a few consistent volunteers for responses and allowing the rest of the class to become spectators.

7. The teacher aims at a balance of high and medium success level in student responses by varying the level of difficulty of questions. For example, the teacher may wish to engage reluctant learners early in the session by starting with questions they can answer easily and then moving them on to more challenging questions.

8. At the earliest grade levels easy, factual questions are

asked at a fairly rapid pace. An occasional alternative to calling on individuals is asking for choral responses. With older students successful responses would often require more time and thought. Recalling that the focus of this module is on sequenced skills, it is important to note that free-ranging discussion is not appropriate in this context, even with higher level skills as the objective. Student initiative should be encouraged at other times but not during focused language and math skills instruction.

9. Students are expected to respond. The teacher probes, restates or simplifies the question for those who do not answer or answer incorrectly, allowing them adequate time to respond. Modeling of correct thinking and responding is considered important for all the class members. An additional benefit of these planned interchanges is quick feedback to the teacher on the effectiveness of the initial instruction for the class and for individuals.

10. Students are provided immediate and objective feedback on their responses. Student errors are corrected in a matter-of-fact way before they can be practiced repeatedly. An error made by an individual may be treated as a group error, and the entire class corrected accordingly. Errors generally are treated as an inevitable part of new learning and no penalties are assessed during practice. This reduces student anxiety and encourages some risk-taking.

11. Praise is used in moderation. The effective teacher praises correct thinking as well as correct response. (See also Module 9, Reinforcing Achievement.)

12. The teacher plans to make sure that students are firm in their mastery of each essential skill by extending practice slightly. Students are given two or three opportunities for errorless practice after they have learned the skill.

13. Independent seatwork, student learning teams or small

study groups are the next opportunity for students to practice or apply new skills. The teacher should move around the classroom, check student work, and answer questions. The teacher continuously signals to the class that they should be on-task.

14. For students or groups of students needing more practice, special homework may be required, perhaps by contract for older students. Homework should reinforce lessons previously taught by the teacher, should be of a manageable amount so that low-motivated students are not discouraged by it, and must always be checked and corrected.

15. Groups may be arranged for reinstruction and practice on particular skills or groups of skills. However, grouping should be flexible and arranged so that no students are permitted to be thought of as "low achievers." Also, no group should be excluded from initial instruction. All should receive the teacher presentation, practice, feedback, and supervision.

16. Increasing skills of the class may be charted and posted on the wall to influence student effort and increase motivation.

Feedback and Corrective/Enrichment Instruction

Corrective instruction is one of the most significant departures from conventional instruction that Learning for Mastery takes. Teachers find it the most difficult, but the most rewarding part of LFM to implement. Many comment that their faster students seem to benefit as much as the slower ones because mastery is not assumed for anyone: it must be demonstrated concretely. Learning errors are caught before they are compounded and for the student, education begins to be a self-correcting process.

1. After initial instruction and controlled practice opportunities, administer the progress or formative test

to students. Remind them that the test is part of student practice.

2. Determine which students have mastered the unit objective(s), and the learning errors of those who have not.

3. Inform students of their mastery level. Tests may be scored (but not used for grades) and returned to students, or discussed with them.

4. For students who have mastered the objective, provide enrichment/extension instruction and activities that will strengthen the learned skill and allow them to apply it in new ways or to new situations. The use of Bloom's taxonomy, is helpful here (reference is included in "Additional Resources" at the end of this chapter). An excellent reinforcement is to create conditions where mastery students can comfortably help others in the class to attain mastery (see Module 8, Student Team Learning).

5. For students who have not yet mastered the objective, provide corrective instruction. Correctives *always* provide additional time, practice, participation and alternative instructional strategies whether they are for the whole class or for individual students.

Correction is done on a personalized basis. The teacher tries to determine the nature of the learning error (or the specific missing prerequisite skill), and applies corrective instruction in a mode different, from that of the initial instruction, using knowledge of the student's preferred learning style when possible.

Some students react to "cues" in different ways. Some students grasp the meaning of a lesson more quickly from touch and manipulation than from hearing and seeing a demonstration of the same thing. In a classroom it is obviously not possible to use the precise best method for each child for each objective. However, it is possible to provide one or two well-selected alternative strategies for each objective. With practice and encouragement students begin to see that they do have alternate ways of learning, that they will get help in finding and using these alternatives, and that they will get results if they put in the extra time they require to achieve mastery.

While there is a wealth of material available for planning alternative strategies, teachers are chronically short of time for finding and organizing such materials. Unless the materials are available in advance, they will not be used when needed. Here is where the value of cooperative effort by a building staff is greatest. A "stockpile" of successful strategies and materials should be maintained and increased annually to save time for all participating teachers.

Ways of managing corrective instruction in the classroom include: small group study and practice, team study and practice, academic games, tutoring (including peer tutoring), assigned homework, and class exercise and drills.

6. Retest students after corrective instruction to determine mastery. Ideally the class moves as a unit after all students have mastered the objective. If handled correctly, this is a powerful motivator for class effort and student cooperation. However, in the best interests of the class, the teacher will have to decide when to move ahead. In making this decision, it should be recalled that if adequate time to achieve mastery is allowed in the early part of the course, the students will probably cover the remaining objectives more quickly. If the press to "cover the course" by the end of the semester or year forces the teacher to move on to a new objective, corrective instruction for non-mastery students should continue as new instruction progresses (see also section on Dealing with Prerequisite Skills and Corrective Instruction).

As a rule of thumb, the teacher should aim for at least 90 percent mastery in the classroom before going on to the next objective.

Mastery Testing and Grading

1. Following completion and review of instructional unit(s), administer mastery or summative tests which measure final mastery of the objectives. They may be used at the ends of the marking periods, or they may be given more frequently and their grades averaged for a marking period report card grade.
2. Grade students according to the mastery performance standard established at the beginning of the course (A or B for mastery). If grades are given for participation, attendance, assignment completion, citizenship, or in other areas, they should be separate from the grades for mastery.
3. Use evaluation of achievement results to plan improvement of instruction in subsequent units or courses.

Review and Retention of Learning

Hunter (1979) has done extensive study of practices which help students to retain what they have learned. Provision is made in our description of effective instruction for these practices. They are briefly restated below:

1. *Meaning.* Students do not remember isolated bits of information which have no meaning for them. Structuring the curriculum and maintaining sequence of objectives lays the base for meaningful learning. Fewer and better objectives are more effective than numerous, trivial ones: concentrate on key concepts and skip unimportant details. In the overview which

Praise a colleague!
Compliment a friend!
Give the KAPPAN!

Celebrate a raise, a completed dissertation, a retirement,
or a special occasion with a subscription to the KAPPAN.

It's a gift that's also an investment in a friend's professional growth.

YES! I want to give a friend a subscription to the KAPPAN.

☒ 1 year, $20   ☐ 2 years, $36   ☐ 3 years, $52   ☐ Payment enclosed   ☐ Please bill me

Send gift to:

NAME Vic

TITLE

ADDRESS

CITY

STATE _____ ZIP

☐ New Subscription   ☐ Renewal
☐ Please send a gift card to the recipient.

MY NAME

TITLE

ADDRESS

CITY

STATE _____ ZIP

Mail to: Phi Delta Kappa, 8th & Union Streets, P.O. Box 789,
Bloomington, IN 47402. Non-U.S. subscription rates are: 1
yr., $22.50; 2 yrs., $41; 3 yrs., $59.50.

BUSINESS REPLY CARD

FIRST CLASS   PERMIT NO. 179   BLOOMINGTON, IN

POSTAGE WILL BE PAID BY ADDRESSEE

KAPPAN

P.O. BOX 789
BLOOMINGTON, IN   47402

NO POSTAGE
NECESSARY IF
MAILED IN THE
UNITED STATES

precedes a lesson, or the review which follows, put what is being learned into the context of larger learning. Relate sub-objectives or lesson content to a main course objective. Occasionally discuss with students the purposes or uses of the learning which is occurring, preferably with relevance to their own lives.

2. *Degree of original learning.* What is not learned well in the first place will not be remembered. The teacher should *assess* the degree of learning on important material before moving on, and reteach the class or correctively instruct individuals as necessary.

3. *Pleasant feeling tone.* The feeling of accomplishment, of "I can do it," helps students to remember and also motivates them to keep moving forward. Successes must be genuine, however small. Unpleasant feeling tone will also help students remember, but probably not what the teacher intends to be remembered. Avoidance behavior is a common student reaction to unpleasant feeling tone.

4. *Positive transfer.* When something in students' past learning helps them to master and retain new learning, it is called positive transfer. This is why newer curricula aim to teach generalizations and principles rather than a string of facts: similarities and relationships between old and new learning help positive transfer, especially if called to student attention. Negative transfer, on the other hand, is interference in new learning by previous learning and results in student confusion. Teachers who try to anticipate student responses will be more aware of the possibilities of either kind of transfer. For example, an experienced math teacher will teach together from the multiplication tables 8 x 4 and 8 x 8, because they are similar, related and "support" each other: the teacher would avoid teaching 8 x 7 and 8 x 9 together because of learning interference and the possibility of "scrambling" answers.

5. *Practice.* At the beginning of any new learning, practice periods should be frequent and closely spaced.
This is called massed practice. Such practice opportunities are described in the sections above. Once the
material is learned, practice continues but the time
between practicing is extended. This is distributed
practice. When using sequential objectives, the
teacher would review or refer back to skills learned
earlier and have students practice them occasionally
for retention. If the skills learned previously must be
exercised to accomplish the new objective, as often
happens, review and practice take place naturally
with just a reminder from the teacher.

Keeping the above factors in mind will assist teachers in
planning their reviews of learning. Students will "test" better at
the end of the year and master later learning more efficiently.

Dealing With Prerequisite Skills and Corrective Instruction

We believe it is possible for teachers to bring most of their
students to mastery of grade level skills under the conditions
described in this module. It may not be possible, however, for
teachers to assume alone the total responsibility for overcoming
critical skill deficiencies which prevent mastery of grade level
skills, especially when these are extensive and of long standing.
The resource staff of the building or district, especially any
compensatory education program staff, should be mobilized to
identify and deal with prerequisites in a planned fashion. The
same should be true of extensive corrective instruction on grade
level objectives, although these would be exceptional cases.

The teacher should selectively identify those skill deficiencies among the students that interfere with mastery of grade
level objectives and then teach the missing prerequisites. If there
are just a few, the teacher can handle these during regular instruction. If there are many skill deficiencies, the teacher may

need the help of resource teachers, student teachers, aides, parent volunteers, a school or community learning center, or older students as tutors. The classroom teacher should still direct the process, assigning the skills to be learned, checking on progress, and evaluating outcomes.

Consistent with improving school learning climate, students should not be "pulled out" of their regular grade level language/math instruction to receive this corrective instruction or help with missing prerequisites. Students deficient in skills must receive regular classroom instruction in an amount equal to or greater than their classmates if they are to arrive at grade level mastery.

Feasibility

The instructional methods described are not meant to make teaching easier but to make it more successful. In the early stages of implementation, extra work and planning time are required. However, there are ways to save time, and there are certain features of these methods that help to make them feasible in the classroom.

For example, a key feature of Learning for Mastery is that it seems to move dependent students in the direction of independent learning. This is due in part to their growing attainment of prerequisite/essential skills and their feelings of academic efficacy, and in part to their "learning to learn." While this is a gradual process, especially at the secondary level, eventually the extra teaching time required for slower students tends to decrease. Most secondary schools have an extremely wide range of student achievement with which to contend because early learning deficits in language and math were not attended to and kept expanding. While it is clear that early experience with LFM is the most productive of overall learning, learners at any age can overcome discouragement and acquire essential skills when this high quality instruction is provided. The sense of renewed hope that students feel on entering a new school can be used to good advantage by beginning LFM at the start of junior and senior high school. Tangible and fairly immediate rewards for mastery help to re-engage the discouraged student in learning. These special external incentives become less important as the students gain in skill and confidence.

In general, most effort and planning in LFM should go into whole-class instruction on common objectives. This is another significant time saver when it is compared to individualized instruction or differential goal-setting and instruction for various groups within the classroom.

Key to the feasibility of building-wide adoption of this approach is coordination and cooperation by the building staff. Grade level or departmental staff, with the support of the principal and any resource staff, can avoid much duplication of effort and develop superior products by jointly undertaking the following activities:

1. Identifying instructional objectives, if not already in place.
2. Arranging objectives in a sequence from the easiest to the most difficult.
3. Scheduling the teaching of objectives so that teachers are operating from a common calendar. (The common calendar, in our experience, is the basis for ongoing joint staff effort.)
4. Lesson planning based on mastery model.
5. Development or selection of supportive materials for initial instruction, student practice, corrective instruction and enrichment/extension. Arrangements should be made for quick accessibility by any participating teacher.
6. Development or selection of any additional tests needed.
7. Identification of skills prerequisite to the selected grade level objectives and a plan to accomplish the teaching of those most needed.

Additionally, the time which is spent in meetings or in the

faculty lounge in providing mutual assistance, advice and encouragement between colleagues should never be undervalued, especially as new approaches are tried. Research increasingly points toward staff cooperation and common goal-setting as a hallmark of good learning climate.

Student Team Learning

Evidence on the importance of student cooperation to achievement is also appearing with increasing frequency (e.g., Fisher, Berliner, Filby, Marliave, Cahen, Dishaw, & Moore, 1978). Practitioners are finding that Learning for Mastery promotes a greater willingness among students to help each other because of its emphasis on group learning of common objectives, as opposed to individual competition for a limited number of good grades or other rewards. To the extent that this is true, the teacher has many teaching allies in the classroom. It is exhausting and perhaps unnecessary for the teacher to have to initiate every motivational or learning contact each day. Some of this can be done by the students themselves during regular team practice sessions if the teacher has made student team learning a basic and continuing part of classroom instruction.

We conclude by recommending that mastery teams be organized wherever possible to support and reinforce instruction by the teacher. We consider the enhanced cooperativeness known to result from student teaming to be a main facilitator of this approach to effective instruction. Four-to-six member teams should be selected carefully by the teacher to include slower and faster students and students of different races and socioeconomic backgrounds. Teams should meet on a regular basis to practice together, using materials provided by the teacher.

Cooperative behavior among teammates should be taught and reinforced. The sensitive teacher will see that each student has chances to help and be helped as the teams study and practice for game or quiz competition. When students with different skill levels can interact comfortably on the material they are assigned, and have learned to use regular team practice time well, the teacher has some time to do corrective/enrichment instruction with individuals, small groups, or one of the teams. Bloom (1978) notes that most students needing corrective instruction require only an additional hour or so every two weeks, the equivalent of six minutes each school day. A few minutes spent on corrective instruction while the teams practice can be highly effective. (See also module on Student Team Learning.)

Summary

The major steps of effective instruction as briefly described above are:

1. Teach common grade level objectives and provide practice opportunities to whole class.
2. Use student learning teams to reinforce instruction by the teacher.
3. Follow up with frequent ungraded progress tests.
4. Provide personalized or group corrective instruction to non-mastery students before moving on: provide enrichment instruction to mastery students and/or the whole class.
5. Using mastery test results, give grades of A or B to students meeting an established mastery performance standard.

Staff coordination and enhanced student cooperativeness lessen the burden on individual teachers.

Although the full potential of this combination of effective instructional methods takes some time to be realized, the immediate gains have convinced many teachers to adopt these methods. While we have emphasized in this module the building of basic skills that enable students to become independent and lifelong learners, mastery instruction has been used with equal success in many subjects and from the elementary school through the graduate school level.

This approach provides an excellent framwork for decision-making by teachers. The planned verbal and written feedback from students provide clear "stop and go" signals for both short range and long range instructional decisions. At the same time, no limitations are placed on the strengths, creativity and ingenuity of the teacher or the capabilities of the student. Teaching must have variety and interest and suit the teacher as well as the learner.

Suggested Activities

1. Discuss concepts
   - normal curve
   - J curve
2. Assess current instructional practices and results
   - success-failure rates of last year
   - standards for grading
   - common objectives
   - special groupings, tracking
3. Establish a common expectation (or performance standard) for learning in your building for the current year, such as: _____ percent of students will master _____ percent of grade level skills. This is the goal to which planning, instruction and evaluation all relate. It should be based on a collective staff decision and commitment.
4. Review district basic skill program. Place objectives in sequence and schedule time for teaching basic skill objectives for the semester or year. Establish a common school calendar for teaching grade level objectives to facilitate joint efforts of staff.
5. Individual teachers, dyads, or small cooperating groups of teachers can begin to adopt the techniques

of Direct Instruction with only a limited amount of advance preparation. These techniques are used for whole class instruction and controlled practice: see pages 133 - 136 in this module for description. Results of such use should be shared with colleagues.

6. Individual teachers, dyads, or small cooperating groups of teachers can begin to implement the corrective/enrichment instruction phase of Learning for Mastery as they choose. Wider adoption demands more lead time for preparation and staff coordination.

7. Form grade level or subject area committees to plan mastery teaching units for objectives, to be shared by all participating teachers. Units should include:

   a. Lesson plan for whole class instruction;

   b. Progress or formative test; mastery or summative test if needed;

   c. Alternative strategies for reteaching or for corrective instruction, at least two;

   d. Enrichment/extension strategies for individuals (Use task analysis and taxonomy for steps c and d.);

8. Use and experiment with mastery teaching units. Evaluate results, plan improvements and additional units in preparation for wider implementation in following year.

9. Discuss ways to use student team learning to support basic skills instruction. Plan and implement team selections, practice sessions on content, and team competition with some appropriate rewards.

10. Identify critical prerequisite skills for grade level instruction. Decide who is responsible for teaching skills outside the regular grade level program.

Additional Resources

Block, J. H., & Anderson, L. W. *Mastery learning in classroom instruction.* New York: MacMillan Publishing Co., 1975.

This is the most complete "how to" source on implementing a groupbased mastery learning instructional system. It is essential reading for effective implementation of a mastery learning program.

Bloom, B. S. *Human characteristics and school learning.* New York: McGraw-Hill, 1976.

Annotated in Introduction.

Bloom, B. S. *All our children learning: A primer for parents, teachers, and other educators.* New York: McGraw-Hill, 1981.

Bloom's recent book describes further work on the theory, research, and implications of mastery learning with respect to the ability of all students to learn well.

Fisher, C. W., Berliner, D. W., Filby, N. N., Marliave, R., Cahen, L. S., Dishaw, M. M., & Moore, J. E. *Teaching and learning in the elementary school: A summary of the Beginning Teacher Evaluation Study.* San Francisco: Technical Report VII-1, Beginning Teacher Evaluation Study, Far West Laboratory for Educational Research and Development, 1978. (ERIC Document Reproduction Service No. ED 165 322).

This summary of the extensive BTES research on effective teaching is a major contribution to the work on direct instruction, time-on-task, emphasis on academic achievement, and other characteristics of successful practitioners.

Good, T. L. Teacher effectiveness in the elementary school *Journal of Teacher Education,* 1979, *30*(2), 52-64.

This article gives a thorough review of the literature on

direct instruction, concluding that this style of teaching promotes higher achievement.

Keller, F. S. Good-bye teacher . . .*Journal of Applied Behavior Analysis* 1968, *1,* 79-89.

A second branch of work on learning for mastery is Keller's Personalized System of Instruction, a student-paced individualized approach. While the principles of feedback and correctives are included in this system, it lacks the whole group, direct instruction and common attainment of objectives which are consistent with an effective school learning climate.

Rosenshine, B. Content, time, and direct instruction. In P. L. Peterson & H. J. Walberg (Eds.), *Research on teaching: Concepts, findings, and implications.* Berkeley, Cal.: McCutchan Publishing Corp., 1979.

A review and analysis of direct instruction in which Rosenshine notes that the concept is still loosely defined but refers to "academically focused, teacher-directed classrooms using sequenced and structured materials" (p. 38).

Note: See also references in Module 8, Student Team Learning.

Module 6

Academic Engaged Time

- **The Concept of Academic Engaged Time**
- **Research on Time and Student Achievement**
- **Relation of Academic Engaged Time to Other Factors**
- **Strategies for Increasing Academic Engaged Time**
- **Suggested Activities**
- **Additional Resources**

Educators and researchers have long recognized time as an important factor in learning. The direct relationship between achievement and active learning time has become firmly established both for individuals and for groups of students. Numerous studies have demonstrated that a consistent difference of just a few minutes in active learning time will show up clearly in achievement differences between otherwise comparable classrooms. Studies done in Learning for Mastery (Bloom, 1976) show that, on the average, the difference between mastery and non-mastery for a student needing corrective instruction is about an hour of extra instruction every two weeks: this is the equivalent of six minutes per school day (see Module 5 on Effective Instruction for an explanation of this process).

This module, and the accompanying activities, will focus upon increasing the amount of time spent in instructional activity as opposed to that spent in non-instructional activity. Improving achievement by increasing active learning time is a task the principal and staff should be involved in together.

The Concept of Academic Engaged Time

The concept of Academic Engaged Time (AET), as used in this module, refers to the amount of time devoted to instruction and learning. This time is largely determined by the teacher. It involves 1) the time allocated or planned for instruction, 2) the time actually spent on instruction, and 3) the time the student is actively engaged in learning (time on task).

Academic Engaged Time is not synonomous with allocated time, which is the time scheduled for instruction in a particular subject area. Our position is that maximum classroom time should be allocated to academic instruction. Our concern is that actual time spent in classrooms is often much less than intended or planned. For example, the teacher may allocate one hour a day for reading instruction. However, if reading instruction follows a recess, as much as ten minutes of the allocated time may be lost while students settle down to work. If they are assigned to small groups after the teacher presents a lesson, another few minutes may be lost as they move to new locations. Normal classroom problems, such as minor misbehavior, interruptions, misplaced materials, materials distribution, and so on, further intrude on the allocated time and reduce the potential for Academic Engaged Time. Some of this loss of time is avoidable or can be minimized.

One serious detractor from academic time in most schools is discipline problems. As we note in Module 7, discipline largely depends on the level of expectations for conduct and the consistency with which this role expectation is carried out in the school social system. These expectations are alterable, and will be reflected in improved discipline if the school as a unit decides to upgrade expectations for student behavior.

Increasing school attendance can help to increase your school's achievement. Increasing the Academic Engaged Time of a class will not help those students who are absent from the class. Stated simply, if students are not in school they are not on task.

In order to increase Academic Engaged Time, the assumption under which we must operate is that teaching does make a difference in the achievement of students. Thus, the more teaching that occurs, the more learning will result. Our position that schools can make a difference in student learning is supported by the fact that the school and, in particular, the teacher directly control the teaching process. The teacher can plan the school day to maximize the time devoted to teaching and learning the specific academic objectives for each day. This is the Academic Engaged Time.

The time students are involved in active learning may be decidedly less than the time allocated to instruction. The active learning time is frequently identified as "time-on-task." This includes the time students attend to the instruction given, practice on the learning tasks, recitation, testing, and other learning activities.

This actual time-on-task for each student is critical in the learning process. It is therefore important that we determine what percentage of time the student is actively engaged on-task during the instructional period. For example, daydreaming, sleeping, misbehaving, and the like reduce both the academic engaged time and the time-on-task. The goal is to maximize the amount of the school day used for Academic Engaged Time.

Research On Time and Student Achievement

Several studies now clearly demonstrate that the level of student achievement is clearly related to each of the time dimensions noted above. Another factor that affects each of these dimensions, however, is the attendance of students. Wiley and Harneshfeger (1974) found that the level of school attendance explained a significant proportion of the variance in school achievement. Absent students generally receive less instruction and devote less time to learning the desired skills and knowledge than students that attend school.

There is not much differnce between schools in the amount of time in the total instructional day. Most schools schedule between five and six hours of daily instruction. Only when schools are on split or half-day sessions does the allocated time vary greatly between them. However the small variations in total instructional time are related to resulting levels of achievement, (Wiley & Harneshfeger, 1974).

Although the length of the school day varies little, the amount of time allocated to academic instruction varies markedly. This is a function of the school social system and expectations regarding learning. If the school staff believes students are unlikely to achieve grade level skills in reading and math, time allocated for these subjects is likely to be less than in schools where the staff expects mastery of those skills. Doss and Hester (1978) found that Title I schools, as a group, spent more time in activities which did not involve direct instruction (assemblies, school fairs, field trips, etc.) than did non-Title I schools. Students served by Title I and bilingual programs received substantially less reading instruction than did students not served by these programs.

Also, Rosenbaum (1976) indicates that academic instructional time differs among various groups within a school. He noted the number of hours of academic work (reading, math, science, etc.) college-bound groups received was higher than vocational and other student groups received. He concluded that the sorting of students into different groups reduces the total amount of time allocated to academic learning for at least some groups.

Although allocation of time for instruction does not guarantee that full time will be devoted to teaching and learning, high levels of learning do not occur when most of the school day is devoted to other activities.

Time-on-task or active learning time research requires good technique and considerable time. Numerous researchers have found that teacher reports of time-on-task are not adequate measures of time usage. So far only observations of classroom activities by an objective observer seem to give valid measures of time usage. Studies recording actual engaged time and time-on-task have consistently found that the greater the time-on-task the greater the level of achievement (Anderson, in press; Bloom, 1980). The Beginning Teacher Evaluation Study (Fisher et al., 1978) reports that seatwork is one of the periods in which students are frequently not on task. Ironically, independent seatwork is a major instructional activity in most classrooms today. While seatwork can be beneficial, the absence of direct teacher-student contact during independent work time increases the opportunity for students to become disengaged from learning.

The evidence supporting the relationship between time and achievement is so conclusive that schools wanting to improve the achievement of their students should examine carefully the ways in which the Academic Engaged Time can be increased.

Relation of Academic Engaged Time to Other Factors

Improvement in the amount of time devoted to teaching and learning the desired outcomes is highly dependent on the other factors discussed in these modules. Significant increases in Academic Engaged Time are not likely to occur if other changes do not occur.

Expectation and Time

As we have noted in Module 2 teachers and other staff who believe students are unable to learn and for whom they hold low expectations are less likely to devote as much time to instructing them as they do students they expect to learn. This occurs in many ways. The amount of time they give the student to answer (wait-time) frequently varies with teacher expectations. The number of cues or prompting given and the reinstruction given during recitation time varies with teacher expectations. Also students from whom little is expected are more likely to be given irrelevant seatwork to occupy their time than are students for whom high levels of learning are expected. These and other activities suggest that teachers must think students can learn what they teach, and expect them to do so, or they are unlikely to see that students are productively engaged in learning during the time available.

Time and Effective Instruction

Academic Engaged Time is essentially the time devoted to academic teaching and learning. The Effective Instruction module outlines a direct instructional method based on mastery learning which will help plan uses of instructional and active learning time. As Bloom (1980), a leading developer of mastery learning, notes, if two students are in the same classroom and one is actively engaged for 90 percent of the hour while the other is actively engaged for only 30 percent of the same period, there will be significant differences in their learning during that hour. Both the previous module and this one are designed to assist in the effective use of time allocated for academic instruction.

Time, Discipline and Classroom Management

As we noted earlier, major detractors from Academic Engaged Time are transitions (e.g., getting a class ready for instruction) and various discipline problems. The following module dealing with these topics is also an essential part of a program to increase time devoted to academic learning tasks. The classroom management portion of that module emphasizes the management of time.

In fact, essentially all the modules in this set have some relation to time devoted to learning. Therefore, increasing time allocated or time-on-task should not be seen as a separate or independent activity. The strategies for enhancing learning time are intertwined throughout the training package. The Effective Instruction module exemplifies the particulars of good planning, managing and instruction. The team learning module attempts to increase active learning time by mobilizing the peer culture toward achievement. Proper use of rewards can decrease discipline problems and thus increase both instructional time and time-on-task. Use of assessment information can be helpful in organizing for instruction by identifying subject areas that need more time for mastery to be achieved. These are but a few examples which highlight the interrelatedness of the training package. Use of this set of modules will directly result in an increase of time spent on academic instruction.

Strategies For Increasing Academic Engaged Time

Attendance

Obviously, students absent from school are not likely to learn as many academic skills as they do when attending school the need to maximize attendance by all students is therefore apparent. Some features of an effective plan for improving attendance are listed below. Of course, these suggestions must be combined with an effective school learning climate in which students learn well and are positively rewarded for doing so (see section on Reward Structures in Module 3).

A parallel program to that outlined below can be implemented for tardiness.

1. *High expectations:* teachers must clearly communicate that good attendance is important and that the school and the teacher expect this.

2. *Agreement on procedure:* schoolwide agreement on the sequence of steps taken for absenteeism, including reporting and follow-up.

3. *Consistency:* consistent application of the plan by all staff (monitored by the principal).

4. *Written signed excuses:* requirement of parental excuse for returning students, with medical excuse for extended absence.

5. *Data on absences:* strict record keeping for each student of why, as well as how often, absence occurs.

6. *Student conferences:* personal conference with students upon returning from absences, in which concern for the student, the reason for the absence, the importance of the missed work, and the need for good attendance are the focus. This surveillance of students should become progressively forceful as the number of absences increases, especially if it appears that the absences are not legitimate.

7. *Parent contacts:* parental phone calls or conferences, paralleling those for the student, should be instituted when a record of poor attendance is forming. This should be started before the student has already become a problem.

8. *Truancy proceedings:* truancy proceedings, in line with the state or county regulations, should be instituted for problem students.

9. *Competitions between rooms:* positive school incentive programs of competition between rooms for highest attendance should be implemented (the procedure and strategy for this are similar to that described for Student Team Learning, Module 8).

10. *Encouragement through peer pressure:* the school attendance competition by rooms provides an opportunity to utilize positive peer pressure to change student behavior. This should be encouraged.

11. *In-school programs:* suspension from school is NOT recommended for serious truancy or tardiness problems. This defeats the goal of having students in school. Rather, for severe problems some form of in-school suspension with strict supervision and academic instruction, preferably remedial for objectives not yet mastered, may be used (see Frith, Lindsey, & Sasser, 1980; Garibaldi, 1979).

Except for a few chronic problem students, the level of expectations and the extent of surveillance regarding attendance will be a major factor in the degree of absenteeism and school experiences. When Students are not held accountable for their attendance, it becomes very easy to skip school or class.

Total Allocated Time

This dimension was referred to previously as time scheduled for instruction. It is necessary for teachers to become highly conscious of the amount of time allocated for grade level basic skills instruction and the amount of time allocated for other instruction and non-instructional purposes. Without careful advance planning, the more time devoted to other activities, the less time there is available for basic skill instruction. For example, if compensatory education students are "pulled-out" for special instruction they lose time going to the special room, getting started, returning to their regular classroom and getting prepared for the next instructional session, as well as missing the regular instruction that took place in their absence.

Total allocated time in the school social system is related to the overall patterns of organization which characterize a school. Individual teachers cannot affect much change in this organization: this must be a process in which the entire staff participates, with leadership from the principal and the building leadership team. The above examples, for instance, show how allocated time varies with group placement. This should be taken into account when organizing the building for instruction. If we don't expect certain groups of students to do well, we may not allocate as much time for teaching them the academic subjects as for other less meaningful activities.

Planned change in the allocation of instructional time should have as its starting point the teaching of grade level skills in reading or language arts, math and other academic subjects. The creation of a common school instructional calendar, explained in Module 5, Effective Instruction, helps to focus total staff attention on time requirements, particularly for students needing extra instruction to attain master and of needing help with prerequisites. Time allotted for remediation must supplement, not supplant, regular grade level instruction. Only in this way will we end the massive and systemic loss of instructional time frequently imposed on those students who most need time to learn.

Time allocated for academic instruction can be increased by:

1. Adding on instructional time by lengthening the school day, extending the days of instruction, or extending instructional activities outside the regular school day, e.g., homework, tutoring, etc.

2. Reallocating existing time by reducing/eliminating time spent on non-academic activities.

Increasing allocated time is difficult and, at best, limited. The most productive approach for dealing with allocated time is for the school staff to protect and manage whatever time is available. While to the businessman time is money, for the teacher and student time is learning. Today, faced with the difficult tasks of erasing cumulative learning deficits for large numbers of students and bringing all students to high levels of achievement, the school staff must squeeze the most learning it can get from each school hour and day. Now, more than ever before, the school must learn to "beat the clock."

Suggestions for Managing Allocated Time

1. Consistent with the expectations of high academic achievement for all students, model and develop an awareness for students of the importance of using time productively.

2. Within allocated time, the teacher must deal with three kinds of activities: a) academic (reading, math, etc.); b) non-academic (sharing, social relations, physical activities, etc.); and c) non-instructional (transitions, waiting, housekeeping, disruptions, etc.). To the extent possible, reduce time devoted to non-academic or non-instructional activities so that time for academics is maximized.

3. The principal and the teacher should protect classroom instructional time from interruption and erosion.

   a. Schedule the maximum number of minutes each day for academic instruction and hold to the schedule.

   b. Start and end classes on time.

   c. Avoid interrupting classes for general announcements or special requests.

   d. Discourage "drop-in" visitors, including staff members and students, during instruction time.

   e. Reduce passing time between classes.

   f. Reduce transition time between instruction periods, when switching from one activity/class to another.

   g. Reduce loss of instructional time due to clerical activities, such as taking attendance, collecting money, issuing tickets, passes, etc. Some suggested ways to do this are:

      1) Start instructin first and then do necessary clerical tasks while students are working;

      2) Get someone else to do clerical tasks (e.g., stu-

dents, aides, volunteers, etc.) so instruction isn't delayed;

3) Streamline clerical techniques so tasks are performed more efficiently;

4) Develop routines;

5) Deter or eliminate tasks that are not absolutely necessary during instructional time.

   h. Reduce total time allocated to "special" activities that erode instructional time, such as breakfast program, lunch, recess, loading and unloading buses, etc.

4. Coordinate the pace of instruction through common calendar scheduling of skill instruction for classes that deal with the same content, e.g., all mathematics or language arts classes at the same grade level. Common scheduling encourages teachers to get the most achievement allocating time to keep up with the schedule. It also helps to insure that teachers will cover all the required materials during the time allocated to the course.

5. Coordinate compensatory education scheduling so that no students will be pulled out of their regular instruction on grade level basic skills.

The principal should frequently monitor the level of student mastery progress for basic classes. Each review should be followed by appropriate feedback to the teacher from the principal. This process reinforces accountability for achievement with both the teacher and the principal.

Time-on-Task

Increasing time allocated for instruction does not mean that student time-on-task will automatically increase. However, increasing learning time will result in greater student achievement. Time-on-task is probably the most significant single factor in raising student achievement. Increasing active learning time must be a priority for every teacher. While the teacher cannot do the learning for students or dictate it by decree, the teacher, through his/her attitudes, expectations and behaviors determines the amount of active learning in the classroom. The teacher must be aware of what the students are doing and recognize the characteristics of students on task, some of which are:

    a. spends considerable time working on tasks directly related to the subject matter to be learned;

    b. pays attention;

    c. shows some enthusiasm;

    d. keeps busy on assigned tasks;

    e. spends a lot of time practicing and reviewing skills;

    f. enjoys learning;

    g. frequently experiences success in learning;

    h. understands the instructional task; and

    i. knows that he/she is expected to show results for work time to the teacher.

There are many things a teacher can do to increase time-on-task, even within a limited amount of allocated time. Proper use of student time in the classroom depends on careful advanced planning, consistent management, focused instruction and a very large measure of teacher modeling on how to use academic time.

Instructional Planning

This has been the subject of reams of material. While we have no wish to restate the obvious here, it has been shown time and again that good planning, management and instruction are interdependent. A good instructor seldom "wings it" but has planned in advance for the immediate and long-term needs of the class. He/she can state succinctly at any given time the objective which is to be learned this is communicated to the class so that students can manage their own time accordingly, without being left wondering what the instructor's point is or what is expected of them. Classroom discussions or questions and answers do not depend on student or instructor interests of the day but revolve around the content to be learned. Instructional materials selected or prepared by the instructor are ready for immediate use or distribution as needed. Various contingencies within the classroom have been anticipated and planned for, so that valuable student time is not wasted while the instructor reacts to new or unexpected situations.

Teaching is one of the few professions which has built-in preparation time. This time should be used to the fullest extent for individual or joint planning of instruction. Preparation is the first step toward increasing student Academic Engaged Time.

Non-Instructional Planning

Non-instructional events take student attention, reduce teaching time and interfere with the best laid plans. Nevertheless, there is an irreducible minimum of time which must be spent on recordkeeping and housekeeping details, in transition from one activity or place to another, in interruptions or P.A. announcements from the front office, in irrelevant questions or disruptions from students, and so on.

However, the teacher does not have to be helpless before this onslaught on instructional time. Advance planning can smooth routines and reduce the amount of time they take. Organization and structure of the classroom can be planned so that students do not need to wait in line for teacher attention, do not need to shift frequently from one place to another or mark time while waiting for materials to be located, and do not have to ask unnecessary questions to learn what they must do. When surprises do occur in the classroom, the teacher can have a planned repertoire of responses to draw from and usually will not need to think long about what to do. Without advance planning, time spent waiting or effecting transitions can be trouble spots for restive students, with a spillover into academic time. Even during the first few minutes of the day, the class can be assigned an appropriate task while attendance is taken, papers collected, and so on. In this way, a certain businesslike tone is set which helps students to use their time well.

In anticipating and planning for these necessary non-instructional activities, it is worth remembering that even minutes saved each day for instructional time count toward achievement. A few minutes of planning by the teacher may save 25 to 150 times that many minutes of student time, depending on the number of students taught by that teacher during the school day.

Managing

Consistent management of learning in the classroom can help to increase and sustain student learning time. Routines which are established and practiced by the students save time, particularly those routines which are of a non-instructional nature, such as class roll taking, sharpening pencils, using the lavatory or other behaviors which are potential interruptions of Academic Engaged Time. Management simply is the monitoring of activities and behaviors. Proper reinforcement of appropriate behaviors in the classroom can help to establish an environment where students are on task and interruptions are minimized. For specific information on management to increase active learning time see the activity section following this module.

Instruction

Direct and focused instruction is a necessity for increasing active learning time. Throughout the modules we have stressed the need for establishing common instructional goals for all students. It creates a sense of purpose and accountability for students and thus indirectly increases learning time.

Students who are involved in seatwork activities are more likely to be involved in off-task behavior. When students are working directly with a teacher or other students active learning time is increased. Yet, in the average classroom two-thirds or more of the allocated time is devoted to independent seatwork, resulting in huge losses of active learning time. More ideas for increasing active learning time through instruction are contained in the activities section of this module.

Summary

The primary point is that the amount of time spent actively learning an objective directly affects the outcome for individual students and for the class.

As Bloom (1980) indicated, "Time-on-task is one of the variables that account for learning differences between students, between classes, and even between nations. Time-on-task can be altered positively (or negatively) by the instructional process, and this alteration has direct consequences for the learning that will take place (p. 383)."

The challenge to the teacher is to increase Academic Engaged Time in the classroom. An approach which has proven quite effective is to run a structured, orderly, teacher-directed classroom with an emphasis on academics and with frequent high level monitoring of student task behaviors. In Learning for Mastery classes using this approach, the percentage of class Academic Engaged Time is far higher that the average of 35 percent, with corresponding and measureable increases in achievement. (Hyman & Cohen, 1979).

It must be remembered that the classroom does not stand alone but is part of the school social system. Thus, the entire staff should cooperate in discussing ways to improve allocated and active learning time. Increases in the amount of time allocated to instruction resulting in higher proportions of active learning time—will be greatest if approached and solved through leadership of the principal and joint efforts of the staff.

Suggested Activities

With the aim of maximizing allocated time for all students,

1. the Building Leadership Team of teachers and the principal should assess the existing school time schedule and organizational practices for their effect on student time, teacher time, and overall consistency of scheduling. The team should report its findings to the faculty and recommend changes where appropriate. At least two checkups a year should be made by this committee, one each semester.

2. The principal should establish a time efficient daily schedule for the building and communicate it to staff, students, and parents through the school handbook, newsletters, and bulletins. The principal is responsible for seeing that the schedule is followed.

3. All school personnel must be expected to model a respect for and compliance with the established school regulations for use of time.

4. Because of their great potential for negative effect on student allocated and engaged time, the principal should limit the scheduling of "pull-out" classes and switching of classes as much as possible. If pull-outs and switches must be made, the amount of time allocated for transitions should be minimal and rigidly enforced.

5. Observation-feedback suggestions on individual use of time should be available to all school personnel. Ideas can be communicated by:
   a. Informal cooperative arrangements between staff

members, where one person will occasionally observe another person for a brief period of time (at least 20 minutes) and then report back what was observed;

b. Scheduled observations where an administrator, department head, or specialist teacher will use checklists or video/auditory tape. This type of observation is probably the most accurate, but can also be the most threatening if not used in a supportive manner. The purpose is not to catch people making mistakes, but rather to mirror what they are doing not what they think they are doing.

The use of recording instruments should be employed when making observations to increase the objectivity and, hopefully, the value of the feedback information. In particular, the time-on-task instruments developed by Anderson and Scott (Classroom Process Scale) and Jones (Student Observation Scoring Form) are available upon request from the original authors. See Additional Resources at the end of this module.

c. Occasional assessment of their actual use of time, by teachers and administrators, making notes every 10-15 minutes as to what they are doing. Over time, logs of this kind usually reveal information suggesting where improvements or changes should be made.

6. Being an efficient manager of time and other resources is a critical aspect of increasing engaged time. Lack of planning is the most common cause of poor management for both teachers and administrators. In particular, the failure to make definite written plans about what to do, how to do it, when it is to be done results in low productivity. In the classroom, having well-prepared, written lesson plans are a must. Daily written lesson plans for

teachers should be expected and available for comment by the principal. (See comments below)
7. Instructional behaviors of the teacher are another critical aspect of keeping students on task. (See comments below)

Suggestions for Teachers in Planning, Managing and Instructing to Increase Academic Engaged Time

In addition to modeling a positive attitude toward learning and learners, the teacher can promote active learning by increasing his/her proficiencies in planning, managing, and instructing.

1. *Planning for Instructional Time.*
   a. Make weekly written plans based on the basic skill grade level calendar schedule.
   b. Make provisions for:
      1) Teacher led instruction (directed lesson, lecture, etc.);
      2) Practice activities (assignments, academic games, etc.);
      3) Testing for mastery progress (quiz, informal test);
      4) Correctives for non-mastery students, (alternatives);
      5) Enrichment and extension for mastery students (challenge students that have shown mastery);
      6) Testing for mastery performance (the "biggie," the one that counts).
   c. Share ideas for teaching skills with all teachers of your grade level. This results in better coordination, utilization of materials, and problem solving. In short, more effective instruction results from comprehensive, collaborative planning.
   d. Anticipate off-task activities, such as socializing, daydreaming, and misbehaving, by developing

lessons that provide:

1) Structure (definite activities, procedures);
2) Meaning (ties in with previous learning);
3) Group focus (clear purpose that students understand);
4) Variety (change format occasionally to combat boredom);
5) Lively pace (eliminate drag);
6) Smoothness (avoid jerkiness, stops and starts);
7) Minimal student movements (can lower time on task);
8) Student response (accountablility, assists teacher feedback).

2. *Managing instructional time*
   a. Become a manager of learning.
   b. Develop routines for efficiency.
   c. Establish a minimum number of rules—but rigidly enforce them.
   d. Begin instruction promptly.
   e. Reduce interruptions.
   f. Don't become a disruptor yourself.
   g. Keep breaks to a minimum—both frequency and duration.
   h. Actively monitor students.
   i. Use positive and negative sanctions, but emphasize positive reinforcement.
   j. Increase the frequency of teacher-pupil interactions:
      1) Practice teacher cruising. Circulate among entire class, checking on progress, prompting, and reinforcing. Do not sit behind a desk like an overseer.
      2) Limit help to individual students to a few seconds at a time. The key is to get the student to begin working. Continue to cruise and return to the student with additional help or encouragement. Spending large amounts of

time with "helpless" students reinforces their helplessness and prevents the teacher from working with other students. (See Module 7 also.)

3) Break down learning tasks into smaller component parts to enable the "stuck" student to begin working. Reinforce all correct efforts.

    k. Make students accountable for their use of time. Specify what you expect and by what due date.

    l. Use contingency management techniques.

3. *Instructing*

    a. Establish a goal focus for every lesson.

    b. Structure the lesson and give specific directions on task procedure.

    c. Teach to the whole class initially, but use small group and individual instruction as needs develop for enrichment, extension, or remediation.

    d. Maintain direct teacher involvement (produces the most student engagement).

    e. Provide teacher-student interaction opportunities during the whole class lesson. Specifically, interaction activities consist of questioning, answering, reacting, and explaining. Ask short, clear questions that require short, brief answers. Expect everyone to respond and participate.

    f. Keep independent seatwork to a minimum, to protect against loss of student time on task.

    g. Make student assistance readily available from the teacher, adult tutor, or peer tutors. Assistance should be brief.

    h. Engage in frequent and timely use of student encouragement, reinforcement, and feedback to increase engaged time.

    i. Employ team academic games to develop student interest, cooperation, and skill performance.

    j. Make assignments challenging but not impossible.

Being able to successfully complete assignments motivates students to keep working. Assignments that are too difficult frustrate students and turn them off. Be prepared to vary the level of difficulty of assignments so that all students experience success.

Suggestions to the Principal for Support of Academic Engaged Time

1. Model behavior that communicates to teachers and students expectations for high performance.
2. Establish operational schedules that maximize classroom instructional time.
3. Supervise halls, so students get to class on time and stay in class.
4. Keep classroom interruptions to a minimum, e.g., announcements, requests, unexpected visitations, etc.
5. Support the teacher's discipline plan.
6. Expect high level of follow-through from teachers:
   a. Good use of preparation period(s)
   b. Written lesson plans
   c. Punctuality
   d. Student discipline
   e. Student attendance
7. Visit classrooms every day to keep abreast of what's happening and to let teachers and students see that you are interested.
8. Monitor classroom progress of student mastery of basic skills on a regular basis. Establish a schedule and process.
9. Be a good manager of time yourself; set an example by practicing what you preach.

Additional Resources

Anderson, L. W. Instruction and time-on-task: A review with implications. *Journal of Curriculum Studies,* in press.

Anderson provides an excellent review of five different strands of research on time-on-task. He then suggests further work in the field based on his synthesis of the common findings.

Anderson, L. W. & Scott, C. C. The Classroom Process Scale (CPS): An Approach to the Measurement of Teaching Effectiveness.

The CPS places measurement of student time-on-task into the context of classroom instructional activities. Type of content presented and type of teaching method employed are also examined.

Inquiries can be directed to either fo the coauthors:
Lorin W. Anderson
College of Education
University of South Carolina
Columbia, S.C. 29208

Corrine C. Scott
South Carolina State Department of Education

Bloom, B. S. The new direction in educational research; Alterable variables. *Phi Delta Kappan,* 1980, *61*(6), 382-385.

Bloom describes characteristics of the learning environment that can be altered to improve learning and increase achievement. Time-on-task is one of the alterable variables presented in this short, but very important article.

Frith, G. H. Lindsey, J. D., & Sasser, J. L. An alternative approach to school suspension: The Dothan model. *Phi Delta Kappan,* 1980, *61*(9), 637-638.

This article describes an in-school suspension program

which has decreased dicipline problems and improved attendance while providing academic instruction and remediation to suspended students.

Jones, F. H. Classroom Management Training Program. Data System and Scoring Manual. *Observation of Student Behavior.* 64 Alta Vista Drive, Santa Cruz, Claifornia 95060.

This instrument is designed to obtain information on two types of problem behaviors: 1.) disruptions and 2.) time off-task.

Rosenshine, B., & Berliner, D. Academic engaged time. *British Journal of Teacher Education,* 1978, *4,* 3-16.

This is a basic reference for this concept.

Module 7

School Discipline and Classroom Management

- **The Crisis in School Discipline**
- **Effective School Discipline**
- **Creating Effective School Discipline**
- **Classroom Management**
- **Suggested Activities**
- **Additional Resources**

According to an annual survey of American attitudes toward education (Gallup, 1979), for eight of the nine years prior to 1979, discipline was the number one problem in our schools. The public perceives a need for stricter discipline and a "get tough" policy. In many schools teachers have given up trying to discipline effectively or have resorted to increasingly punitive techniques, including corporal punishment, in order to maintain control.

This dismal state of affairs is not inevitable. Some schools and teachers DO have effective discipline. Furthermore, higher achievement is associated with effective management of behavior. This module will outline the problems and suggest solutions based on techinques and principles of effective classroom management that are used by successful schools and teachers. The relationship between the school learning climate, time-on-task, and achievement will be stressed. The module will conclude with specific strategies for improving norms of behavior in the school and skills of classroom management for the teachers. These strategies and skills will focus on the gains in achievement that come from improved discipline in the schools.

The Crisis in School Discipline

One of the few topics which produces consensus of opinion in America's schools is the problem of discipline. The Gallup surveys of public concern are reinforced by the troubled response of educators themselves. Many teachers see discipline as their number one problem. This focus on "discipline" leads all to often to a narrow definition of the problem and to "solutions" which treat symptoms rather than causes. "Discipline" and "classroom management" are often used interchangeably. We reject that interpretation. Discipline in the schools is clearly a major problem, but that problem is a reflection of the social norms of the overall school learning climate and the specific techniques of classroom management. For our purpose, "discipline" refers to dealing with student behavior with respect to manners, following instructions, disruption of routine, and consideration of the rights of others. "Classroom management" refers to the entire range of teacher-directed planning, managing, and monitoring of student learning and behavior. The school learning climate incorporates not only collective classroom management by the staff but also schoolwide rules and norms for defining and enforcing proper student behavior. We are concerned with the effect of these classroom and building practices upon academic performance.

This chapter will examine the problem of discipline in more detail, noting the close connection to student time-on-task. The question of why so many teachers feel that nothing can be done about the problem is addressed in terms of myths and negative, self-fulfilling prophecies.

The Problem Defined

The popular conception of our schools is that they are increasingly out of control. Violence, vandalism, and disrespect for authority are often highlighted as the major factors. While these factors contribute to the general disruption of schooling and, when present, create situations that often imperil the safety and welfare of those involved, these serious acts are only one aspect of the overall discipline problem. We are not downplaying the importance of these acts. Where serious disruption exists, it must be dealt with. But, as Jones (1979) notes, the major factor in school discipline is the continual, often trivial, undertone of inattention, talking, and interruption that occurs in most classes. The spectacular nature of more blatant offenses distorts our perception of their importance, compared to the seemingly innocuous misbehavior that is irritating but not dangerous (and consequently often ignored). It is, however, precisely these minor misbehaviors that create the greatest barrier to effective education: time spent misbehaving or goofing-off is time not spent in active learning.

Jones (1979) ties these minor interruptions directly to time-on-task. In the average class, disruption results in 45-55 percent of time-off-task. The implication for the percentage of time-off-task in poorly managed classrooms is staggering. Considering that many schools in low income or urban areas have a "discipline problem," it is little wonder that achievement is low: students in these schools are seldom on task!

Furthermore, Jones (1979) and Canter and Canter (1976) both suggest that teacher stress and burn-out are associated in large part with the energy drain of trying to manage and cope with continual disruption in the learning process, producing feelings of hopelessness about the possibility of effective instruction.

The problem, concerns not only the safety and welfare of students and teachers along with costs of personnel and maintenance to control serious violence and vandalism, but, more importantly, disruption of the learning process through incessant minor misbehaviors.

Beliefs, Myths, and Self-Fulfilling Prophecy

Despite the tremendous amount of attention given to the problem, poor discipline continues as a major force in American education. Many educators believe that little can be done to resolve the problem, short of increasing the use of authoritarian and repressive control tactics. Several beliefs have become prevalent. Some of these myths, in close parallel to the reason often given why poor or urban children cannot learn well, are listed below (Canter & Canter, 1976; Jones, 1979; Lyles, 1973).

Myths that teachers and schools cannot maintain good discipline:

1. "Those kids"—low achieving, low SES, minority, the emotionally disturbed—are "different;"
2. Children in general are uncontrollable because of the permissiveness of society;
3. Parents are no longer supportive of the schools;
4. Parents cannot control their own children;
5. Court cases, giving due process to students, have tied the hands of the schools; and
6. Teacher training institutions do not deal adequately with the problem.

Teachers who believe in myths of this nature set up a self-fulfilling prophecy. Such beliefs result in lower expectations for behavior, often reflected by such remarks as, "Nothing I try makes any difference. These children just will not listen!" Weiss and Weiss (1975, cited in Brophy & Putnam, 1978) document a lowering of standards and increased tolerance for misbehavior by teachers for low SES students compared to middle class students. Brophy and Good (1974) also found this phenomenon in their extensive review of research on teacher expectations. Canter and Canter (1976) described how teachers interpret continued misbehavior as shortcomings of students rather than inconsistency of their own classroom management. This displacement of the perceived source of the problem often results in trying one "gimmick" after another, without using any one strategy consistently. Subsequent failure of each new plan, for want of consistent enforcement, then confirms in the teacher's mind the hopelessness of trying to deal with "problem" children.

The process by which erroneous beliefs and myths become self-fulfilling prophecies has been described in detail in Module 2. The mechanism is similar, whether for academic or behavioral outcomes. But these negative expectations and failure are NOT inevitable. Positive, effective discipline without repressive actions is possible with all kinds of students. In the next section, we examine evidence for that claim.

Effective School Discipline

The need for information on successful and positive programs cannot be over-emphasized. Unless schools and teachers are aware of what can be and has been done, there is the very real possibility of overreaction. As Ianni and Reuus-Ianni (1980) state in NEA *Today's Education:*

> At present we are faced with a very real danger. Despite research indications to the contrary, the public continues to believe that school crime is escalating at an alarming rate. Until public opinion catches up with research, the schools may be tempted to turn increasingly to criminal justice instead of educational solutions (p.23G).

Extensive evidence exists that effective school discipline is a result, not of composition of the student body or of repressive and law enforcement type strategies, but of the educational practices and techniques of school and classroom management used by the staff. Furthermore, these effective practices are associated with increased achievement.

Schools and Teachers DO Make A Difference

Some schools have an effective school learning climate with an industrious working atmosphere in which discipline is not a problem. Some teachers use effective classroom management practices which result in good discipline. Other schools and teachers have poor discipline and little learning. Three points reflecting this variance between schools and teachers stand out.

1. A common myth which should be dispelled is that discipline problems cannot be avoided in low SES, minority, or urban schools. This clearly is not the case. Although many urban schools do have discipline problems, some have been able to provide effective programs of discipline. Duke (1978) found differences in the level of discipline problems in both urban and suburban schools. (Reports of successful programs can also be found in Elardo, 1978; Urich & Batchelder, 1979; Wint, 1975.)

2. Closely related to the above is the feeling that "problems" strike only in large city or low income schools. The Senate Subcommittee to Investigate Juvenile Delinquency (Bayh, 1978) and Duke's (1978) survey both unequivocally state that discipline problems are found in all kinds of neighborhoods—rural, small town, suburban, and white as well as large, inner city schools.

3. The norms of accepted behavior in the school, not the students, make the difference. In short, it is the behavior and techinques used by the school and the teachers which are the primary determinant of the level of discipline, and not the community or composition of the students attending the school. This position is summarized by the Senate Subcommittee to In-

vestigate Juvenile Delinquency (Bayh, 1978), noting that schools that have reduced violence and vandalism have programs that ". . . are not based on the premise that we should confront these problems by turning our schools into armed fortresses. Instead, they are educationally oriented strategies that can succeed in enriching the classroom environment and creating the kind of atmosphere in which education can best take place (p.130)."

Relation to Achievement

The problems of school and classroom discipline cannot be understood fully apart from their relation to achievement. There is considerable evidence that educationally-oriented strategies and positive learning environment are associated with better discipline. The following points support this.

1. The school learning climate, the focus of this set of modules, must be the emphasis of the school. When learning and achievement are not the priority goal, other behaviors detract time and effort from that fundamental purpose. In essence, school discipline can and often does become an end in itself, rather than an aspect of the school learning climate which facilitates learning.

2. We sometimes become so involved in how to deal with problem students that we forget why misbehavior occurs. Overwhelmingly problem children are those pupils with learning problems whom we are not reaching. This has been documented by numerous researchers (Bloom, B., 1976; Bloom, R., 1978; Duke, 1976, 1978; Glasser, 1969; Kindsvatter, 1978). Students know that they go to school to learn. When they are unsuccessful in this realm, they turn to other means of satisfying needs for success and attention. Any effective program of school discipline must meet those educational needs.

3. Edmonds' (1979) review of studies of effective low income schools indicates that these high achieving schools have an orderly, industrious and well behaved student body.

4. The relation between achievement and teachers' effective management skills has been thoroughly demonstrated. Much of this work involves the amount of time-on-task in well managed classrooms compared to poorly managed ones. (Brophy & Evertson, 1976; Good & Brophy, 1977; Good & Grouws, 1975; Jones, 1979; McDonald & Elias, 1976; Rosenshine & Berliner, 1978).

5. Kounin (1970) and Jones (1979) stress that the major difference between effective and ineffective classroom managers is in the use of pedagogical practices that provide a positive learning atmosphere and prevent inattention, talking, and misbehavior from escalating into time-wasting behavior and class disruption. While response to misbehavior is important, these studies show that it is the actions taken by teachers *before a problem occurs which control* the level of discipline and separate good from poor classroom managers.

In summary, discipline cannot be divorced from concern for achievement and learning. Effective school and classroom learning climate go hand in hand with effective discipline practices.

Creating Effective School Discipline

This section will present a framework for setting up an effective program of discipline and will offer specific guidelines for classroom management that complement the school effort aimed at high achievement.

Many educators think of classroom practices when discussing discipline. Our approach, while not neglecting the individual classroom, stresses the priority of an effective schoolwide program. Students pass through the halls to recess, lunch hour, rest room, and assemblies, all activities that occur outside the classroom. Schools must have rules and standards of behavior for these common activities. Behavior in the wider milieu of the school creates a norm which is reflected in the individual classrooms. Serious problems that begin outside the classroom often appear in the classroom as spillovers.

Faculty and administration must share the responsibility for creating an orderly learning climate in which academic pursuits are not disrupted. The leadership for building a schoolwide environment must come from the principal, but the entire staff, including grade levels and departments, must develop written policies and procedures for the staff to deal with student behaviors that adversely affect the building climate and individual achievement. The following problems should be addressed: truancy, excessive absenteeism, tardiness, fighting, insubordination, cheating, and failure to complete assignments.

Just as in academics, the key to effective school discipline is the level of expectation which the staff holds and the consistency with which it is upheld. Expectations for behavior must be related to the learning process. Decisions on which behaviors are appropriate or inappropriate must be based on how they affect the learning climate. In too many instances, educators have allowed behavior that interferes with learning.

The School Plan

The school plan for discipline should include two aspects, in-class and out-of-class behavior. This plan represents the basic expectations of a school staff for student behavior within the building or on school grounds. The essential features of both the in-class and out-of-class parts of the plan are 1) identification of specific required behaviors and 2) consequences, both negative and positive, that result from non-compliance or compliance. The challenge for the principal and teachers is to agree on a minimum number of essential rules (e.g., five rules for each area) that must be followed by all students and then to specify what will happen as a result of breaking or following those rules. In short, students who break essential rules receive negative consequences (e.g., penalties, loss of privileges, detention, etc.). Students who comply with the rules receive positive consequences (e.g., praise, complimentary notes, rewards, etc.). While the in-class rules for behavior should be consistent from class to class, each teacher should be allowed to modify the classroom plan to meet his/her needs.

Steps for Setting Up the School Plan

1. A committee of teacher representatives, with the principal, develops a draft of a schoolwide discipline plan.

2. The draft is presented to the total staff for reaction and suggestions.

3. The committee prepares a final draft.

4. The total staff is presented with the final draft for approval.

5. The adopted plan is presented to parents through special meetings, bulletins, and the Parent Handbook.

6. The principal and teachers of the committee presents the plan directly to students in an assembly.

7. Follow-up discussions with students are conducted in classrooms.

8. Regular discussions of how to handle special discipline problems should take place either as part of whole staff meetings or grade/department meetings.

Following Through on the School Plan

Once a discipline plan has been established and communicated to students and parents the difficult part—follow through—must be accomplished. A schoolwide discipline plan is worthless unless it is carried out by *all* teachers. A complete plan not only specifies what students are required to do, it also specifies what teachers and the principal are expected to do. Rigid enforcement is essential.

When negative consequences are to be employed, a critical part of making the procedure successful depends on making *prior* arrangements with other adults who are expected to participate in resolving behavior problems. If, for example, a teacher expects to involve the principal in handling discipline problems, this intervention should be identified as one of the systematic steps of the classroom plan. The principal should have full knowledge of and approve the steps the teacher will follow, if necessary, to deal with offenders. In this context, a student referral to the principal for improper behavior occurs according to agreement by the teacher and the principal. In short, intervention of the principal is one step, like others, in the classroom discipline plan. In like manner, the point of requesting parent intervention should be set and explained to parents ahead of time.

Teacher Responsibilities

1. Determine wants/needs
2. Establish EXPECTATIONS for behavior/teaching
3. Establish minimum classroom rules
4. Set up classroom Discipline Plan: rules, negative and positive consequences
5. Get principal's approval of plan
6. Explain expectations, rules, and plan to students (give copy)
7. Send copy of expectations, rules and discipline plan home to parents. (Suggest requirement of parent signature)
8. Give POSITIVE REINFORCEMENT to students

who comply with rules
9. FOLLOW THROUGH by consistently and calmly carrying out a plan of negative consequences for students who choose to misbehave/disrupt
10. Revise plan and consequences if disruptions continue (get tougher)
11. PERSIST and behave consistently according to expectations, rules, and plan. Don't give in.

Principal Responsibilities
1. Review, modify, and approve classroom discipline plans
2. Check to see that teacher responsibilities are carried out
3. Support teachers as they carry out their plans.

For a more detailed explanation of how to establish a schoolwide discipline plan, see Canter (1979).

The elements above form a planning framework for effective discipline. No matter how thorough the planning, success will require consistent implementation. Jones (1979) and Canter and Canter (1976) have identified three typical modes of response to discipline problems. The effectiveness of the school plan depends on which of these modes of enforcement is employed.
1. *Avoidance.* Ignoring the behavior in the hopes that it will go away (it will not). By ignoring misbehavior, teachers communicate that the stated rules are not the actual definition of appropriate behavior. Students perceive that the staff either does not know what is going on, does not care, or is unable to stop it. In any case, the students soon control the situation, often pushing limits of tolerance to the point at which a staff member will explode, call the principal or react in some other drastic manner—but at a level far beyond what is necessary or acceptable for a positive learning climate.
2. *Punitive Action.* Because of frustrations growing out

of the situation noted above, or as a means of enforcing the rules to prevent this development, schools may resort to legalistic solutions or use of outside security personnel, while teachers and principals may resort to verbal abuse, screaming, threats, or physical punishment.

3. *Firm and Consistent Assertive Response.* Effective schools and teachers respond to infractions firmly, immediately, but without harsh action. The key to this firm assertive response is communicating clearly, through both verbal and non-verbal channels, that the students are there to learn and that interruptions of that learning will not be tolerated. The rationale is thus reasonable, the manner relaxed, calm, firm, and most important, consistent.

Most educators and communities would clearly prefer the firm and assertive response. The preponderance of discipline problems shows that many schools fail to achieve this. Yet the existence of schools and classrooms with an orderly, positive learning climate show that this response can be achieved.

Attending to Problem Behavior

In achieving desired response to inappropriate behavior, the staff must be aware of three distinctions: 1) preventing misbehavior, 2) responding to misbehavior, and 3) obtaining help for the few students with serious problems. Each of these will be considered in turn.

1. *Preventing Misbehavior.* As noted earlier, efficient and well-organized schools and classrooms prevent many of the problems that plague most schools and teachers. Keys to preventing problems include the following:

   a. *Thorough Planning.* Poor planning for instruction is one of the biggest contributors to poor student behavior in the classroom.

   b. *Appropriate Instruction.* The planning must be

accompanied by an academic program in which students' educational needs are met. Appropriate reteaching, remedial work, and enrichment must be provided as needed for all students. (See modules on Effective Instruction and Reinforcement).

c. *Positive Reinforcement.* Proper use of timely verbal and written statements of positive reinforcement helps to motivate students to perform as the teacher desires. The use of incentives or contingency management techniques may be in order if other approaches do not work.

d. *Daily Organizational Activities.* Every school must attend to certain organizational requirements: taking attendance, lunch, recess, changing classes, rest rooms, and assemblies are a part of school. Wide variations exist in how schools manage these functions. For example, some schools and teachers waste as much as 15-20 minutes in the complex of morning activities in which students have nothing to do. Other schools utilize this time to have students do silent reading, work on handwriting skills, etc., while teachers complete required record keeping. This is prime time in which students are fresh and alert. The staff should plan independent instructional activities that take advantage of this often unused time. Other aspects of the school day are also likely to subtract from time-on-task, thus providing instances where unoccupied students create disturbance. Each school should monitor carefully these activities, setting procedures which streamline them and reduce the chance of problems.

e. *Contingency Plans.* Emergency plans for rainy days, substitutes, assemblies, and last minute schedule changes should be prepared in advance. (Murphy's Law: Whatever can go wrong will go wrong.)

    f. *Effective Supervision.* Most behavioral problems occur in unsupervised situations. The staff has a shared responsibility to monitor the school. The very process of close supervision communicates to students that the expectations for good behavior will be enforced consistently—by everyone on the staff.

    g. *Consistent Rules Between Classrooms.* Individual teachers should adopt rules that are consistent with the overall school plan. This action will reinforce the norms of the school learning climate. Enforcement of rules within classes should also be carried out consistently in accord with the school plan.

2. *Responding to Misbehavior.* Despite the most careful planning, students will inevitably "test" the system. It is the response to this testing of limits that determines the norm for school and teacher handling of discipline. The key to the school's response is *consistency.* The principles below (see Canter & Canter 1976; Jones, 1979) are effective in helping the staff to achive the needed consistency.

    a. *Setting Limits.* Enforcement must be consistent. Jones (1979) speaks of two stages: training a class and maintaining a class. While training students, the staff is setting and enforcing the limits of acceptable behavior. Until this process is complete, students will test these limits, trying to find out how firmly the line of resistance is set. During this time, the staff must meet each and every infraction. Generally, a simple warning is sufficient, but it may require stronger non-verbal procedures (backing the student down with eye-contact while moving closer, perhaps speaking the student's name with a firm request to desist at the same time). If the staff is consistent, this testing will gradually subside as the students accept the now firmly established line.

NOTE: Consistency is the major difference between effective and ineffective disciplinarians. Effective disciplinarians meet each challenge until the limits are accepted. Ineffective staffs allow some misbehavior to go unchallenged or give up before the limits are accepted.

Once limits have been set, the staff will occasionally have to remind the students of those limits. This can be done with a simple verbal or non-verbal cue (e.g., snapping the fingers, softly speaking the pupil's name, walking toward the offender, etc.), which does not disrupt the on-going class. However, teachers must continue to meet infractions quickly and firmly with the message that, even though a simple cue is now all that is usually necessary for enforcement, they are prepared to go further if needed.

b. *Choice.* Inevitably, there will be some students who either do not stop their disruptive behavior when confronted or who repeatedly exceed the acceptable limits. The student must realize that his/her *choice* to continue misbehaving results in a *consequence* that is self-inflicted. This is an important aspect of the student's learning responsibility. Cause and effect must be clearly established in the student's mind.

c. *Consequences* (Negative Reinforcement). Consequences must be planned in advance. The consequence should be reasonable and capable of being carried out. It should also be something the student does not like, yet is not psychologically or physically harmful (sarcasm, corporal punishment, or personal condemnation are not appropriate). Finally, the consequences should be given in terms of the student's actions, "Since you chose to continue your actions, you have chosen to receive . . ." (Canter & Canter 1976).

Some effective consequences can be: loss of privileges, restitution of damages, isolation, calling parents, making up wasted time, etc. Whenever possible, the consequences should follow logically from the action, e.g., paying for a broken window, cleaning up a mess, sanding a name off a desk, etc.

d. *Incentive Systems* (Positive Reinforcement). In situations where negative consequences do not produce the desired change in student behavior, switching to the use of positive reinforcements may work. Setting up special incentive programs involving rewards for acceptable performance may be motivating for the student whereas continuous negative consequences may be a turn-off and cause more and greater non-compliance. Usually, alternating a negative consequence with a positive incentive approach is more productive than a steady diet of totally negative consequences. It is important for the teacher to emphasize and reward appropriate behavior with positive consequences while providing negative consequences each time a student chooses to misbehave.

e. *Additional Follow-Through.* The process of enforcing limits, providing choice, and giving consequences will work for most students. For some students, further action may be needed. Parents and the principal should be involved in setting up further procedures and consequences. In addition, students who need this extra attention also need supportive counseling, remedial academic work, and a caring teacher. Students who continue to act out can learn to control their behavior. But they often require help in learning appropriate responses and in meeting their needs for success and attention.

   f. *In-School Suspension.* Sometimes students may
      have to be removed from class because they en-
      danger other students, show flagrant disrespect,
      or engage in other serious misbehaviors. These
      same students are often in need of remedial
      educational help. Suspension may be just what
      the student wants. More and more schools are
      recognizing the need for alternatives to suspen-
      sion.

      An in-school suspension room, staffed with
      counselor and/or teachers to provide intensive
      remedial academic work and firm behavioral
      limits can be one possibility. The Dothan,
      Alabama (Frith, Lindsey, & Sasser, 1980) pro-
      gram is an example of this type of program.
3. *Obtaining Help for Non-Conforming Students.*
   Students are not evil by nature. Individuals who have
   trouble conforming to established limits use acting
   out behaviors to satisfy their social, academic, and
   emotional needs for success, recognition, and attention. These problem students must learn to meet their
   needs in acceptable ways. Additional help in
   socialization or academics may be necessary. For the
   vast majority of students, firmly set and enforced
   limits in a positive learning climate enable them to
   function successfully. For the generally small number
   of students that are serious, chronic discipline problems, the teacher and/or principal should refer the
   student to specialized agencies or trained personnel
   for professional help.

The staff which consistently follows these guidelines
should be able to maintain successful discipline as a part of a
positive school learning climate.

Classroom Management

Classroom management and classroom discipline need to be consistent with schoolwide programs. Because the principles of setting and enforcing consistent limits for behavior were discussed above, under the school plan this section will address specific time-saving and instructional techniques that imporve discipline and raise achievement. Much of this section on classroom management focuses on management of time. It complements Module 6, Academic Engaged Time.

Time-Saving Techniques

The following techniques have been shown to improve the instructional process, increase time-on-task, and prevent behavior problems. They are consistent with research on effective instruction that results in better achievement.

1. *Planning and Preparation.* Well planned lessons improve the quality of instruction and reduce boredom and restlessness. Advance preparation of materials avoids delays for duplicating and assembling. Teach by design—not by improvisation.

2. *Fluency of Transitions.* Much time is wasted switching from one subject or class to another. Teachers who can move a class easily from one topic to another or students from one class to another increase time-on-task and reduce behavior problems.

3. *Monitors.* Student helpers can ease the burden of trivial paper work, distribution of materials, and errand running. Student monitors save the teacher time during transitions and learn personal responsibility. Being a monitor is a reward to many students.

4. *Routines.* Early in the year students should learn acceptable ways of dealing with daily routines, such as orderly entering and leaving class, getting ready for

instruction, moving into groups or teams, sharpening pencils, etc.

5. *Traffic Patterns.* Classrooms should be arranged to permit easy movement in and out of class and to areas for activities. Arrangement of furniture and desks so the teacher has quick access to every student is essential.

6. *Enrichment Activities.* Audio-visual materials, instructional games, and learning centers should be available for students who finish their work ahead of the rest of the class. Instructions on how to use such materials independently and quietly must be provided.

7. *Attendance Taking.* Much time can be wasted during necessary administrative details. Classes should have standing instructions to be working on some form of independent material or project as soon as they enter the class, so instruction can proceed as attendance is taken. For secondary teachers, this time saver can occur from 4-6 times a day.

8. *"Tired" Time.* The period of time just prior to lunch or dismissal is often wasted because students and teachers are hungry and tired. These are excellent times for academic games, stories, silent reading, or group-response activities.

Instructional Techniques

Studies have shown that certain techniques used during instruction may improve time-on-task and prevent disciplinary problems. Kounin (1970) suggests that the biggest difference between good and poor classroom managers is their skill in using the following preventive techniques:

1. *"Withitness."* The "with-it" teacher is aware of all class activities even during individual and small group

instruction, and intervenes to prevent misbehavior from escalating to disruption. Withitness includes clear vision of the entire classroom and frequent scanning of the class.

2. *"Overlapping."* The skilled teacher has the ability to do more than one thing at a time, such as conducting a study group and helping a single student.

3. *Group Focus.* Establishing clearly a single purpose for student activity, then not allowing other activities to compete for student attention, is an important teacher task.

4. *Maintaining Smoothness and Momentum.* The teacher's careful attention to transitions, maintaining continuity of thought, and avoiding jerkiness of sudden stops and starts, helps instruction proceed in a deliberate, orderly fashion.

Jones (1979) describes two common classroom activities that waste time:

1. *Seatwork.* The rate of time-off-task is 2-3 times as great during seatwork as during whole-group instruction. Seatwork must be challenging, varied, and easy enough to permit independent work. It must be perceived as important by students rather than as a filler of idle time.

2. *Helping Contacts.* Helping contacts average 4 minutes per student. At this rate, in a 30 minute session only 7 students are helped. Students who work independently are ignored, while students who depend on assistance from the teacher are rewarded with attention. Jones suggests improving helping contacts by reducing them to 20-30 seconds. During that time the student is rewarded for completed work and is given cues for the next step. Thus the number of contacts can be increased and students are rewarded for independent work. This technique has shown success with slow and learning-disabled students.

These are sample classroom management techniques. Many others exist in the literature and in the repertoires of skilled teachers. Classroom management is a learned skill. Self-evaluation, peer and principal observation, staff discussion, and time-use analysis are all means of discovering and correcting weaknesses in efficient use of time. All effective teachers are good managers of instruction. No teacher, even the most popular and talented, is immune from the need for management skills.

Summary

This module has addressed the problem of poor discipline and its effects on achievement. We defined the problem, concluding that, although violence, vandalism, and disrespect must be dealt with, more important factors are continual disruption, talking, and inattention: all distractions of a "minor" nature which prevent or impede academic process. Myths and beliefs were presented which perpetuate the "inevitability" of discipline problems for "certain" students—low SES, low achieving, minority, the emotionally disturbed—which often result in a self-fulfilling prophecy. However, effective school and classroom discipline is possible. Evidence was presented that schools and classes with good discipline exist and that these schools are associated with higher achievement. Students have the right to an education free from fear or worry about their safety or their psychological and physical well-being, including the trauma of destructive verbal and/or corporal punishment.

Finally, a frame work and principles for actually improving school discipline and management were given. This model stressed increasing time-on-task by cutting down on minor disruptions which interfere with learning. The increase in time-on-task is accomplished by setting and consistently enforcing limits on behavior, providing positive incentives and success, and improving classroom management and instructional skills.

Schoolwide programs to improve behavior must accompany efforts to improve discipline and time-on-task in the classroom. Building-wide efforts must be a collective staff effort led by the principal.

Suggested Activities

School Discipline Planning

1. Establish a schoolwide plan for discipline that is consistent with and supportive of individual classroom plans. This is an operational plan that provides a systematic, orderly, and effective method of reacting to acts of student misconduct.
   Suggestion:
   a. Review guidelines on pages 10-15 of module.
   b. Read *Assertive Discipline* text and *Competency-Based Resource Materials and Guidelines* by Lee Canter.
   c. Use other media identified in the Resource section of this module for additional information/ideas that can be built into the school or classroom discipline plan.
2. Make the schoolwide plan for discipline available to teachers, students and parents. This plan should be included in the school handbook for teachers and also in handbooks for students/parents.
3. Copies of the school discipline plan should be sent home with provisions for parents to sign and return to the principal a slip indicating they have received and read the plan. Expect all students to return a signed parent slip. Follow up meetings with parents should be scheduled to discuss the plan and promote support.
4. The principal should explain the school discipline plan to students: what it is, how it will operate, and how the staff will follow through on the plan. Con-

ducting grade level assemblies for this purpose is suggested.

5. Check up on yourself periodically by evaluating your
    disciplinary techniques.
6. Discussion of discipline problems should be a regular
    feature of whole staff meetings or grade/department
    meetings. Individual students should not be iden-
    tified; rather, emphasis should be placed on a specific
    behavior and how to remedy it. Sharing and making
    suggestions are encouraged.

Classroom Management

1. Review the factors for improving the use of teacher
    and student time identified in this module (pp. 16-17).
2. Thoughtful advance planning for operating your
    classroom and delivering instruction will eliminate
    many problems for maintaining an orderly, produc-
    tive classroom. At least, two (2) kinds of plans should
    be made:

    a. General Operational Plan, establishing the
        routine daily operation of your classroom, in-
        cluding starting and ending times, procedures and
        time for taking role, grouping schemes, sequence
        or flow of activities, subjects, etc. Describe any
        special or specific procedures you expect to be
        followed.

    This plan should be placed in the front of your lesson
    plan book (for substitutes) and posted in the
    classroom for students to read.

    b. Specific Instructional Plan, indicating how you
        will spend time and deliver instruction. Merely
        recording times and page numbers from text
        books is not sufficient. This does not give ade-
        quate information about what you intend to do

during a time period, what you expect students to do, and how you expect instruction to proceed (e.g., grouping, activities, units, content development, etc.).

The instructional plan should serve as a record of how you intend instruction to proceed, which can be reviewed for future planning and shared with other teachers, if you desire.

Note: Although it has not been mentioned, daily instructional plans should evolve from a longer range plan for instruction (e.g., semester, month, week) that attends to concerns of subject scope and sequence as well as time/task requirements. (See "Suggestions for Teachers in Planning, Managing and Instructing to Increase Academic Engaged Time" in Suggested Activities for Module 6.)

3. Use audio and visual recordings to extend your understanding of classroom management concerns. These can be effective discussion starters for grade level or departmental meetings. The use of audio/videotape by a teacher to record classroom events is recommended as a means of getting a true picture of what is actually happening.

4. Cooperative observation of classroom instruction by other staff members is also encouraged. This should be followed up with adequate discussion between the teacher and observer to identify strengths and weaknesses.

5. As with discipline problems, discuss and seek solutions to problems of classroom or building management in staff meetings or in the smaller grade/department meetings.

Considerations for a School Discipline Plan

Potential Payoffs

1. Staff can increase their positive influence on students.
2. Staff can reduce tension, strain and confusion for self and students.
3. Staff will be less likely to make hasty and improper decisions in correcting behavior problems.
4. Staff use of positive reinforcements will help motivate students to behave and learn.
5. Everyone knows what to expect.
    - Teacher
    - Students
    - Principal
    - Parents
6. Student learns to be responsible for own behavior (Choices - Consequences).
7. Climate improves
    - no surprises
    - systematic resolution of conflict
    - order established
8. Behavior problems reduced.
9. Time on task increased.
10. Students learn more; achievement goes up.
11. Staff and students happier.

Pitfalls

1. Staff fails to construct adequate plan for in-class and out-of-class behavior.
2. Principal's approval of plan not requested or received
3. Students not informed properly.
4. Parents not informed.
5. Staff establishes plan but doesn't follow it.
    - inconsistently applied

–non-assertive reaction (threatens instead of acting)
–hostile reaction (uses "heavy" negative consequences first instead of last)

6. Staff fails to use positive reinforcement and only emphasizes negative consequences.
7. Belief that a quiet, orderly classroom in itself ensures
a positive learning climate.

Additional Resources

Brophy, J. E., & Putnam, J. G. *Classroom management in the
elementary grades.* East Lansing: Institute for Research
on Teaching, Research Series No. 32, Michigan State
University, 1978.

This is an excellent review of the literature on effective
classroom management in which principles of control are
synthesized from various researchers.

Canter, L. *Competency based resource materials and
guidelines.* Los Angeles: Canter and Associates, Inc.,
1979.

This is resource material and instructions for implementing the school discipline program of Canter's Assertive
Discipline, based on the book annotated directly below.

Canter, L., with Canter, M. *Assertive discipline: A take charge
approach for today's educator.* Los Angeles: Canter and
Associates, Inc., 1976.

This is the book which describes Canter's method of
assertive discipline. This approach, which has helped
schools around the nation improve discipline and get on
with the business of teaching, is essential reading for any
school haveing discipline problems.

Frith, G. H., Lindsey, J. D., & Sasser, J. L. An alternative approach to school suspension: The Dothan model. *Phi
Delta Kappan,* 1980, *61*(9), 637-638.

Annotated in Module 6.

Jones, F. H. The gentle art of classroom discipline. *The National Elementary Principal,* 1979, *58,* 26-32.

Jones' work on discipline should be required reading. He incorporates principles of classroom management with techniques for increasing time-on-task, thus tying improved discipline to increased achievement.

Module 8

Student Team Learning A Cooperative Learning Model

- **Groups, Group Values, and Group Reinforcements**
- **Team Learning Techniques**
- **Essential Characteristics of Team Games**
- **Some Basic Formats for Team Learning Games**
- **Suggested Activities**
- **Additional Resources**

Throughout our training modules we have emphasized the importance of changing the learning climate in the classroom and in the school. One important aspect of the learning climate of a classroom consists of the norms, values, and behaviors that students express in the classroom setting. Team or cooperative learning has proved successful in involving students in the instructional process and in mobilizing powers inherent in the peer group.

We often talk about peer power but usually fail to use it effectively. The intent of this module is to present a rationale for team learning with an instructional method for its accomplishment so that student groups can be a significant part of their reading and math instruction. We will illustrate what research at Johns Hopkins University (Slavin and DeVries, 1979) has shown:

that team learning can be used as a regular part of instruction in skill areas.

Groups, Group Values, and Group Reinforcements

People belong to groups because membership enables them to achieve goals that would be difficult to obtain if they were functioning individually. We join groups to play sports, produce things, meet community needs, and exercise shared interests. The most important quality of a functioning group is the set of values or goals to which all members of the group subscribe.

Groups have powerful techniques for reinforcing the attitudes, actions, and behaviors of their members. For most of us it is important to be an accepted member of a group. All of us are sensitive to rejection or disapproval by our peers or fellow group members. Correspondingly, all of us are extremely receptive to praise, being liked, and other signs of approval by our peers. This is, in fact, how groups "keep their members in line." If a group member acts of talks in a way contrary to the group values or norm, he or she is likely to be given negative sanctions. By the same token, if a group member subscribes to and acts upon the shared values and norms, he or she is likely to be popular, well-liked, praised, and positively rewarded. By these techniques groups tend to persist, show consistent patterns of behavior and attitudes, and produce very powerful "shaping" of members' actions.

In any classroom, students form friendship groups, common-interest groups, boy groups, girl groups, and sometimes racial groups. These groups will pursue various goals and hold special values. One group may be interested in trading bubble gum football cards, another may be interested in talking about dolls and doll clothes, and still another group may exist primarily to get into trouble while in school. In very few cases are student groups organized around academic values or the reinforcement of learning.

McDill and Rigsby (1973) found thatpeer relationships strongly influence student feelings about the importance of academic performance and about the appropriateness of such behaviors as studying, cheating, skipping school, and going to college. Coleman (1961) indicates that student norms often oppose academic achievement and penalize students who strive to do their best. Students are likely to develop feelings of futility or hopelessness in school when they are neither expected to achieve well nor rewarded for doing so (Brookover et al.,1979).

The task, then, is to find ways that student groups may be used to pursue learning as an important shared goal which can prove instrumental to other goals.

Benefits of Team Learning

Research on team learning provides us with evidence that this technique is valuable for a number of reasons, all of which relate to improving the academic learning climate and overall student achievement in a school. In extensive reviews, Slavin and DeVries (1979) and Slavin (1980) conclude that research on cooperative learning techniques shows them to be effective in increasing academic performance, mutual concern, and pro-academic norms. Slavin and DeVries also noted definite improvements in race relations, in attitudes towards school, and increases in active learning time. These results indicate the importance of their use for developing an effective learning climate. A study conducted by Aronson, Blaney, Sikes, Stephan, and Snapp (1975) indicates that some cooperative techniques positively affect self-concept or self-esteem. (See Johnson & Johnson, 1975, for description of techniques.) Although additional research needs to be done on the total effects of team learning, it seems to be a valuable tool. Like all tools, it must be used correctly to produce desired results.

Team Learning Techniques

The Importance of Team Rewards

Most of the learning games that will be described below rely on team competition. In order for group learning games to work, teachers must create symbolic or tangible team rewards that will be attractive to the student peer culture.

Generally, students are in touch with the symbolism, language system, and reward structure of competitive team sports. When organizing a class for team games, begin with the sports analogy and then modify it as necessary to insure that the goal of achievement by all students is advanced. Team names, standings, and percentages form a part of the analogy. Reward systems similar to those utilized in team sports have been used. Teachers may obtain inexpensive trophies that can be passed from one winning team to another at various stages in competition. Pennants or flags are indicators of group success. A newsletter highlighting team standings is attractive to the students and their parents.

Teachers and principals may also use tangible rewards. The parent-teacher organization may raise money for group prizes such as movie tickets, sporting events tickets, or coupons for hamburgers and milk shakes at a local fast-food restaurant. Second and third place groups, or teams showing improvement ought to receive lesser rewards occasionally to recognize their efforts.

Symbolic and tangible rewards for distribution in classrooms should be kept readily available. Pennants, trophies, coupons, jacket patches, team photographs, posters and recognition assemblies are rewards that the school staff can employ at little cost. Students also may be asked to indicate their preference for various rewards. Frequent non-tangible favorites are "free time" or a weekend without homework.

Time and Team Learning

The learning that occurs in team games does not differ greatly from that observed in more traditional types of teaching. What does differ is the source of the rewards of reinforcements. The power of the peer group can be extremely important here. In many classrooms, a teacher instructing the whole class may be interacting with only one or a few students at a time, while the other students are expected to listen or follow along. To the extent that other class members attend to the lesson or pay attention to the teacher-student interaction, learning is active and productive. However, unless students are motivated to pay attention when not being called on by the teacher, engaged time drops and learning decreases.

Well-structured team learning offers two distinct advantages to time-on-task. The first is that teams practicing for competition are likely to spend all their available time working hard to learn the material. The second is that during such practice sessions, the teacher has the opportunity to work closely with individuals, small groups or particular teams without the rest of the class engaging in off-task or disruptive behavior. In effect, the team structure absorbs some of the instructional, reinforcement, management and discipline functions of the teacher, giving him/her time to work at a higher level of teaching skill in providing corrective or enrichment instruction.

Cooperative Learning

Student team techniques change both the task and the reward structure of a classroom. Rewards given to students are based on the performance of the team as a whole. Slavin (1977) notes that team learning can be called a cooperative task structure and the reward structure can be called a cooperative reward structure. Students performing well in a team help improve the functioning of their teammates by modeling and encouraging positive attitudes and correct responses.

The traditional classroom uses an individual task structure

(students work independently or listen to the teacher) and a competitive reward structure (grading on a curve) where students seldom help each other, but compete instead for a limited supply of good grades (Slavin, 1977). The personal attention each student receives is necessarily limited. Students compete against one another because everyone cannot get an A. In fact, with curve grading, to help or encourage another student to get better grades is to reduce one's own chance of a good grade (see also module on Effective Instruction).

Team learning research has shown that student prefer and learn better in settings in which they teach and learn from each other (see Devin-Sheehan, Feldman, & Allen, 1976).

Built into every learning game should be time for practice, peer tutoring and modeling. This practice is imperative for effective instruction. If the team game is some sort of spelling bee or math fact drill, members of the team should have a considerable amount of time to spend practicing together on the content of the competition. Tutoring may consist of peer-to-peer drill, a form of modeling, or having one of the students function as a quasi-teacher for the rest of the group.

The exact nature of peer-to-peer teaching ought to be left to the group so that it develops spontaneously its own instructional dynamics. However since we cannot assume that students automatically will use the most productive means of teaching and helping each other in their teams, teachers need to give strategies and techniques for helping individuals and working cooperatively in groups. This will not hinder the internal dynamics of the group, but will give the team members more effective options from which to choose.

If the team games are perceived by students as important activities, a peer reinforcement system usually will emerge. The "academic heroes" of the day will come to receive more and more praise and adulation by their peers as they lead their groups to victory in group games and tournaments.

The peer group will reward academic performance as well as other successes (i.e., sport performance). On the other hand, it is likely that some negative reinforcement will be aimed toward team members who bring down team scores and fail to do well on the team competition learning tasks. This should not be construed in a negative mannner by the teacher. Such peer-to-peer reinforcers are likely to "motivate" the team members to work harder and to increase their performances. The team-mediated positive and negative reinforcements should be allow-ed to flourish, as long as they are within the bounds of good sportsmanship.

Team learning sessions should become part of the regular classroom routine. These are not the kind of activities which are done once in a while "to give the kids something fun to do." Team learning is an instructional technique which maximizes peer encouragement, social relations among students, time ac-tively spent in learning, self-concept, and academic perfor-mance. Growth occurs only when team games become part of the classroom operation, and are tied closely to the main course objectives.

Essential Characteristics of Team Games

Several team games below include essential game features. There are many commercial pre-programmed learning games for both reading and math but certain of their characteristics differ from the ones suggested below. For example, some com-mercial games suggest homogeneous teams to ensure "fair" competition, or allow only the most skilled members to com-pete. This is contrary to our view of effective grouping (see Grouping and Differentiation module for explanation). Consis-tent with the goal of high achievement for all students, the point of team learning is not to "select out" the best, but to make each student a participant and a winner.

The important features to remember in selecting and developing team games are:

1. Teams are not used for initial instruction but for sup-plementing instruction presented by the teacher and practice on common grade level objectives. Students are not expected to learn on their own in teams but to

practice, drill, study, and apply; also to encourage, correct, tutor and help each other on learning objectives and materials provided by the teacher.

2. Teams should be formed that are heterogeneous in terms of performance. The teacher may divide the class into teams in any number of ways, balancing academic strengths and weaknesses, race and sex, and breaking up undesirable behavior combinations. The teacher makes the team selections rather than permitting students to choose their teammates. (The latter method might be quite appealing in terms of the team sports analogy that it represents, but it can damage self-esteem of those chosen last, or restrict participation to a select group of "buddies.") In competition of team against team or room against room at the same grade level, the competing groups ought to be heterogeneous and matched against roughly equivalent competing teams. In other words, teams should have a fairly equal chance to win so that it is their own effort that makes the difference.

3. Teams should be together for a period or time, at least six weeks, which allows members to come to know and trust each other and work well together. If the teacher has made careful selections, he/she should simply ignore initial protests on team assignments and move ahead. If teams are formed and reformed too frequently or have frequent "substitutes," team spirit does not build. Experience in districts with poor attendance suggests the wisdom of increasing slightly the size of the teams (6 instead of 5, 5 instead of 4) so that teams can function without missing members. At the same time, tardiness or absence would put the team at some competitive disadvantage so the errant member will receive group pressure to attend (e.g., bonus points may be awarded to teams with perfect attendance).

4. Prior to every competition, time ought to be devoted to practice. The full strength of the peer culture will be

mobilized only if students have an opportunity to teach one another and exert group pressure upon team members in ways that cannot be used in the context of the game itself. The teams should have regular structured practice time to drill on the learning materials that will be used in the game, using the same kinds of information, spelling lists, number facts, or learning objectives that will be used in the contest.

It is in team practice sessions that peer instruction and encouragement influence learning. The actual contest or competition provides the incentive for students to improve skill performance, but it is the practice in teams that makes the greatest contribution to improved achievement. Practice and drill on academic subjects are necessary but can be less than exciting. Just as in sports, the academic contests with their intrinsic and extrinsic rewards provide the motivation for students to practice and improve.

5. Rules should be developed to ensure orderly and sportsmanlike competition. Cooperative behavior is not learned immediately in sports or in academics: it is acquired gradually. As in teaching classroom behavior, this instruction takes place every day until the appropriate behavior becomes routine. Observe how the teams operate as you circulate around the room, and sit in with the teams occasionally as they practice. The teacher should reinforce strongly all examples of cooperative or helping behavior and bring them to the attention of the class. For example, during the first few contests, points can be awarded or taken away from teams on the basis of sportsmanship and conduct; or a special trophy may be awarded for exemplary team behavior.

6. In any of the learning games extensive use should be made of both symbolic and tangible rewards to the teams. The teams ought to feel that performance is important and instrumental to learning (i.e., mastery of grade level basic skills). The use of external rewards

such as pennants or trophies adds to the intrinsic reward of peer encouragement.

7. Contests can be oral or written and can contain questions for individual team members or for the entire team, either as a deliberative body or in sequence for multiple operations or parts of a problem. Teachers should consider and balance several factors in determining the type of contest or question format. For example, younger students have shorter attention spans while older students can be "contested" over more objectives. Short, right answers, as in spelling or number facts, call for a different setting than complex problem-solving. An oral contest may generate more excitement and motivation while a written contest may increase time-on-task by requiring all students to participate in providing answers. Alternatively, the "challenge" process may be used in oral contests to induce all students to work each problem or answer each question in order to win game points.

8. All students should have frequent successes in practice and in competition, as individuals and as teams, if maximum learning is to result. Some points to keep in mind:

    A. Encourage all team members to contribute to the learning of the team. If the teacher assumes, and acts on the assumption, that only the most advanced students can help others, much of the potential of team learning is lost. For example, a common error is to appoint permanent "captains" who are the most advanced students on their teams and to give them great leeway for making decisions, assigning tasks and so on. This tends to lessen the sense of responsibility of the other team members and may even arouse their resentment if the captain usually insists on being "teacher." Jobs such as captain, scorekeeper, answer checker, drillmaster or resource gatherer, where necessary, should be rotated among team members. Slower students often surprise the class with their ability and willingness to help others if the structure and operation of the teams gives them, as well as the faster students, the opportunity.

B. If you have individuals in the class who consitently fail to answer questions correctly, vary the difficulty of the questions. In some contest, students could choose the kind of question to answer. For example, the difficulty of questions might vary according to getting a single (easiest question) to scoring a homerun (hardest question) where the risk of "striking out" is greater. Students may select a level of risk and still add points to the team total.

C. If you have a team that remains in last place for weeks, with no sign of improvement, it is probably time to reshuffle the teams to give them an even chance at winning. Alternatively, the team might be given advice and help on how to proceed in mastering the material on which they will compete. It is usually possible to spot the problems of a losing team by closely observing their practice sessions for awhile.

Some Basic Formats For Team Learning Games

Spelling Bee or Number Facts Bee

The bee is a classical game that has been used for generations. The past focus has been on individual competition. We suggest that this be modified to a team format. Academic contests are easily arranged for short-answer learning drills such as spelling, number facts in addition and subtraction, multiplication and division, etc. The stimulus materials may take the form of spelling lists, flash cards, etc., to be used during practice sessions.

During the competition, the teacher presents questions to team members, who have a limited time to respond. A right answer will give the team a point and a wrong answer will give the team a zero. Each team should present a "batting order" to the teacher at the beginning of the game. A variation on the above format is to give the next team an opportunity to answer a question missed by the previous team. Such a "corrective"response may be given two points in scoring. To facilitate the game, a student score keeper should keep point scores and make sure that the questions are being directed to individuals in the pre-determined order.

The bee may be used with spelling and number facts. It is a fast verbal drill and is likely to be accompanied by a great deal of spontaneous interaction, cheering and group excitement. However, for older students written tests can be employed and the same kind of scoring used. One school had students spell the word or solve the problem on a transparency and then display the answer on an overhead projector. This allowed contestants to write their answers, which many found more comfortable than verbalizing them. The transparency allows the audience, and the scorekeepers, to see the answers more clearly than a chalkboard does, and is easily erased after each contestant is finished.

Team Games Tournament (TGT)
(Source: The John Hopkins Team Learning Project)

Note: We recommend that schools considering Team-Games-Tournaments contact The John Hopkins Project for its manual and directions as well as Grade-appropriate learning objectives in reading and math. These are complete with practice and game questions, answer sheets, scoring sheets and so on. The following brief description introduces the reader to this technique.

In TGT one member from each of several standing teams goes into a new group for the tournament and competes there for points to take back to his/her team. Each of the standing teams should have practice time in which to study the same stimulus materials and prepare all team members for the competition.

The game works through a set of question cards that are in the middle of the table. A student picks a question card from the shuffled pile in the middle of the table, reads the question aloud, then arrives at and announces an answer. The rest of the people at the table, in turn, may challenge the answer if they believe it is wrong and refer to a common set of answer sheets (or the teacher) to check for correctness. The correct answer or correct challenge earns one game point. The student with the right answer keeps the question cards as a tally. The game proceeds for a specified length of time or until all the question cards have been used up. At the end of the game individual standings at a given table are computed on the basis of total game points. These places, in turn, earn team points for an individual's team. For example, with four players, the winner at a table will get eight points for first place, the second place person will get six points, the third place person will get four points and the lowest scoring member gets two points. These team points will be summed from all tables in the class and then applied to team standings. Note that every player takes adjusted points back to his/her team. Quizzes may be substituted for the game occasionally with teams points determined as indicated.

Rutabaga
(Source: The John Hopkins Team Learning Project)

Rutabaga is a form of TGT that is used for building oral reading skills at any grade level. In practice sessions, team members read aloud to each other. On game day, students are assigned to 3-6 member tournament tables as in TGT and compete for points to take back to their own teams. Students take turns reading aloud to the other players who have the same reading material in front of them. The reader substitutes the word "rutabaga" for words of his/her choice and the first player to fill in the missing word gains a point. A wrong guess loses a point.

Jigsaw II
(Source: The John Hopkins Team Learning Project)

Jigsaw II can accommodate complex learning tasks. Each team member is designated "expert" for his or her team on one part of the material to be learned, although all team members read the material. The "expert" studies the assigned section and meets with the experts from all the other teams who have responsibility for the same material. The experts discuss the material in detail and make sure they have mastered it well, because their job is to go back and teach it to their own teams to prepare them for competition.

Twenty Questions

This is a team game version of the well-known TV game. It is particularly appropriate for complex "reasoning" tasks.

The teacher identifies a person, place, or thing which the various teams are to identify through a series of questions that receive yes-no answers from the teacher. Each team will identify an interrogator to ask the questions of the teacher. The teams rotate their questions and may ask only one question at a time. For every question that is answered "yes" the team receives points; for every answer that is answered "no" the team loses points. Prior to each question by the team "interrogator," the members have an opportunity to caucus among themselves and come up with a question selected by the group. If a team identifies correctly the person, place, or thing, it receives a set number of points.

Between-Classroom Contest Formats

Most team learning games will occur within a single

classroom. Occasionally teachers may wish to challenge another classroom or even have a grade level contest. Although other formats can be devised, two that we have used successfully are described briefly below.

a. Winning Teams Compete: A week before the grade level contest, each room has its own contest. The team that wins the room contest then competes for the grade championship. If the contest is held in the gym or auditorium, all other students in the rooms can be spectators, cheering their own teams on to victory. The cheering by spectators often reaches great intensity. Under these conditions, practice and learning are facilitated by a team's strong incentive to be the room representative, then the grade champion. Cheering of classmates can also be a strong factor in promoting a sense of room spirit and pride. *Caution:* the pressure to win is great enough that some rooms may be tempted to send as their "representative team" the 5 or 6 fastest students in the class. This defeats the entire dynamics of team learning as described in this module. Teachers must police themselves against such an eventuality.

b. All Teams Compete: In this format, all of the teams from each room compete. This intramural style has the advantage that all students compete in the grade level contest as well as in the room contests. A seventh grade at one school illustrates this format.

Each of 5 classrooms had 5 heterogeneous teams of 5-6 members. The week before the grade contest, each classroom had its own contest to determine within-class ranking. On the day of the grade contest, the #1 ranked team from each classroom went to one room. Likewise each of the #2 ranked teams gathered in another room and so also for #3, 4 and 5 ranked teams. Prior to the contest, the five teachers had prepared common questions covering the agreed-upon learning objectives. The 5 teams in each room, representing 5 different classrooms, competed for points under the direction of one of the teachers. The teams were awarded points based on order of finish (e.g., 10, 8, 6, 4 or 2 points). Team points were added up for each of the classes, and the top scoring room became the grade grand champion.

The all-team competition system eliminates spectators and makes every student a participant. We feel that both of these methods facilitate common planning of grade level objectives by teachers at any one grade level. Teachers work together to establish standards of behavior, contest rules, award assemblies, and so on. One teacher commented that the sharing of ideas and instructional techniques that resulted from such a contest was the most positive experience of his teaching career.

Summary

In this module we have presented methods of student cooperative learning which increase basic skill achievement and improve the school learning climate. These strategies, like those suggested in other modules, need structure, collaboration, and joint decision-making that are consistent with emphasis on student achievement. Team learning furnishes practice opportunity in the mastery learning strategy and should not be seen as separate from regular instruction. It is a motivating technique which keeps students on task. It is an efficient means for practice and reinstruction on skills which have been introduced by the teacher to the whole class. In team learning students get immediate attention from their group members and are kept interacting with the learning material. Module 5 puts student team learning into the context of "effective instruction."

The team learning approach can improve the effectiveness of a class or school program significantly and reduce the amount of time it takes for some students to master grade level skills. Team learning should become part of the school social system, used by all teachers. (If only a few teachers employ this method, the effect on the total school will be reduced.)

Finally, the motivational power of the peer group and the team model may be used to "turn on" students who might not ordinarily be excited about academics. This makes team learning an important strategy by which teachers can structure learning so that changes in student attitudes and academic motivation are likely to occur.

Suggested Activities

1. Read *Using Student Team Learning* by Robert Slavin (1980) for information and ideas on using team learning successfully. Teams-Games-Tournaments (TGT), Jigsaw I and II, and Rutabaga are explained.

2. Grade level teachers should develop an approach to team learning games with which they feel comfortable and can support. Come to agreement on:
   a) Areas or subjects for competition
   b) Composition
   c) Schedule of interclass competition
   d) Rules for competing
   e) Sportsmanship requirements
   f) Format of competitions
   g) Rewards

3. Discuss with students the concept of team learning, team competition, and sportsmanship. Developing an appreciation for being a team player and a good sport are critical to the success of using team learning. Being a good winner and good loser are attitudes that must be taught and modeled by the teacher. Slighting this important topic can easily destroy your team learning program. (See Suggested Sportsmanship Rules.)

4. In forming teams:
    a) Each team should reflect the range of perfor-
        mance, and the ethnic and sex mix of the class.
    b) Equalize teams for performance.
    c) Teacher places students on teams rather than hav-
        ing students pick teammates.
    d) Team decides on name.
5. Schedule team practice at least once a week—more
    often if possible. Practice is where the greatest poten-
    tial for team learning payoffs is found. Don't neglect
    this vital element.
6. It is suggested that team competition be held regularly
    within a classroom. Treat this like regular competi-
    tion, with standings and appropriate rewards.
7. In setting up an interclass contest:
    a) Teachers decide the content to be used and supply
        all teams with the same information to study.
    b) Establish the date of the contest in advance so
        teams can have sufficient practice beforehand.
    c) Specific rules should be decided and discussed
        with students.
    d) The object of the competition is to identify the
        winning class in the grade level that is involved.
8. Team learning games can follow a variety of formats:
    verbal, paper and pencil, simulation, etc. Alter the
    game format occasionally to maintain student in-
    terest.

Suggested Sportsmanship Rules
for Team Learning Games

Note: These rules were compiled by one school's 6th
        grade students. Rules were then enforced during
        the contests by the teachers.

1. Come into room in an orderly way.

2. Stay in seats.
3. Avoid distracting all players while they are thinking and taking tests.
4. Avoid laughing at wrong answers.
5. Avoid arguing over answers, points, and accusing people of cheating.
6. Have a good attitude toward others such as: Tell others they have played well, avoid bragging, and try to have fun even if you lose.
7. Don't tease others when they lose.
8. Follow directions.
9. Congratulate the winning team.
10. Be respectful when others are talking.
11. Don't make fun of your own teammates when they don't get any points for the team.
12. If any of these rules are broken 5 points will be taken off the teams' score for each rule broken.

Suggestions To Teachers For Interclass Contests

1. Agree on all rules prior to practice sessions and the contest.
2. When reading results to students, be positive in announcing positions and giving standings of teams.
3. Have answer sheets available ahead of time to facilitate scoring.
4. Have extra ditto copies of materials on hand to prevent problems due to faintness of copy.
5. Penalize points for talking, etc. Decide on consistent enforcement among teachers before the contest.

Additional Resources

Aronson, E., et al. *The jigsaw classroom*. Beverly Hills, Cal.:

Sage Publications, Inc., 1978.

Rationale, explanation, and description of the jigsaw approach to student team learning.

DeRoche, E.F., & Bogenschild, E. G. *400 group games and activities for teaching math.* West Nyack, N.Y.: Parker Publishing Co., 1969.

Gibbs, G. I. (Ed.). *Handbook of games and simulation exercises.* London: E. & F. N. Spon, Ltd., 1974.

The Johns Hopkins Student Team Learning Project. Baltimore: Center for Social Organization of Schools, The Johns Hopkins University.

Materials for Student Team Learning may be purchased at cost. A teacher's manual, overview filmstrips, and curriculum material packets for math, language arts, and other subjects at various grade levels are available. (3505 N. Charles St., Baltimore, MD 21238.)

Johnson, D. W., & Johnson, R. T. *Learning together and alone: Cooperation, competition, and individualization.* Englewood Cliffs, N.J.: Prentice-Hall, Inc., 1975.

This is an excellent review and analysis of the advantages of cooperative team learning.

Metzner, S. *77 games for reading groups.* Belmond, Cal.: Fearon Publisher, Inc., 1973.

Although some of these games are oriented toward individuals, many can be used with groups or adapted to team competiton.

Slavin, R. E. Classroom reward structure: An analytical and practical review. *Review of Educational Research,* 1977, *47,* 633-650.

This review focuses on reward structures and their use and effectiveness in changing classroom behavior.

Slavin, R. E. Cooperative learning. *Review of Educational Research,* 1980a, *50*(2), 315-342.

Good overview of the literature on cooperative team learning.

Slavin, R. E. *Using student team learning: The Johns Hopkins Team Learning Project* (Revised ed.). Baltimore: Center for Social Organization of Schools, The Johns Hopkins University, 1980b.

Slavin provides an overview and directions for team learning as a classroom instructional technique for improving student achievement and intergroup relations.

Slavin, R. E., & DeVries, D. L. Learning in teams. In H. Walberg (Ed.). *Educational environments and effects: Evaluation, policy, and productivity.* Berkeley, Cal.: McCutchan Publishing Corp., 1978.

This review and analysis of the literature on student team learning is a thorough treatment of the topic.

Zuckerman, D. W., & Horn, R. E. *The Guide to simulations/games for educational training.* Lexington, Mass.: Information Resources, Inc., 1973.

Module 9

Reinforcing Achievement

- **Basic Reinforcement Principles**
- **Types of Rewards**
- **Some Classroom Examples**
- **Suggested Activities**
- **Additional Resources**

In attempting to develop an effective school learning climate, with high expectations for all students, we should be aware of various reinforcement techniques which will help motivate and sustain the student behaviors which are consistent with these expectations. The following techniques provide a general framework of reinforcement principles which are applicable to student learning and student conduct.

This module will focus on the proper use of reinforcement so that desired student behavior, both social and academic, may be realized. It will cover the principles and values of reinforcement, types of rewards, proper use of rewards, praise and encouragement in the classroom, and the qualities of reinforcements which make them most effective. In addition, we will present specific examples of proper reinforcement during oral and written drill.

Basic Reinforcement Principles

The Stimulus: In a learning situation we must reinforce responses, but responses by students can only occur in relationship to something that is presented to them. This "something," in the literature of reinforcement theory, is the stimulus. An example of an academic stimulus would be a flash card shown to a student for a correct number fact response. It also may be in the nature of a verbal or written question, an exercise in a book, a word presented on a spelling test, or a subtraction problem. We present these stimuli to students, and either by example, lecture or a variety of creative teaching techniques, we provide our students the information needed for a correct response.

One point to bear in mind is that students must be clear about what is being asked of them. Thus, the subtraction problem that is being presented to them must stand out from the general classroom hubbub. The word that they are being asked to spell must be understandable. The question that has been verbally directed to them must be unambiguous, and should generally have no more than one correct answer. The problems, questions, and exercises that we present to students must be ones that enable the student to distinquish relevant information from background information.

The Response: The response is the answer that the student produces in relation to the stimulus that is presented. It is the verbal, written, or overt behavior that the student produces when asked a question, given a problem, or asked to spell a word. One of the things we often forget as teachers is that a response should be either right or wrong, or at least, acceptable or unacceptable. Teachers must make a discrimination between answers that are right and answers that are wrong. Thus, not only must students discriminate among possible answers to the question asked, but teachers must also determine the correctness of the response given by students.

Reinforcement: after a stimulus has been presented to a student and the student has produced a response, what happens next? This is where the teacher, if he/she chooses, can reinforce the answer or behavior exhibited by the student. Reinforcements can be either positive or negative in nature. A positive reinforcement (sometimes thought of as a "reward") is likely to cause the response to be strengthened in a student. Reinforcement is like psychological glue; every little dab that we use is likely to attach the answers more firmly in students' minds. This simple fact is both the strength and the danger of reinforcement. When we positively reinforce something—no matter whether it is right or wrong— we are likely to increase the probability of its being repeated. Sometimes teachers reinforce wrong answers. Sometimes teachers reward incorrect behavior. Usually, this is done inadvertently, or because a teacher feels it is important to be always warm and accepting of students. Unfortunately, the frequent result is that students unintentionally "learn" to be poor students.

Negative reinforcement is the reverse of positive reinforcement. Sometimes we can motivate student behavior by withdrawing something that students value. For example, if students value the teacher's praise when answering questions, withholding that praise for incorrect responses can be a powerful motivator. This is analogous to parents withdrawing an allowance from children who refuse to do their dishwashing chores. This type of reinforcement can be as effective as positive reinforcement.

Most of us prefer to be "positive people" and so may avoid using negative reinforcement. We must be aware that sometimes telling a student, "No, that's not correct," while providing support and encouragement, "Now try again, I know you can do it," will help the student learn the correct response. By telling students they are wrong and providing encouragement for the correct response, students will feel that learning is possible and thus be more motivated to respond correctly. Any reinforcement used in a non-discriminating manner is likely to impede student learning.

If a reward or reinforcer is to be effective in controlling or modifying behavior it must be delivered *contingently;* that is, the reinforcer is not given until the desired behavior occurs. The individual or group receiving the reward must clearly understand that the reward is given only on the performance of correct behavior. In a school or classroom these behavioral expectations should be clearly understood by the students. They should know what is expected of them academically and socially. Rewards or punishments should then be consistent with the expectations for all students.

Types of Rewards

In the classroom or school there are two basic types of reinforcers which can be delivered: tangible and social rewards. Tangible rewards are typically associated with items such as snack treats, free time, etc., which are given for appropriate responses. More complex or sophisticated systems, in which the rewards may be points or check-marks that are given at the time of response and then accumulated for exchange or purchase of actual rewards later, are known as token economies. Also, tangible rewards can be symbolic; the use of trophies, banners, honor roll and certificates of merit are a few such rewards. The stars we place on student assignments are another example of a symbolic reward. By using such reinforcers teachers are communicating to students their satisfaction with student performance, by withholding them they communicate dissatisfaction.

Some difficulties in providing tangible rewards should be recognized. They can be expensive and time consuming for the teacher. Also, if a reward is to be effective, students should be responsive to it. A reward for some students may not be valued as a reward by others. The teacher will have to try various types of tangible rewards to identify those most effective for affecting behavior in the classroom. Some rewards lose their effectiveness if used too often or too long. It is advisable to vary the material rewards, or to use them sparingly enough to stimulate desired behavior.

The second type of reward most commonly used is social in nature. Praise given by the teacher or student peers has been advocated as a useful method. Praise is relatively easy to apply and is a direct statement of the contingency between the behavior and the reinforcer (Brophy, 1981). Yet praise does not always operate as a reinforcer. For example, students may see it as embarrassing and thus undesirable. Teachers should be sensitive to situations in which praise will be valued as an effective reward.

Brophy (1981) found that when intrinsic motivation does not exist, extrinsic rewards, both social and tangible are appropriate. Yet, research by Crandall (1963) and Crandall, Good, and Crandall (1964) indicates that intrinsic motivation (enjoyment of achievement) is a more lasting and powerful motivator. Thus, the teacher should be concerned with helping the student make the transition from extrinsic to intrinsic rewards, gradually reducing or "fading" the number of extrinsic rewards. Calling students' attention to "how good it feels" and to their sense of personal accomplishment, and relating classroom learning to the outside world of jobs and later education, are some strategies that can be used to make this transition.

In Brophy's (1981) review of teacher praise, he finds that generally praise does not function as a reinforcer because it is often misused in the classroom. Another review of studies of praise in *Learning* (Martin, 1977) details many of the negative effects of improperly applied praise. Harris and Kapche (1978) note that most praise is non-contingent on the child's prior behavior. As mentioned above, for a reinforcement schedule to be effective, it must be contingent upon behavior. Teacher praise, however, is often given inappropriately, as in the case when an incorrect student response is praised or rewarded verbally. This inappropriate praise is often found among teachers who have low expectations for student learning (Weinstein, 1976; Brookover et al., 1978). Teachers sometimes use it as an attempt to encourage students or to reward them for simply participating in the class. It is seen by many as a way of getting low achieving students to feel good about themselves. Yet as Brophy (1981) notes, to the extent that students recognize what the teacher is doing, the result will be embarrassment, discouragement, and other undesireable outcomes.

For example, if your child walked up to a table with four legs and petted it saying, "Nice kitty," would you reward him/her for that response? This may seem simplistic, but there is little difference between that and praising a child for an incorrect math or spelling response. Are these the kinds of behavior we want to encourage in students? If academic learning is the goal, then only behavior which approximates that goal should be rewarded.

Another problem with typical classroom praise is its lack of specificity. Anderson, Evertson, and Brophy (1979) found that only five (5) percent of teacher praise followed good work or good answers by students. As they note, this seems unacceptably low, since praise is intended to motivate desired responses, either academic or other behavior, from students.

Another factor which reduces the effects of teacher praise is lack of credibility. In other words, the verbal content is not supported by, or is even contradicted by, non-verbal expressive behavior (Feldman & Donohoe, 1978; Friedman, 1976). Students are very aware of the sincerity or credibility of teacher talk; praise which is seen as insincere is often not functional. Brophy, Evertson, Beam, Anderson and Crawford (1979) found that troublesome students received as much praise and access to classroom rewards as did better behaved and more successful students, but that non-verbal cues usually indicated negative feelings in the teacher, the student, or both. In other words, the teacher gave automatic praise but acted negatively, or the student who received the praise reacted negatively to it, or both acted negatively to the verbal reward. In this study they also found that praise was not used as a systematic reinforcement technique with students who were described as uncooperative or disruptive because the teachers wished to minimize their interactions with these students. Thus, the consistent finding is that praise given to students is usually not dependent upon specific academic behavior but rather dependent upon the social attributes of the students. Rewards given in this manner are not consistent with the proper use of reinforcement and may in fact lead to undesirable outcomes.

Studies of teachers indicate that praise when used properly, is related to student achievement most consistently in low SES or low achieving classrooms. (Good, Ebmeier, & Beckerman, 1978; Murname & Phillips, 1978). This is explained by the fact that teachers' praise for academic progress is more meaningful to low achievers than to high achievers who are accustomed to consistent success. This does not mean we should praise low achieving students for every single response: the reinforcement must be contingent upon specified correct performance. But teachers should reinstruct and encourage slower students until the correct response is given; then the praise should be given sincerely and in the tone of "I knew you could do it! See how your hard work paid off!"

As summarized by O'Leary and O'Leary (1977), to yield positive reinforcement, praise must have the following characteristics:

1. *Contingency:* praise should be contingent upon performance of the behavior to be reinforced;
2. *Specificity:* praise should specify the particular behavior being reinforced;
3. *Sincerity/variety/credibility:* praise should be sincere and convincing. This means that the verbal content should be varied according to the situation and to the preferences of the student being praised.

Contingency

In a program to improve school learning climate, the contingent behaviors which should be rewarded are mastery of basic skill objectives at age grade level, progress leading to such mastery, and classroom conduct which supports many varied types of learning behavior; thus, the teacher should focus on a few important common behaviors for the whole class, as well as for individuals.

Since expectations for basic skills achievement should be the same for all students, this is an appropriate place to begin, remembering that praise should be awarded only to those who meet the common expectations for the class. Teachers should use rewards only following performance of the desired behavior.

Specificity

It is important to specify the particulars of the behavior being rewarded. This makes it more significant to the student(s) being praised and tends to reinforce the specific desired behavior. For example, if a student thinks through and follows the steps to solving a problem as he/she has been taught, it is the thinking through that is praised, not just the right answer. There are other ways to get a right answer (estimating, guessing, cheating, and so on). The teacher makes sure that no misunderstandings occur about what is praiseworthy and desirable behavior for members of the class by finding and rewarding that specific behavior.

A further consideration here on specificity: if a teacher applies negative reinforcement to stop an undesirable behavior, it is important to follow up by identifying to the student(s) a substitute desirable behavior. For example, "John, you have not done well on your assignment today because of carelessness. You can prevent this by taking time to check your work before handing it in. Do you understand how to check your work? Good, now check this paper over and make the necessary corrections before returning it to me today." The new behavior would then be strongly reinforced, or praised, using the principles of contingency and specificity.

Sincerity, Variety, Credibility

To determine which positive reinforcement techniques serve as rewards for students' reaction to them, observe how the student responds to the reinforcer, verbally or non-verbally, and make adjustments accordingly. The aim is to identify those rewards toward which students react favorably. One simple method is to ask students what is rewarding or not rewarding to them and try to note individual differences. The negative reinforcement of being placed in a chair next to the teacher may be humiliating and upsetting to one student, but a reward to another who enjoys the extra attention. Ware (1978) found that in some instances teachers acted on the assumption that students liked extrinsic rewards, while the students actually preferred intrinsic rewards.

Teachers can utilize students' preferences for free time activities as a positive reinforcer. Assuming that those activities which students choose to engage in during free time are intrinsically satisfying, teachers can use those same activities as rewards for completing work or doing well in academic areas. For example, puzzles are a source of attraction to all ages and many students eagerly seek them when they have a chance; allowing students to work on these same puzzles can then be used as rewards for academic accomplishment.

Praise, to be effective, must also be sincere. Positive rewards that are accompanied by negative non-verbal cues such as facial expressions are received negatively by students. Some consistency in the use of praise and related behaviors, within and between classrooms, is also required if students in the school social system are to accept it as credible.

One further consideration should be kept in mind. Crandal et al. (1964) note that teachers and parents generally have a particular style of praising. The amount of praise given is usually consistent for an individual. Students soon learn a teacher's style and adapt to it. The point is that "no praise," a neutral area between positive reinforcement and negative reinforcement, may not really be neutral. Students regard silence or lack of praise from a "heavy praiser" as criticism, while no praise from an "infrequent praiser" is perceived by students as usual behavior. Heavy praise can lead to dependency, frequent checking with the teacher, and student insecurity, or it can become like "water off a duck's back" and lose all effectiveness. This is further reason for giving praise only in an appropriate manner; that is, contingent, specific, and sincere.

Frequency of Reinforcement

Teachers have only so much time to attend to a classroom of students. A teacher cannot expect to be able to reinforce all the responses students make. Meacham and Wilson (1971) provide some general rules to follow regarding how much, how often, and when we should reinforce.

1. Teachers should reinforce most heavily when the student is learning a new task and less when he/she is maintaining a behavior that has been well learned.
2. When the desired behavior is social and to be maintained over a long period of time, it is recommended the teacher use an intermittent schedule of reinforcement. In this method, several correct responses may be required for a reinforcement (ratio schedule) or a given time may elapse before it is given (interval schedule).

Some Classroom Examples

The following examples are based on our intital framework of stimulus, response, and reinforcement. They should provide further clarity of the principles of praise and encouragement discussed above. These are practical examples which are encountered in most classrooms. Note that in these examples, the teacher is seen as the reinforcer, but the peer group can also be motivated to follow these principles. They may be an even stronger force in maintaining or sustaining appropriate behavior. Just as in team learning, the group can be mobilized to reward or sanction the behavior of students in the classroom.

Stimulus—Asking Questions: Questions, whether verbal or in a written form, should be asked in such a way as to enable the student to understand and discriminate what is being asked. Generally, there are two types of questions, or learning stimuli, that we present to students. One type of question calls for a short factual answer. These convergent questions often deal with matters of fact which a student either knows or does not know. For students this questioning process is in essence, an exercise in memory. Examples of convergent questions include those involving famous dates, state capitols, number facts, presidents of the United States, etc. Convergent questions often begin with "when," "where," and so on.

One thing to remember in asking this type of question is not to ask two questions at the same time. For example, we should not ask, "Who was the first governor of Michigan and how many terms did he serve?" Double questions tend to confuse both students and teachers.

Generally, questions of this type can be asked or presented in a very rapid manner (see Module 5, Effective Instruction). Thus, if we are involved in an oral drill on number facts, we should pace ourselves fairly rapidly. Correspondingly, we should not allocate a great deal of time for similar written exercises.

A second type of question involves a reasoning process on the part of students. These questions, divergent in nature, not only include who, what, where and when, as before, but they also include how and why. In responding to such a question, the student must become involved in more complex thought processes and more complex answers. However, the same guidelines about clarity of the question and the associated clarity of the answer suggested for convergent questions also apply to divergent questions. Just as in rote or mechanical learning, the student must understand what is being asked.

These types of questions, of course, should be paced more slowly than rote learning questions as students will need more time to think over their responses.

Responses—Correct and Incorrect: Unless the student does not respond at all, (s)he is likely to give a response that can be evaluated in terms of its "rightness" or acceptability. As implied in the above discussion, most questions should have clear, unambiguous, right or wrong answers. Factual-memory questions are definitely of this sort.

When questions are more complex the teacher's evaluation may be that an answer is "mostly right" or "mostly wrong." This demands more elaborate feedback on the part of the teacher, and a more astute application of reinforcement principles. This process resembles that of reinstruction, with teachers providing encouragement and support, but at the same time insuring that students know whether their answers are basically right or wrong.

Reinforcement and Feedback Behavior on the Part of the Teacher: Whatever a student does, whether he/she answers correctly or incorrectly, or doesn't answer at all, some reciprocal response is demanded on the part of the teacher. Let us consider for a minute a situation in which a student does not respond. If the question is a simple factual one, such as a math or work drill, the teacher should encourage the student, wait a few seconds, and then give the answer. However, if the question is more complex, involving reasoning, the teacher should give the pupil time to think over the answer and should try to ascertain whether the student does or does not know the answer. If a student does not respond to a complex question, the teacher should always attempt to get a correct or nearly correct response from the student. This may involve simplifying or restating the question, or breaking it down into its component parts.

What happens if the student gives a wrong answer? If we are talking about a factual question, presented in a rapid-paced learning session, the teacher should indicate that the answer is incorrect, give the correct answer, and either move on or immediately reinstruct and requestion. The student should clearly understand that the answer given was wrong. However, it is important that this information be given to the student in a positive, instructive manner. The teacher should matter-of-factly point out the error, give the correct answer and move on. Whenever an incorrect answer is given, the teacher must be very careful to avoid either discouraging the student or reinforcing incorrect answers.

What about situations where an incorrect or mostly incorrect answer is given to a reasoning quesion? In these circumstances, a more complex process is called for on the part of the teacher. On the one hand, the feedback should be elaborated with attempts to nudge the student into giving a fully correct answer. This may involve restatement in a different vocabulary, or a shortening of the question itself. Another strategy is to provide the student with hints or prompts, or to break the question into smaller, shorter questions. If attempts to simplify the question do not yield a correct response from the student, the teacher should point out the incorrectness, possibly advise more study, and move on to the next question and/or student.

The strategy of "staying with" a student in order to help him/her come up with the correct answer is a part of the process of "probing" that follows questions. This practice is especially necessary for students who are behind in their work, or who lack confidence. Probing must be done in an encouraging and supportive manner while communicating clearly the expectation that the student can and will learn. As noted earlier, this is necessary in order to insure that the students will receive reinforcement. Unless you probe or stay with students who have not mastered the material, they are unlikely to receive the kind of success and reinforcement that helps to motivate and sustain appropriate behavior.

Let us now consider the happy situation in which the student produces a correct response. It is here that a clear, positive reinforcement should be given. At the very least, the student should understand that a correct answer has been given. In other words, the correctness of the answer must be acknowledged. It should be clear to both the student who produced the answer and to the rest of the class that this was the correct answer to the question. This type of reinforcement may be supplemented by more elaborate use of praise, or even tangible rewards. Thus, the teacher may comment "Very good" or "Exactly right" as a quick acknowledgment for factual questions but give a longer, more complete response for reasoning questions, significant accomplishments, and extra efforts. This allows the teacher to differentiate the level and quality of praise in response to the difficulty of the questions and thus prevent praise from becoming so commonplace that it is no longer effective. The teacher should attempt to give praise that is varied and individually oriented. Thus, rather than saying, "That's good" to everybody's correct answer, the teacher can individualize it by adding the student's name to the comment or praising the specific skill the student exhibited, e.g., "That's excellent work, Janice! You have shown you now understand how to write topic sentences."

Using Reinforcement with Written Exercises: Often teachers use correct reinforcement in verbal learning situations but not when students are involved in written exercises. Reinforcement principles are equally valid here. Thus, if students are being asked to perform a set of math problems at their desks, the teacher should be circulating around the room, pointing out wrong answers, possibly restating questions, acknowledging correct answers, correcting errors, occasionally giving praise, and so on. If students merely work by themselves on workbook drill, with no involvement on the part of the teacher, their active learning time is reduced. Furthermore, they may not be aware of the rightness or wrongness of their responses.

Summary

Teachers and principals often praise incorrectly or fail to

praise at all.

1. The school staff needs to be reminded to praise when praise is earned.
2. If staff members are unsure of the effects of praise, they should be shown why, when, and how to use it for best results.

   A. Positive reinforcement of correct student responses with encouragement and support will result in:
      1) Mastery of intended behaviors;
      2) Feeling that learning is possible and valuable;
      3) Ability to appropriately assess one's functioning in school social situations;
      4) Positive perceptions of self and sense of well-being.

   B. Positive reinforcement of incorrect response, without reinstruction, results in:
      1) Incorrect knowledge, skills, and behavior;
      2) Confused self-assessment and feelings of futility regarding school;
      3) Inability to apply basic skill principles.

   C. Negative reinforcement of incorrect student responses, with reinstruction, results in:
      1) Feeling that learning is possible;
      2) Learning correct behavior;
      3) Acquiring reasonable perceptions of self;
      4) Ability to perceive accurately and respond appropriately to others.

Reinforcement which is misused can have disastrous effects on learning and conduct. It is our contention that teachers and staff can improve learning through the proper use of reinforcement techniques in the classroom and in the school generally.

Suggested Activities

1. Examine your current level of use of reinforcement practices using General Observations on Reinforcing Achievement and the Teacher Check List. (See below, these Activities.)

2. Periodically, take a look at what you're actually doing in the classroom with students to reinforce achievement. This can be done by use of audiotape or videotape recordings or by getting another teacher to observe your reinforcement practices. The use of audiotape can be done by yourself, placing the recorder next to a desk where students come to you for assistance. If desired, video recording can also be done without having someone to operate the equipment, providing the camera is positioned to cover teacher - student interaction. If this approach is too restrictive or does not produce the recording quality you desire, consider using a student to operate the camera. Otherwise, ask a staff member or volunteer to videotape for you.

3. Involve other staff members in looking at reinforcement practices by using role playing to illustrate correct - incorrect techniques. This can be fun and very informative at the same time. If time allows, pre-record the role playing on videotape so only the best "takes" are presented at meetings of the whole staff or smaller grade/department meetings.

4. Survey your students to find out about their likes and dislikes. You may be surprised to find that something you are using as a positive reinforcer is actually viewed negatively by some students. Also, there may be some actions or activities preferred or valued by students which could be more effective. (See Suggested Survey below.)

5. Determine how you can best use tangible rewards to

reinforce achievement in your class. Remember, tangible rewards can be very motivating for students to improve behavior or performance but you must use them appropriately:

a. contingently – awarded only for desired performance;

b. selectively – used when social reinforcers cannot produce the desired results,

c. temporarily – used only as long as students need it. Don't condition students to expect tangible rewards for every effort.

Reinforcing Achievement

Teacher Check List

Positive Reinforcement

_____ Do you positively reinforce every student in your class at least once each day?

_____ Do you give positive reinforcement immediately, or as soon as possible, after a desired response has occured?

_____ Do you give students positive reinforcement for correctly doing things you expect them to do?

_____ Do you use positive reinforcement in a planned way?

Negative Reinforcement

_____ Do you use negative reinforcement with students to initiate a change in behavior?

_____ Do you use punishment to suppress undesirable behavior?

_____ After using negative reinforcement do you identify an alternative desirable behavior for the student?

_____ If so, do you then encourage the student to achieve the desired change by using a regular schedule of positive reinforcement?

Extinction

_____ Do you ignore undesirable responses that are new or occur infrequently?

_____ If ignoring doesn't eliminate the undesirable response, do you switch to using negative reinforcement?

_____ Do you understand why ignoring academic errors of students is inappropriate?

Schedule

_____ Do you use a regular schedule of reinforcement during the initial steps of learning?

_____ Do you continue to use a regular schedule of reinforcement up to the point at which learning occurs?

_____ Do you reinforce learned behavior periodically to sustain it?

Social Rewards

_____ Do you know your students well enough so you can utilize their likes and dislikes?

_____ Do you know your students well enough to determine the sources of approval they value most and least?

_____ Do you use verbal praise often with students?

_____ Is your praise contingent, specific, and sincere?

_____ Do you deliberately position/locate yourself or students in the room as social reinforcement? (Proximity)

_____ Do you purposely use body language as a positive or negative reinforcer?

_____ Do you allow your students to participate in activities of their choosing?

Tangible Rewards

_____ Do you provide special rewards to students to encourage desired behavior?

_____ Do you make sure all students clearly understand that acceptable or specified behavior will be rewarded and other behavior will not be rewarded?

_____ Do you reward students only when they perform in the manner specified?

_____ Do you avoid making students dependent on artificial reinforcers by giving tangible rewards only when necessary or appropriate?

_____ Do you attempt to switch your students from tangible rewards to social rewards?

Performance Feedback to Students

_____ Do you check and return student work promptly?

_____ Do you give every student a clear picture of his/her performance status?

_____ Do you offer performance feedback to every student every day?

_____ Do you use feedback language that is easily understood, not complex?

_____ Do you give feedback information that is specific or related to particular errors, correct responses, or accomplishments?

_____ Do you provide opportunities for performance feedback from peers? (e.g., Student team learning practice, group checking, peer tutoring, etc.)

_____ Do you select or structure your teaching materials so students can evaluate their own work without teacher assistance?

_____ Do you utilize other adults (aides or volunteers) to provide performance feedback to students?

Suggested Student Survey   Name _____

Concerning this class, I am a person who . . .

likes _____

hates _____

can _____

cannot _____

would never _____

would rather _____

wants to learn how to _____

would be better off if _____

is really good at_____

gets really angry when _____

"bugs" other people when _____

has the good habit _____

has the bad habit of _____

wishes I could change the way I _____

wishes I could change the way other people _____

Outside of school, I am a person who . . .

never misses watching the TV show entitled _____

will someday _____

enjoys doing _____

Additional Resources

Brophy, J. Teacher praise: A functional analysis. *Review of Educational Research,* 1981, *51*(1), 5-32.

This is an excellent review of the literature on reinforcement and praise.

Hunter, M. *Reinforcement theory for teachers.* El Segundo, Cal.: TIP Publications, 1980.

This is a highly readable and useful review of reinforcement theory and practice which explains major concepts and principles.

Module 10

Use of Assessment Data For School Improvement

- Types of Evaluation
- Types of Assessment Tests
- Record Keeping
- Improving the Quality of Assessment
- Evaluating the School
- Suggested Activities
- Additional Resources

In order to develop and maintain an effective learning climate, the frequent evaluation of instruction is essential. This module focuses on the use of assessment data as an important tool for evaluating instructional effectiveness and to aid in decision making regarding curricular change and program improvement. The availability and use of assessment data should be an integral part of the school operation. Teachers and other staff can increase the level of student achievement in their classroom when they use assessment data to guide needed curricular and instructional modifications.

Types of Evaluation

Most educators are familiar with the evaluation processes

generally found in schools. Teacher are familiar with the teacher evaluation procedures that are used to make judgements about tenure status and job performance. Usually such procedures are required as district policy. Teacher evaluations are usually completed by the principal and the formal evaluation report becomes a part of the teacher's personnel file. The teacher evaluation process usually focuses on the behaviors of the teacher and the instructional processes carried out by the teacher.

A second common type of assessment procedure evaluates student progress or mastery of learning objectives. Virtually every school district has some form of student evaluation. The information gathered by the use of student evaluation instruments is extremely useful in helping teachers to better understand which students have learned, or failed to learn which material. Not only do such instruments help to objectively assess individual student progress but they are sometimes used to compare students of the same grade level.

Evaluation procedures are also commonly used to assess program effectiveness. The instruments used to assess individual student progress are often used in an *aggregated* way to evaluate program effectiveness. For example the assessment results for a group of students who receive the services of a special program are compared to the assessment results of similar students not receiving the same services. The differences in the aggregated performance for the two groups may be one indicator of the effects of the special program.

Another important use of aggregated student assessment process is that of monitoring progress for special groups in the classroom or school. This use of assessment results is extremely informative and should be routinely undertaken by teachers and administrators. An example of such an application of this evaluation process might be used to answer the following question, "Is out math curriculum equally effective for boys and girls?" To answer this question, teachers would simply aggregate math assessment scores for the boys and girls separately and then compare the results.

Another extremely valuable application of the aggregated assessment process is to examine the rates of progress for youngsters from advantaged and disadvantaged backgrounds. The goal of this application is to be sure that the full range of students (advantaged and disadvantaged) are progressing satisfactorily in their mastery of essential skills. As educators attempt to assess this instructional effectiveness and school climate it is critical that they pay close attention to whether all students, regardless of family background, are benefiting equally from the school experience.

The percentage distribution of the poor and/or minority students who master the objectives of reading and math compared to the percentage of other students who master the same objectives will reveal the effectiveness of the instructional program for both groups. The table of 6th grade reading test scores prepared by the Connecticut State Department of Education on the following page illustrates a method of comparing the reading achievement of low-income and other students. Such division or disaggregation of the test results for various groups in the student body is helpful for assessing the school's effectiveness for all students.

DISTRIBUTION OF SIXTH GRADE READING SCORES OF LOW-INCOME AND OTHER STUDENTS

Connecticut State Department of Education   READING

19% Others are below 30%ile
47% Low-Income are below 30%ile

	N	Percentage
OTHERS	116	53%
LOW-INCOME	102	47%
	TOTAL 218	

Downtown Elementary School   California Achievement Test (77)   Test Date 3/80   Grade 6

Reproduced by permission of Joan Shoemaker
Connecticut State Department of Education

Types of Assessment Tests

Norm-Referenced Tests (NRTs)

Although norm-referenced or standardized tests such as the Metropolitan Achievement Test (MAT) and Scholastic Aptitude Test (SAT) can identify persons with different levels of achievement, they are of questionable utitlity in school program evaluation. Often the tests do not measure what the local educational programs are designed to teach. Since the items are designed to differentiate between the "best" and the "worst" students, writers of norm-referenced tests are likely to exclude test questions that measure the common skills most students have learned. Also, such tests are not designed to reveal particular problems that are keeping pupils from achieving at a mastery level. Thus, they provide little information which a teacher or a school staff can use to improve the instructional program. They are useful, however, if used as a general assessment of the school, as it compares to national norms on the content the test measures.

Objective-Referenced Tests (ORTs)

These tests are meant to determine whether or not a student has mastered the specified knowledge or skills identified as objectives, rather than how he/she compares to some norm group. The tests reveal what students have or have not accomplished in specified situations. Related to ORTs are the criterion referenced tests (CRTs) which have built-in mastery indicators. The items selected for objective-referenced testing should measure those objectives which the school program emphasizes. Items used in the tests should match the set of student skills called for in the objective itself and should not be eliminated (as they are in the norm-referenced tests) merely because most students answer them correctly. Objective-referenced tests can be a sensitive measure of what has actually been taught to the students. These tests have become popular in instructional settings because they indicate the kind of instruction that is needed by the students, and also when the students are ready to proceed to other tasks.

Teacher-Made Tests (Objective-Referenced)

Because test results reported once or twice a year are not sufficient for measuring student mastery of specific objectives, teacher-made tests must supplement the district or state assessment program. The major reason for using objective-referenced teacher-made tests is to enable more frequent modification of instruction by furnishing measurements of classroom achievement of specific objectives over shorter periods of time. It is suggested by Block and Anderson (1975) that progress (formative) testing be carried out at least every two weeks for best results. Teacher-made tests can be both written and oral, or the student can demonstrate the target behavior to the teacher's satisfaction. Oral testing is an effective means of assessing student learning particularly for students who are having reading difficulties. Oral testing also helps with students who react negatively or nervously to the written test.

Teachers at the same grade level should, whenever possible, construct common instructional materials and common tests to faciliatate teaching and assessment of mastery in basic skills at grade level. This helps to assure congruence in objectives, materials and tests, and considerably reduces the workload on any one staff member.

The use of frequent progress tests is beneficial in a number of ways. First, it familiarizes the student with testing through practice. Second, it provides assessment information more frequently. Finally, frequent progress checks reduce anxiety regarding how well students will perform on the final overall mastery tests or end-of-year tests.

Recordkeeping

If instructional improvement is to result, recordkeeping is

an indispensable part of testing for progress and mastery. It provides the teacher with ongoing objective information, in writing, on the progress or lack of progress each child is experiencing. It serves to jog both memory and teacher judgement. It is an important vehicle for providing accurate and comprehensive academic feedback to students and their parents, and to other teachers if necessary.

In some districts computerized scoring partially replaces the teacher's hand recording and summarizing of test results, particularly for annual pre-and post-tests and school-wide interim tests. We refer in this section to the more frequent testing done within the classroom. In particular, we refer to the ungraded progress tests given approximately every two weeks which are considered part of student practice, and to the mastery tests which cover the same material but are final tests, used for grading. (In the language of Learning for Mastery, these tests are called formative and summative respectively.) These are the tests which directly reflect what is being taught in the classroom. The results should be used for daily and weekly lesson planning and student work assignments.

We suggest two basic recordkeeping forms, a student form and a teacher form.

1. Generally, each student has a folder, notebook or other location where samples of work, completed assignments, notes, homework and so on are kept. This folder should also contain a simple form for listing essential course objectives and recording the results of progress and mastery tests. A sample is shown on the next two pages.

Additionally, wall charts and other observable recordkeeping devices are excellent examples of symbolic rewards for achievement. Some kind of check mark or symbol is used each time a student masters one of the objectives or units. Student names may or may not be used on such charts. If they are used, chalking up successes publicly can be a real stimulus to student. If the teacher feels this would upset rather than encourage students, names can be eliminated altogether. The chart would then measure movement of the total class toward mastery, and individuals could still assess privately how they compare to the class.

Parents, as well as students and teachers should be kept informed of students' progress in mastering the basic skills. The teacher should provide parents with information about their child's performance in a format which parents well understand and which will facilitate discussion at parent-teacher conferences. A letter like the one following may be used to serve this purpose.

Record Keeping Regarding Achievement in Math

Your Name _____

Hour _____

(Not Used for Grading) 85% = Mastery

Whole Numbers Units	Progress Tests	Date	Mastery Tests	Date
(Use for objectives)				
Multiplication				
1 digit				
2 digit				
3 digit				
Division				
1 digit				
2 digit				
Rounding Off				
Inequalities				
Greater Than				
Less Than				
Equal To				
Averages				
Story Problems				
Factors				
Prime Factors				
Factor Trees				
Prime Factorization				
Greatest Common Factor				
Multiples				
Least Common Multiple				
Expanded Notation				
Roman Numerals				
Principles				
Commutative				
Associative				
Distributive				
Functions				
Bases				

Sample Teacher Chart

CODE:

◻ Introduced

⊠ Needs Corrective

■ Mastery

(USE FOR OBJECTIVES)

Student
  Monitoring
    Record
    Unit _____

Name	1	2	3	4	5	6	7	8	9	10

A Suggested Report To Parents

Your student is in a mastery lear___ _ does this mean? It means that for each unit of work, stuucιιιs are told the skills they will review or learn. Each skill is taught to the class and then an ungraded practice test is given to everyone. Those who "master" skills (get 85%) can do extra things that extend or apply the skills. Those who do not "master" skills get a second chance to learn, using a different lesson. Then a final test is given for a grade. Sometimes a student needs extra time and help outside of class to really master the skills.

Listed below are the units we have worked on so far. Your child's scores on the final test are given. Remember: a score of 85 indicates mastery.

UNIT:	Place Value	Rounding	Add/Subtact	Multiplication
Final test:	75 %	85 %	95 %	85 %

We are working on a division unit now. The skills your child will be reviewing or learning are:

1) Know division facts
2) Divide by a number from 1-9 and check answer
3) Divide by 10, 20, 30, 40, 50, 60, 70, 80 or 90 and check
4) Divide by a number from 11-99 and check
5) Divide by 100, 200, 300, 400 . . . 900 and check
6) Divide by a number from 101-999 and check
7) Estimate the answers to division problems

In order to do well in division, a student must know the multiplication facts, how to subtract and how to round numbers.

Improving the Quality of Assessment

By improving the quality of tests and testing, we can be sure that assessment results are representative of what the students have learned and are not due to extraneous factors. It is important that the test be a valid measure of the student's actual state of knowledge. For example, we know that some students do poorly because they are not comfortable in a testing situation. Nervousness and anxiety can lessen a student's motivation and thought processes. Furthermore, we cannot assume that students are equal in their understanding of how to take a test, their motivation to do their best, and their understanding of the importance of the test. Thus, not only is it important for the tests to be technically sound, but the testing situation itself must not be neglected. The following suggestions can help to ensure that all students are prepared to perform to the best of their ability.

First, the teacher must believe that the test is important and must communicate this to students. Students should be told that the results will be used to help them learn and to improve their instructional program. Frequent ungraded progress tests should be considered part of practice and used to give the student feedback regarding his/her learning, without using results for final evaluation of learning. When test results are explained and used positively instead of negatively (to help rather than punish), and students get lots of practice in taking tests, they become more comfortable and perform better on tests generally. Second, it is important that teachers cover the material in class in the same form to be used for testing. This means they must be fully acquainted with the test items. For example, if the test uses a horizontal format ($25 + 5 = N$) for addition, students must be taught this format. There should be no surprises in item format. This has been found to cause unexpectedly poor results on the part of students, even those the teacher knows have mastered the material in class.

Another problem is caused by computer-scored answer sheets which are typically used with assessment instruments.

Some children put answers in the wrong places and their poor results are due to this mistake rather than not knowing the material. Also the failure of students to erase completely when changing answers, or neglecting to erase all stray pencil marks, may lower test results. Students should be taught the format and method of using test answer sheets so these problems will not occur. Some schools have purchased stand-alone scanners (non-computer) for teaching the use of answer sheets as well as scoring tests. These are passed from classroom to clsssroom so that all students can learn the correct techniques. Students are given directions, take a test and then run it through the scanner themselves. Bells or buzzers sound, sheets are scored incorrectly or not at all when directions have not been followed. Students enjoy and are not likely to forget this lesson.

It is unfair to penalize students for not knowing proper test procedures and for not being comfortable and familiar with a test format. Since testing is school-related practice, it is the job of the school staff to see to it that test-taking skills are developed.

Finally, be sure to let students know the test is coming and when it will be given. Arrange for any review necessary on objectives or material covered by the test.

Evaluating the School Program

Responsibility for assessing the effectiveness of the school instructional program should be shared by the principal and teachers in a building. The school principal must be the facilitator of school program evaluation. This means it is the responsibility of the principal to be aware of the reported data, to communicate it to teachers, and to see to it that the data is utilized to improve the basic skills program. Further, he/she should initiate school modifications to overcome major basic skill deficiences made evident by test data. Since more than one staff member may be responsible for the students of a particular age group within a school, evaluation of school effectiveness should be based on the school as a unit. The quality of a school's performance can be determined by the extent to which students are achieving the specified objectives of the school program.

Specifically, the yardsticks for measuring the school's effectiveness in teaching the basic skills should be based on an established building goal for student performance. This is usually expressed in terms of a specified percentage of grade level skills. For example, if the school goal in a particular year is for all students to master at least X percent of the grade level skills, then the match of post-test results to this goal is the basis for evaluating the school's success. It is important to remember, however, that the school goal for mastery performance should be clearly established at the beginning of the school year so students and teachers can work to achieve it. This kind of criterion should not be used to measure the effectiveness of the program unless it was clearly communicated to teachers and students with sufficient time to achieve it.

All students, including those in compensatory education programs, must be expected to master the minimum basic skills objectives. It is not sufficient that only the "average" of "normal" students achieve grade level performance. Compensatory education students are expected to reach normal levels of achievement according to state and federal policy. These students must therefore be included in district-wide evaluation as well as school or classroom assessment. Each school must be responsible for its compensatory education students achieving the objectives specified for all other students. The policy or practice of some districts or schools to exclude certain children from testing suggests that these children are neither expected, believed able, nor (presumably) taught to achieve mastery of grade level objectives. The lack of assessment data for these children provides an incomplete picture of the school's effectiveness, and obstructs efforts to improve the instructional program.

Summary

Assessment data are primarily used to improve the instructional program at the student, classroom and building level. Objective-referenced tests can ascertain the skills students have mastered or not mastered, and instruction can be modified on the basis of the results. The school staff can improve year-end outcomes by making testing a regular routine in the building. It is the responsibility of the principal and staff to see to it that results are used to improve the school's effectiveness.

Suggested Activities

1. The principal should establish and publish the school schedule of formal student testing for the year. This should be done by September, indicating dates for pretesting, interim testing, and post-testing. This information should be communicated to students and parents. Thus, expectancy for both students and teachers to be ready to perform on the indentified dates is established.

2. The principal should familiarize the staff with the types of formal tests that will be used, with the kind of data that will be generated, and how the data can be used to improve student performance. (In too many cases, this step is overlooked or neglected, resulting in little teacher understanding or use of test data. This is a glaring example of educational waste—in dollars, time, and information.)

3. Discuss record keeping at a department or grade level meeting. Ask teachers to share information on what forms or ways they record student progress. If the district provides a record keeping procedure, make sure everyone has copies and understands how to use it. (See example in this module.)

4. The principal should meet with the special education staff members concerning how the grade level basic skills program will be delivered to their students. Also, since these students are expected to learn the same objectives as regular students, communication and coordination between regular education teachers and special education teachers for mainstreamed students is a necessity.

5. Preparing students for testing will help eliminate anxiety and nervousness, and reduce errors. Implement the suggestions in this module. In addition, see attachments concerning additional ways to prepare students for testing.

6. Establish a realistic achievement goal for the school year, while ultimately striving for 100 percent of the students' mastery of basic skills. Examine your school's most current achievement results. How far away are these results from the performance standard you are considering for the school achievement goal? Remember, set your goal above your present level to make teachers and students stretch to achieve it. It you are going to err, err on the high side. The more you expect from students, the more they will give you.

7. Announce your goal to students and parents with resolve and enthusiasm at the beginning of the school year so that everybody understands what is expected. This is an important event and should be treated as such.

   a. Conduct a special assembly for students, to announce the achievement goal and to explain what it expects students to do. Develop understanding and generate a sense of purpose and enthusiasm for reaching the goal at the end of the year.

   b. Conduct a special meeting for parents for the same purposes as above. Issue the School Plan for Parent Support and Involvement and explain how it fits in with the achievement goal. Solicit the backing of parents.

Additional Resources

Block, J. H., & Anderson, L. W. *Mastery learning in classroom instruction.* New York: MacMillan Publishing Co., 1975.

Annotated in Module 5, this is a good all around source for improving the school's overall testing program.

Brown, F. G. *Measuring classroom achievement.* New York: Holt, Rinehart & Winston, 1981.

Brown's textbook is designed for classroom teachers and contains an excellent, short explanation and description of both norm-referenced and objective reference test. The text also discusses rationale for, problems in, and other aspects of testing, including teacher made tests.

Module 11

Parent Support and Involvement

- **Appropriate Parent Involvement**
- **Parent Support**
- **Parent Involvement**
- **Improving Parent Participation**
- **The School Plan**
- **Suggested Activities**
- **Additional Resources**

Traditionally, parent involvement in schools has centered around management or organizational concerns. In this context, parents represent "helping hands" to deal with activities or problems of running a school, e.g., supervision, maintenance, coordination, and service. In most cases, parent involvement in schools provides "extras" or special services the local school cannot afford. Parents are invited to school to perform many and varied tasks: make popcorn, sell baked goods, provide treats, run room parties, and supervise extracurricular activities. Parents are also asked to attend P.T.A. meetings, parent-teacher conferences, and the annual open house. Frequently, parents are asked to volunteer their services at school to help with pupil supervision during lunch, recess, bus duty, and dismissal. Also, parents are asked to work in the library, media center, or school office so additional services can be provided for students, teachers, and parents. In other instances, parents are asked to serve on advisory committees as required by state and federal programs. In essence, traditional parent involvement is focused on help from parents with matters not directly related to the main business of the school—student achievement.

Appropriate Parent Involvement

While the intent of parent involvement has been to keep parents informed about what the school is doing and to insure support, the result has amounted to a public relations effort by the school to make parents feel good about the school and to project an image of an effective, well-run organization. Although these are not improper purposes, the extent to which the time and energy spent by the staff promoting and conducting parent involvement activities carries over and impacts on improving student achievement is questionable. As we have stated earlier, the first order of business of the school is teaching for high achievement for all students. Efforts of teachers and parents must serve this purpose first and other purposes second. It is the direct responsibility of the principal and staff to keep the energies and efforts of parents focused on academic concerns at all times. Since it is our belief that the attitudes, expectations, and behaviors of the staff do, in a large part, make the difference between a high and low achieving school, the decisions the staff makes about what people should do to promote student achievement are very important. This is true not only of what the staff does at school, but also what the school should expect from parents at home. In too many instances, the school does not clearly explain to parents how they can assist in raising their child's achievement or firmly communicate that parents are expected to support their child's academic efforts and the school program. In short, the school staff must decide what it wants parents to do to enhance their child's learning in the classroom or the home. This message must then be communicated with conviction to parents.

Parent Support

The issue of how parents can best assist in raising achievement must be discussed by the principal and teachers and should result in a concise school plan for parent support. (See discussion on The School Plan which follows.) In particular, the distinction between parent involvement and parent support should be understood.

As used in these modules, the term "parent involvement" refers to ways parents show support by participation at school or in school sponsored activities. Parent involvement in this sense means coming to school or helping with a school project or concern outside regular family life or home activities. Parent involvement activities include things like attending parent-teacher conferences, acting as a volunteer tutor, assisting the teacher in the classroom, etc. In general, involvement is direct contact between the parent and the school.

The term "parent support," on the other hand, refers to any means by which parent actions or attitudes reinforce the academic program of the school at home. For example, parents can show support for the school at home by following through on requests or instructions from teachers or the principal, such as contacting the school when a child is absent. Parents can also support the school by modeling and reinforcing academic behaviors valued by the school (e.g., using time wisely, doing best work, showing responsibility, etc.). Parent support may be shown by all parents, including those whose work schedules or family responsibilities make it difficult or impossible to come to school. While parent support in some instances may not be conspicuous, it is a mainstay of the school and it is essential for its smooth operation and ultimate success.

The importance of distinguishing between support and involvement activities require parents to come to school. Support activities can be done at home. Our purpose is not to place value judgments as to whether parent involvement activities are better than those of parent support. However, the number of parents that can or do come to school is limited due to work schedules, family obligations, etc. Many parents for example, never, or at best infrequently, come to school. For the school to place its main thrust with parents on a "you must come to school" basis will result in a limited and diffused impact. While parent involvement at school should always be encouraged, the greatest potential for increasing student achievement through parent efforts resides in the home. Parents can influence their children in ways not available to the teacher or school. The family relationship is unique and the most influential force in shaping a student's attitudes and habits. What the school must do is to determine significant ways to use the family relationship to support student achievement.

It is essential at this point to make one thing clear. The emphasis of the school on parent support does not relieve the school of its responsibility to produce achieving students. Parents and home conditions, good or bad, are not the determining factor in student achievement. With or without overt parent support, the principal and teachers can still improve achievement and are obligated to do so. Improvements, however, will come faster and easier if strong parent support exists at home.

Parent Involvement

Parent involvement activities usually take place at school and, therefore, include a limited number of parents. The school must be concerned with developing both parent support and parent involvement, with emphasis on parent support. However, a significant number of parents do have the time and wish to be involved at school. This is an important group as their volunteer services are very helpful and their physical presence is an obvious direct link between home and school. Also, these parents can be a valuable resource for special helpful roles, such as tutors, aides, P.T.A., etc.

The extent of parent involvement in schools varies considerably. Examination of the nature of existing parent involvement will reveal a school's attitude toward it. Parents respond according to the ways schools ask them to respond. If parents are not asked, they cannot respond. If what the school is asking parents to respond to is unclear, unreasonable, or menial, parents will choose to ignore the request. Also, if parents are asked to fill specific needs as opposed to being given a general invitation to come to school and help out "some time," parents are more likely to volunteer. For example, "We need two parents three times a week for 2 hours a day to tutor students in reading in Mrs. Smith's room" is much clearer and more specific than "We need parent volunteers." Parents want to know what the school wants then to do and that their services will be put to good use. If parents perceive school requests as sincere and important, they will make greater efforts to fill them. Otherwise, parents will choose to ignore the call for help, or else their participation will last only a short time. In short, the attitudes and actions of teachers and administrators in the school can make or break parent involvement. The attitude of the school staff toward parent involvement is the determining factor regarding what kind of involvement will exist and how important or successful it will be. In addition, the principal and teachers reflect their attitude toward parents in both the type and amount of parent involvement they choose to encourage.

In some communities, parent attendance at school functions and participation in the daily school program flourish with or without the encouragement of the school staff. (Often it is in spite of it.) In schools, parents individually and collectively have decided they will be involved—and they are!

Recently, federal and state funds have provided many resources to schools for improving services. For example, Title 1 and CETA have placed many people in schools to improve programs and provide employment opportunities. While many excellent benefits have resulted to schools because of these and other categorical programs, they have also replaced many volunteer services of the past. In many cases since the availability of paid services through federal and state funds, principals and teachers have reduced their requests for help from the community. This fact is unfortunate, since parents quickly get used to letting paid workers assume volunteer tasks. In addition, if parents feel that people who are paid to help at school do not do important tasks or do not appear busy, it creates the impression that additional volunteer services are not really needed.

In many schools, parent involvement is low because the staff does not value it. In these schools, the staff lacks confidence in parents. Teachers are often unsure of the reactions and effectiveness of parents. In other cases, teachers and principals talk like they support parent involvement but they fail to specify conditions, accepting only help that is convenient and nonthreatening.

Although parents can be active at school in a variety of ways, the principal and teachers should encourage involvement in ways directly related to instruction. Parent involvement efforts should facilitate the teaching-learning process, first and foremost. It must be understood, however, that involving parents in this manner requires teacher planning and direction to be successful. Parents should not be expected to be teachers. They are not trained for that. Therefore, teachers must identify suitable and realistic ways for parents to assist the teacher. In most instances, the school should carefully train parents in what to do and supervise their efforts. Without proper training a parent can become a liability to the teacher instead of an asset, adding to the teacher's worries and responsibilities—with little educational return.

In particular, parents should be asked to perform important tasks such as:

1. *Assisting the handling of instructional materials.* (duplicating, filing, locating sources, correcting, etc.)

Assisting a teacher or the school to develop and maintain an up-to-date instructional resource file is a time consuming task and can be of invaluable assistance.
2. *Supervising students working independently.* As noted in the module on Academic Engaged Time, student time-on-task usually suffers greatly during independent seatwork due to lack of adult supervision.
3. *Tutoring.* Assisting students to correct skill deficiencies through tutoring can be effective if conducted properly. In particular, recent studies have shown that well-planned, structured tutoring is highly effective whereas informal tutoring has questionable value (Von Harrison, 1975). This approach could be carried out largely by volunteer parents if the required training and supervision is provided.

Obviously, opportunities for parent involvement are many and varied. The school staff must decide what it wants parents to do and then provide several options for parent response. Additional suggestions for parent involvement can be found in an extensive bibliography from the Midwest Teacher Corps Network (Barletta, Boger, Lezotte, & Hull, 1978).

Improving Parent Participation

Parent support for schools usually suffers from staff neglect. In particular, the failure to assign responsibility for developing a school-wide approach to a specific person or committee results in no one being responsible and, consequently, little or nothing gets done. Too often, it is not clear whether anyone is in charge—or what they are responsible for. For example, teachers may feel developing parent support is the principal's job. The principal, however, may feel this is the responsibility of the teachers or a parent organization such as the P.T.A. The parents, on the other hand, expect the school staff to take the lead so they sit back and wait to hear from the school. The net result is minimal parent participation at best, probably of a superficial nature to maintain the appearance of a home-school relationship. If the school is to shape its own destiny, the school must provide leadership in organizing parental support of academic goals.

The acceptance of specific responsibility (by a person or a group) for heading up parent support should not exempt the rest of the staff from involvement. It must be clearly understood that getting parent support is everyone's responsibility and everyone is expected to do his/her part to make it successful. In most schools, the principal is the ideal person to provide the leadership, impetus, and coordination required for mobilizing teachers and parents. In any event, the issue of parent support for improving achievement should be thoroughly discussed by both staff and parents; priorities and needs must be identified, a program of action planned, and specific duties assigned. Obviously, for greatest results, this should be done early in the school year so plans can be formulated, communicated, and implemented in time to make an impact on student achievement.

We have advocated that the school staff should communicate clearly and simply to parents its needs for support and involvement that can facilitate high student achievement. The staff should initiate this communication by designing a school plan for parent support and involvement that coordinates the efforts of school and home to improve achievement. The plan should establish a norm for parent behavior that will facilitate and promote student success in school. This norm, expressed in parent beliefs, expectations, and actions, is, in effect, a home learning climate.

It is not intended that the school should dictate to parents how they should live or behave at home in order to be "good" parents. Rather, the school should express to parents what they can do to increase their child's chances of being an academic success. As the agency responsible for formal education, he school should be able to communicate to students and parents what it takes to be an achieving student. In order to do this, the school staff must explain exactly what it does; what the curriculum is all about; what the achievement expectations are for all students; what the homework, attendance, and discipline policies are etc. Having done this, the school plan for parent support and involvement should represent specific ways that parents can create a home learning climate that is consistent with and supportive of the school program.

The School Plan

The school plan should encompass both parent support and parent involvement, but emphasis should be on parent support since all parents can be expected to give support but not all parents can be involved at school. It should be simple and easily understood, identifying clearly what parents can do at home or school to promote student achievement. Also, it is important that the school plan be brief and concise. This will facilitate understanding of what is being said and help teachers and parents to remember the scope of the message.

In drafting the plan, the following guidelines should be considered:

1. Clearly state what you want and expect parents to do. (Spell it out—use action words)
2. Be realistic in terms of demands upon parent time. (Keep it simple)
3. Identify a variety of ways parents can help either at home or at school. (Offer choices)
4. Conceive the plan so that everyone can do something. (Expect every parent to help)

Although the school plan must be acceptable to parents, the staff should assume responsibility for drafting the plan. It is important that ownership be shared by the whole staff. Ownership comes from involvement in a process of staff interaction. This interaction is critical and must not be circumvented.

The process of drafting a plan should provide ample opportunity discussion, brainstorming, expression of feelings and attitudes, presentation of information, identification of needs and expectations, and resolution of conflict. This process may take several meetings, so provision should be made for adequate discussion time. Failure of a staff to invest sufficient time in exploration, planning, and communication will lesson the probability for genuine acceptance or ownership by the staff.

An organizational time/task chart should be developed so the plan can proceed in an orderly and definitive manner. Once the plan is acceptable to the staff it should be presented to a representative parent committee for review and preliminary reactions but not approval. If serious concerns are identified in the parent review process, the staff should consider the advisability of revising the school plan. However, it must ultimately represent the needs of students, consistent with a positive school learning climate as described in these modules. Hopefully, there will not be any serious differences between the school plan and parent needs. If so, an effort to educate parents on the efficacy of improving the home learning climate will be needed.

A distinction is made between the school plan for support and involvement and the school plan for discipline. In the parent plan, the staff specifies what parents should do to support the school and student achievement. The school plan for discipline, however, informs parents of what the school will do to maintain order. (Refer to Module 7 for discussion of discipline plan.)

The mere distribution of a school plan to parents will not result in significant changes in parent or student behavior. The plan only represents an attempt at clarity of purpose and coordination between home and school. For maximum success, provisions must be made by the school to promote parent understanding and follow-through. It is suggested that following distribution of the plan to all parents, meetings should be held at school and in neighborhoods to explain:

1. The school program for improving achievement;
2. The plan for parent support and involvement to reinforce the school program;
3. The parent actions requested by the school.

Requesting the help of parent groups, such as the PTA/PTO, Title 1 or special advisory committee, homeroom parents, block clubs, etc., to set up meetings will be of great assistance. The principal and teachers should be present to answer questions and demonstrate their sincerity and desire to work cooperatively with parents. Failure to conduct discussion meetings with parents in addition to merely sending the plan home will have little impact. An example of a school plan for parent support follows.

(SAMPLE)

School Plan for Parent Support Involvement

Having each student achieve high levels of academic performance is the most important goal of our school. Having parents that support this goal will make it happen. We need the help of every parent. The school must have your support and involvement this year if we are to be successful.

The _____ School staff is counting on you to SUPPORT your child in becoming a high achiever. As a parent, the school, expects you to show your child, through words and actions, that you SUPPORT:

A. School Program
   1. The student achievement goal.
   2. The school homework policy.
   3. The school attendance policy
   4. The school discipline plan
   5. Parent-teacher conferences.
B. Home Learning Climate
   1. Encourage and expect high performance from

your child for school work, household duties, and other responsibilities. Insist on accountability.
2. Show interest in what your child does each day in the classroom—know what is going on.
3. Provide proper conditions for home study:
   a) definite study time
   b) quiet and non-distracting conditions
4. Limit time spent watching TV.
5. Provide supervision to ensure your child receives adequate rest, nutrition, and physical exercise.

To the extent your schedule permits, we encourage you to be INVOLVED in the school by:
1. Contacting the school for information or to resolve a concern.
2. Volunteering to help with at least one(1) school activity.
3. Attending at least one (1) P.T.A. meeting a semester.
4. Visiting your child's classroom at least one (1) time during the year.

The _____ School staff has high expectations for your child's academic achievement this year. We need your cooperation and support!

Summary

Traditionally, parent involvement in school has largely consisted of activities outside the main purpose of the school which is student achievement. While it is true that parents collectively provide hours of important service every day to schools for a wide variety of purposes, the largest proportion of parent involvement supports things other than achievement (i.e., fund raising, supervision, recreation, parties, etc.). It is also a fact that parent participation in volunteer activities or parent-teacher organizations, such as P.T.A. or P.T.O., has declined in many schools in recent years. The net result is that parents, representing a potentially powerful force for improving student achievement, have been conspicuously absent from the educational scene. Both parents and schools offer many "reasons" for the decline in parent involvement: "too busy," "not my job," "not important," "waste of time," etc. In short, while it is customary for schools and parents to talk about involvement, talk is not converted to action to support student learning. This is the fault of the school. A well-organized school, concerned with improving its learning climate and raising student achievement, can lead by example in moving from talk to action.

The school can have effective parent support if it wants it and if the school clearly communicates to parents what it wants them to do. The school staff must identify its needs and expectations for parent assistance. Time for staff discussion must be allocated early in the school year so a school plan for parent support and involvement can evolve with sufficient time for implementation. The school plan should represent agreement by the staff as to the most important ways parents can support their child and the school as a whole to achieve high levels of learning. The critical actions for the staff are:

1. Deciding how parents can help most effectively,
2. Communicating in clear, uncomplicated language what it wants them to do, and
3. Expecting parent follow-through on the plan.

The school staff must take the initiative and leadership for making parent support a reality. Just as the school should set clear expectations for student learning, it must specify concise expectations for parental support.

The list of reasons why parents aren't involved in the school program is endless but the potential to turn it around is as great today as it has ever been. All parents, low or high income, black, white, brown, or red, deprived or advantaged, share a strong common desire: success for their children. As Marva Collins, a successful teacher in the inner city of Chicago, stated on *60 Minutes* (CBS, 1979), "I have never met a parent yet that wants her child to fail." This desire for student success is the same as the goal of the school and the purpose for which it was created. However, parent support and involvement do not come easily. The challenge for the school is to take the initiative and tap parent concern for student success, providing many options for effective support of student achievement.

Suggested Activities

Parent Support and Involvement

1. Select a planning committee of parents and staff members (including the principal) to head parent participation thrust for the year. Representatives from parent groups, such as P.T.A., Title I, etc. may be asked to join the committee. A chairperson should be identified to provide leadership. This group should be formed at the beginning of the school year and act as a standing committee.

2. Discuss topics of parent support and involvement in a whole staff meeting early in the school year. Brainstorm on best and most feasible methods of utilizing parents to improve achievement. Narrow choices down to not more than a few items each for support and involvement. Write these ideas in the form of a simplified, one-page School Plan for Parent Support and Involvement. (See sample, in this module.)

3. Review the draft of the School Plan with the official, representative committee of the parents of the school. This review is for parent reaction as to the appropriateness and clarity of the plan. Parent suggestions for modification of the plan should be accommodated as long as the concerns of the staff are not diverted. Obtaining the support of the parent committee will be of considerable help when the plan is presented to the total parent group.

4. Decide on methods of distributing the School Plan and discussing it with parents. Face-to-face meetings are essential, as parent reactions must be encouraged and opportunities for answering questions should be accomodated. Plan for maximum parent participation, meeting both at school and in the community at hours convenient to parents. The principal and teacher representatives should attend all meetings.

5. Methods of keeping the attention of parents on the School Plan throughout the year should be identified by the planning committee. Activities planned in conjunction with regular school events at least three (3) times a year should suffice, e.g., fall open house (October), end of semester (February), and spring parent conferences (April). Some possible activities are:

   a. Recognition awards presented at school activities:
   b. "Thank you for your support" communications.
   c. Reports concerning the School Plan highlighted in the school newsletter and at monthly parent meetings.
   d. Arrange for publicity about the School Plan with local newspapers and radio/TV stations.
   e. Periodic reminders about following through on the School Plan sent to parents (e.g., a particular item could be featured).

The school planning committee should decide early in the year how to enlist parent participation and when special activities will occur to maintain parent interest. The important thing is to make parent follow-through on the School Plan a major—and regular—thrust of the school.

Additional Resources

Barletta, C., Boger, R., Lezotte, L., & Hull, B. (Eds.). *Planning and implementing parent/community involvement into the instructional delivery system*. East Lansing: Midwest Teacher Corps Network, Lansing/Michigan State University Teacher Corps Network, 1978.

This is a very complete and informative resource on parent/community involvement as related to improving instruction in the home and the school This source also contains a lengthy annotated bibliography of research and resources and is a primary reference for this area.

Von Harrison, G. Structured tutoring: The key to effective use of human resources. In C. Barletta, R. Boger, L. Lezotte, & B. Hull (Eds.), *Planning and implementing parent/community involvement into the instructional delivery system.* East Lansing: Midwest Teacher Corps Network, Lansing/Michigan State University Teacher Corps Network, 1978.

Von Harrison's structured tutoring program provides specific training and instructions for parents, volunteers, or students in how to tutor effectively. This program has been found to be more effective than traditional, non-structured tutoring.

References

ABC News (Producer). *The eye of the storm.* New York: ABC Merchandising, Inc., Film Library, 1970.

Allport, F. J-Curve hypothesis of conforming behavior. *Journal of Social Psychology,* 1934, 5, 141-181.

American Institute for Research. *Impact of educational innovation on student performance,* Project LONGSTEP. Final Report: Volumne I, Executive Summary, Palo Alto, California: American Institute for Research, 1976.

Anderson, G. J. Effects of classroom social climate on individual learning. *American Educational Research Journal,* 1970, 7(2), 135-152.

Anderson, L., Evertson, C., & Brophy, J. An experimental study of effective teaching in first-grade reading groups. *Elementary School Journal,* 1979, 79, 193-223.

Anderson, L. W. Instruction and time-on-task: A review with implications. *Journal of Curriculum Studies,* in press.

Anderson, L.W. & Scott, C. C. The classroom process scale (CPS): An approach to measurement of teaching effectiveness. Paper presented at American Educational Research Association, Toronto, 1978.

Aronson, E., Blaney, N., Sikes, J., Stephan, G., & Snapp, M. The Jigsaw route to learning and liking. *Psychology Today,* 1975, February, 43-50.

Aronson, E., et al. *The Jigsaw classroom.* Beverly Hills, Cal.: Sage Publications, Inc., 1978.

Barletta, C., Boger, R., Lezotte, L., & Hull, B. (Eds.). *Planning and implementing parent/community involvement into the instructional delivery system.* East Lansing, Mich.: Midwest Teacher Corps Network, 1978.

Bayh, B. Seeking solutions to school violence and vandalism. *Phi Delta Kappan,* 1978, 59(5), 299-302.

Berry v. School District of Benton Harbor, Mich. 505 F. 2d 238 (1974).

Block, J., & Anderson, L. *Mastery learning in classroom instruction.* New York: MacMillan Publishing Co., 1975.

Bloom. B. S. Learning for mastery. In B. S. Bloom, J. T. Hastings, & G. F. Madaus (Eds.), *Handbook on formative and summative evaluation of student learning.* New York: McGraw-Hill Book Company, 1971.

Bloom, B. S. *Human characteristics and school learning.* New York: McGraw-Hill, 1976.

Bloom, B. S. New views of the learner: Implications for instruction and curriculum. *Educational Leadership,* 1978, *35*(7), 563-568, 570-575.

Bloom, B. S. The new direction in educational research: Alterable variables. *Phi Delta Kappan,* 1980, *61*(6), 382-385

Bloom, B. S. *All our children learning: A primer for parents, teachers, and other educators.* New York: McGraw-Hill, 1981.

Bloom, R. B. Teachers and students in conflict: The CREED approach. *Phi Delta Kappan,* 1980, *61*(9), 624-626.

Bowles, S., & Gintis, H. *Schooling in capitalist America.* New York: Basic Books, Paperback, 1977.

Brameld, T. Education as self-fulfilling prophecy. *Phi Delta Kappan,* 1972, *54,* 8-11, 58-61.

Braun, C. Johnny reads the cues: Teacher expectation. *The Reading Teacher,* 1973, *26*(7), 704-711.

Brookover, W., Beady, C., Flood, P., Schweitzer, J., & Wisenbaker, J. *School social systems and student achievement: Schools can make a difference.* So. Hadley, Mass.: J. F. Bergin Co., distributed by Praeger Publishers, New York, 1979.

Brookover, W. B., Brady, N. M., & Warfield, M. Educational policies and equitable education: A report of studies of two desegregated school systems. In R. L Green (Project Director), *Procedures and pilot research to develop an agenda for desegregation studies* (Final Report). East Lansing, Mich.: College of Urban Development, Center for Urban Affairs, Michigan State University, 1981.

Brookover, W. B., Ferderbar, J., Gay, G., Middleton, M., Posner, G., & Roebuck, F. *Measuring and attaining the goals of education.* Alexandria, Vir.: Association for Supervision and Curriculum Development, 1980.

Brookover, W. B., & Lezotte, L. W. *Changes in school characteristics coincident with changes in student achievement* (Executive Summary). East Lansing, Mich.: Institute for Research on Teaching, Michigan State University, 1977.

Brookover, W. B., & Schneider, J. Academic environments and elementary school achievement. *Journal of Research and Development in Education,* 1975, 9 83-91.

Brookover, W. B., Schweitzer, J. H., Schneider, J. M., Beady, C. H., Flood, P. K., & Wisenbaker, J. M. Elementary school social climate and school achievement. *American Educational Research Journal,* 1978, *15*(2). 301-318.

Brophy, J. E. Advances in teacher research. *The Journal of Classroom Interaction,* 1979, *15*(1), 1-7.

Brophy, J. E. Teacher praise: A functional analysis. *Review of Educational Research,* 1981, *51*(1). 5-32.

Brophy, J., & Evertson, C. *Learning from teaching: A developmental perspective.* Boston: Allyn & Bacon, 1976.

Brophy, J., Evertson, C., Beam, M., Anderson, L., & Crawford, J. Grade level and sex of student as context variables in elementary school. *Journal of Classroom Interaction,* 1979, *14,* 11-17.

Brophy, J. E., & Good, T. L. *Teacher-student relationships: Causes and consequences.* New York: Holt, Rinehart and Winston, 1974.

Brophy, J. E., & Putnam, J. G. *Classroom management in the elementary grades.* East Lansing: Institute for Research on Teaching, Research Series No. 32, Michigan State University, 1978.

Canter, L. *Competency-based resource materials and guidelines.* Los Angeles: Canter and Associates, Inc., 1979.

Canter, L., with Canter M. *Assertive discipline: A take charge approach for today's educator.* Los Angeles: Canter and Associates, Inc., 1976.

Carroll, J. B. A model of school learning. *Teachers College Record,* 1963, *64, 723-733.*

CBS (Producer). Marva. From 60 Minutes. New York: Carousel Films, Inc., 1979.

Cohen, E. G. Design and redesign of the desegrated school: Problems of status, power, and conflict. In W. G. Stephan & J. R. Feagin (Eds.), *School desegregation: Past, present, and future.* New York: Plenum Press, 1980.

Coleman, J. S. *The adolescent society.* New York: Free Press, 1961.

Coleman, J., Campbell, E., Hobson, C., McPartland, J., Mood, A., Weinfeld, F., & York, R. *Equality of educational opportunity.* Washington, D.C.: U.S. Government Printing Office, 1966.

Conran, P. C., & Beauchamp, G. A. Relationships among leadership, climate, teacher, and student variables in curriculum engineering. Paper presented at the Annual Meeting of the American Educational Research Association, San Francisco, April, 1976. (ERIC Document Reproduction Service No. ED 119 330)

Crandall, V. C. Reinforcement effects of adult reactions on chilren's achievement expectations. *Child Development,* 1963, 34, 335-354.

Crano, W. D., & Mellon, P. M. Causal influence of teachers' expectations on children's academic performance: A cross-lagged panel anaylsis. *Journal of Educational Psychology,* 1978, 70(1), 39-49.

DeRoche, E. F., & Bogenschild, E. G. *400 group games and activites for teaching math.* West Nyack, N. Y.: Parker Publishing C., 1969.

Devin-Sheehan, L., Feldman, R., & Allen, V. Research on children tutoring children: A critical review. *Review of Educational Research,* 1976, 46(3), 335-385.

Doss, D. A., & Hester, J. Compensatory programs do not supplant, they supplement. Right? Paper presented at the Annual Meeting of the American Educational Research Association, Toronto, March, 1978. (ERIC Document Repoduction Service No. ED 155 240)

Duke, D. L. Who misbehaves? A high school studies its discipline problems. *Educational Administration Quarterly,* 1976, 12(3), 65-85.

Duke, D. L. How administrators view the crisis in school discipline. *Phi Delta Kappan,* 1978, 59(5), 325-330.

Edmonds, R. R. Some schools work and more can. *Social Policy,* 1979, 9, 28-32.

Elardo, R. Behavior modification in an elementary school: Problems and issues. *Phi Delta Kappan,* 1978, 59(5), 334-338.

Esposito, D., Homogeneous and heterogeneous grouping: Principle findings and implications for evaluating and designing more effective educational environments. *Review of Educational Research,* 1973, 43, 163-179.

Faunce, W. A. School achievement, social status, and self esteem. Paper presented at American Sociological Association Annual Meeting, Boston, August, 1979.

Feldman, R. S., & Donohoe, L. F. Nonverbal communication of affect in interracial dyads. *Journal of Educational Psychology,* 1978, 70(6), 979-987.

Findley, W., & Bryan, M. *Ability grouping: 1970.* Athens, Ga.: Center for Educational Improvement, University of Georgia, 1971.

Finn, J. D. Expectations and the educational environment. *Review of Educational Research,* 1972, 42(3), 387-410.

Fisher, C. W., Berliner, D. W., Filby, N.N., Marliave, R., Cahen, L. S., Dishaw, M. M., & Moore, J. E. Teaching and learning in the elementary school: A summary of the Beginning Teacher Evaluation Study. San Francisco: Technical Report VII-1, Beginning Teacher Evaluation Study, Far West Laboratory for Educational Research and Development, 1978. (ERIC Document Reproduction Service No. ED 165 322.)

Friedman, P. Comparisons of teacher reinforcement schedules for students with different social class background. *Journal of Educational Psychology,* 1976, 68, 286-292.

Frith, G. H., Lindsey, J. D., & Sasser, J. L. An alternative approach to school suspension: The Dothan model. *Phi Delta Kappan,* 1980, 61(9), 637-638.

Gallup, G. H. The Eleventh Annual Gallup Poll of the public's attitudes toward the public schools. Phi Delta Kappan, 1979, 61(1), 33-45.

Garibaldi, A. M. In-school alternatives to suspension: Trendy educational innovations. *The Urban Review,* 1979, 11(2), 97-103.

Gibbs, G. I. (Ed.). *Handbook of games and simulation exercises.* London E. & F. N. S. Spon, Ltd., 1974.

Glasheen, J. D., Hadley, D. W., & Schneider, J. M. Student adaptation to high school social groupings and normative environments. Paper presented to American Educational Research Association, April, 1977. (ERIC Document Reproduction Service No. ED 143 929.)

Glasser, W. *Schools without failure.* New York: Perennial Library, 1969.

Goldberg, M. L., Passow, A., & Justman, J. *The effects of ability grouping.* New York: Teachers College Press, 1966.

Good, T. L. Teacher effectiveness in the elementary school. *Journal of Teacher Education,* 1979, 30(2), 52-64.

Good, T., & Brophy, J. *Educational psychology: A realistic approach.* New York: Holt, Rinehart and Winston, 1977.

Good, T. L., Ebmeier, H., & Beckerman, T. Teaching mathematics in high and low SES classrooms: An empirical comparison. *Journal of Teacher Education,* 1978, 29(5), 85-90.

Good, T., & Grouws, D. *Process-product relationships in fourth grade mathematics class rooms* (Final Report). Grant NEG-00-3-0123, National Institute of Education, 1975.

Hall, G., & Loucks, S. F. A developmental model for determining whether the treatment is actually implemented. *American Educational Research Journal,* 1977, 14(2), 263-276.

Harris, A., & Kapche, R. Problems of quality control in the development and use of behavior change techinques in public school settings. *Education and Treatment of Children,* 1978, 1, 43-51.

Herriott, R. E., & Gross, N. (Eds.). *The dynamics of planned educational change: Case studies and analyses.* Berkeley, Cal.: McCutchan Publishing Corporation, 1979.

Hobson v. Hansen. *Congressional Record,* 1967, 113(13), 16721-16766.

Hoover, M. R. Characteristics of black schools at grade level: A description. *The Reading Teacher,* 1978, 31, 757-762.

Hunter, M. *Retention theory for teachers.* El Segundo, Cal.: TIP Publications, 1979.

Hunter, M. *Reinforcement theory for teachers.* El Segundo, Cal.: TIP Publications, 1980.

Hyman, J. S., & Cohen, S. A. Learning for mastery: Ten conclusions after 15 years and 3,000 schools. *Educational
Leadership,* 1979, 37(2), 104-109.

Ianni, F. A. J., & Reuss-Ianni, E. What can schools do about
violence. *Today's Education* (General Ed.), 1980, 69(2).
20G-23G.

Jencks, C., Smith, M., Acland, H., Bane, M., Cohen, D.,
Gintis, H., Heyns, B., & Michelson, S. *Inequality: A
reassessment of the effect of family and schooling in
America.* New York: Basic Books, 1972.

The Johns Hopkins Student Team Learning Project.
Baltimore: Center for Social Organization of Schools,
The Johns Hopkins University.

Johnson, D. W., & Johnson, R. T. *Learning together and
alone: cooperation, competition, and individualization.*
Englewood Cliffs, N.J.: Prentice-Hall, Inc., 1975.

Jones, F. H. The gentle art of classroom discipline. *The National Elementary Principal,* 1979, 58, 26-32.

Jones, F. H. Observation of student behavior. In classroom
management training program. Santa Cruz, Cal.: Un-
published manuscript, M.s.

Keller, F. S. Good-bye teacher . . . *Journal of Applied
Behavior Analysis,* 1968, 1, 79-89.

Kindsvatter, R. A new view of the dynamics of discipline. *Phi
Delta Kappan,* 1978, 59(5), 322-325.

Kounin, J. *Discipline and group management in classrooms.*
New York: Holt, Rinehart and Winston, 1970.

Lewin, K. Group decision and social change. In G. E. Swan-
son, T. M. Newcomb, & E. L. Hartley (Eds.), *Readings
in social psychology* (Revised ed.). New York: Henry
Holt and Company, 1952.

Lezotte, L. W., Hathaway, D. V., Miller, S. K., Passalacqua,
J., & Brookover, W. B. *School learning climate and student achievement: A social systems approach to increased*

student learning. Tallahassee, Fla.: National Teacher Corps, Florida State University Foundation, 1980.

Lyles, B. D. Chaos in the classroom—Let's blame somebody, not me. *Illinois Schools Journal,* 1973, 53, 21-24.

Madaus, G. F., Kellaghan, T., Rakow, E. A., & King, D. J. The sensitivity of measures of school effectiveness. *Harvard Educational Review,* 1979, 49(2), 207-230.

Martin, David L. Your praise can smother learning. *Learning: The Magazine for Creative Teaching,* 1977, 5, 42-51.

McDill, E. L., Meyers, E. D., Jr., & Rigsby, L. C. Institutional effects on the academic behavior of high school student. *Sociology of Education, 1967,* 40, 181-189.

McDill, E. L., & Rigsby, L. C. *Structure and process in secondary schools: The impact of educational climates.* Baltimore: The Johns Hopkins University Press, 1973.

McDonald, F., & Elias, P. *Executive summary report, Beginning Teacher Evaluation Study, phase II, 1973-74.* Princeton, New Jersey: Educational Testing Service. 1976

Meacham, M. L., & Wilson, A. E. *Changing classroom behavior: A manual for precision teaching.* Scranton, Penn.: International Textbook Co., 1971.

Merton, R. K. *Social theory and social structure* (Rev. and Enl. Ed.). Glencoe, Ill.: The Free Press, 1957.

Metzner, S. *77 games for reading groups.* Belmont, Cal.: Fearon Publishers, Inc., 1973.

Moos, R. H. *Evaluating educational environments.* San Francisco: Jossey- Bass, 1979.

Murname, R., & Phillips, B. *Effective teachers of inner city children: Who they are and what they do.* Princeton: Mathematica Policy Research, 1978.

O'Leary, K., & O'Leary, S. (Eds.). *Classroom management: The successful use of behavior modification (2nd edition).* New York: Pergamon, 1977.

O'Reilly, R. Classroom climate and achievement in secondary school mathematics classes. *The Alberta Journal of Educational Research,* 1975, 21, 241-248.

Persell, C. H. *Education and inequality: The roots and results of stratification in America's schools.* New York: The Free Press, 1977.

Phi Delta Kappa. *Why do some urban schools succeed? The Phi Delta Kappa study of exceptional urban elementary schools.* Bloomington, Ind.: Phi Delta Kappa, 1980.

Rist, R. C. Student social class and teacher expectations: The self-fulfilling prophecy in ghetto education. *Harvard Educational Review,* 1970, 40, 411-451.

Rosenbaum, J. E. Contest and tournament mobility: Norm, policy, and practice in educational selection. Paper presented at American Sociological Association annual meeting, San Francisco, 1975.

Rosenbaum, J. E. *Making inequality: The hidden curriculum of high school tracking.* New York: John Wiley & Sons, 1976.

Rosenbaum, J. E. Track misperceptions and frustrated college plans: An analysis of tracks and track perceptions in the National Longitudinal Survey. *Sociology of Education,* 1980, 53, 74-88.

Rosenshine, B. Content, time, and direct instruction. In P. L. Peterson & H. J. Walberg (Eds.), *Research on teaching: Concepts, findings, and implications.* Berkeley, Cal.: McCutchan Publishing Corp., 1979.

Rosenshine, B., & Berliner, D. Academic engaged time. *British Journal of Teacher Education,* 1978, 4, 3-16.

Rosenthal, R., & Jacobson, L. *Pygmalion in the classroom.* New York: Holt, Rinehart and Winston, 1968.

Rutter, M., Maughan, B., Mortimore, P., Ouston, J., with Smith, A. *Fifteen thousand hours: Secondary schools and their effects on children.* Cambridge, Mass.: Harvard University Press, 1979.

Slavin, R. E. Classroom reward structure: Analytical and practical review. *Review of Educational Research,* 1977, 47, 633-650.

Slavin, R. E. Cooperative learning. *Review of Educational Research,* 1980a, 50(2), 315-342.

Slavin, R. E. *Using student team learning: The Johns Hopkins Team Learning Project* (Revised ed.). Baltimore: Center for Social Organization of Schools, The Johns Hopkins University, 1980b.

Slavin, R. E., & DeVries, D. L. Learning in teams. In H. Walberg (Ed), *Educational environments and effects: Evaluation, policy, and productivity.* Berkeley, Cal.: McCutchan Publishing Corp., 1979.

Sussman, L. *Tales out of schools.* Philadelphia: Temple University Press, 1977.

Urich, T., & Batchelder, R. Turning an urban high school around. *Phi Delta Kappan,* 1979, 61(3), 206-209.

Von Harrison, G. Structured tutoring: The key to effective use of human resources. In C. Barletta, R. Boger, L. Lezotte, & B. Hull (Eds.), *Planning and implementing parent/community involvement into the instructional delivery system.* East Lansing: Midwest Teacher Corps Network, Lansing/Michigan State University Teacher Corps Network, 1978.

Walberg, H. J. *Educational environments and effects: Evaluation, policy, and productivity.* Berkeley, Cal.: McCutchan Publishing Corp., 1979.

Ware, B. A. What rewards do students want? *Phi Delta Kappan,* 1978, 59(5), 355-356.

Weber, G. Inner city children can be taught to read: Four successful schools (Occasional Paper #18). Washington, D. C.: Council for Basic Education, 1971.

Weinstein, R. Reading group membership in first grade: Teachers behaviors and pupil experience over time. *Journal of Educational Psychology,* 1976, 68, 103-116.

Weiss, M., & Weiss, P. Taking another look at teaching: How lower-class children influence middle-class teachers. Paper presented at the annual meeting of the American Anthropological Association, 1975. (ERIC Document Reproduction Service No. ED 137 223)

Wiley, D. E., & Harnischfeger, A. Explosion of a myth: Quantity of schooling and exposure to instruction, major educational vehicles. *Educational Researcher,* 1974, 3(4), 7-11.

Wilson, B. J., & Schmits, W. What's new in grouping? *Phi Delta Kappan,* 1978, 59(8), 535-536.

Wint, J. Contrasting solutions for school violence: I. The crackdown. *Phi Delta Kappan,* 1975, 57(3), 175-176.

Zuckerman, D. W., & Horn, R. E. *The guide to simulations/games for educational training.* Lexington, Mass.: Information Resources, Inc., 1973.